MW01094867

To Liz—

whose life-loving spirit makes the clouds go hide.

Go Liz!

Love,

Joe

2/21/2010

Bylines

Writings from the American South, 1963-1997

Joseph B. Cumming, Jr.,

Newsweek's former Southern Bureau Chief

Foreword by Doug Cumming, Ph.D.

AuthorHouse™
1663 Liberty Drive
Bloomington, IN 47403
www.authorhouse.com
Phone: 1-800-839-8640

First published by AuthorHouse 1/11/2010

ISBN: 978-1-4490-2311-9 (e)
ISBN: 978-1-4490-2309-6 (sc)
ISBN: 978-1-4490-2310-2 (hc)

Library of Congress Control Number: 2009912189

Printed in the United States of America
Bloomington, Indiana

This book is printed on acid-free paper.

Table of Contents

III. Columns from the Sunday Book Page of The Atlanta Journal-Constitution

IV. On Learning and Education

V. Lessons Learned in Black and White

FOREWORD

Joe Cumming was a most unusual sort of journalist. For twenty-two years he covered the American South for *Newsweek* magazine, the very years when the civil rights struggle (an epic clash in constitutional law, then in soul-force protest) made that territory a beat with as much excitement and consequence as one finds anywhere in the history of journalism. Yet he came to this job with zero training, no college courses in journalism, nor a single day of work at a newspaper or wire service. His preparation was writing poetry and radio dramas, selling building supplies and making commercial films for a few years. His education, from childhood through the University of the South at Sewanee, was a deep liberal-arts immersion in literature and history. An unusual journalist, yes, but then, he is a most unusual sort of person.

Joseph Bryan Cumming, Jr., grew up on genteel, easygoing Cumming Road, a world that looked down a little, in physical elevation as well as social class, on the rest of the historic river city of Augusta, Georgia. This world was at once vanishing to the tiny phosphorescence of a firefly, and looming large as the harbor view from a tall ship's topmast. It was a micro-world filled with historic time. Family stories harked back to when President Buchanan made Uncle Alfred Cumming governor of the Utah Territory or the night President Taft dropped in on the Cumming house for dinner.

Born on February 26, 1926, Joe was the only son of two strong leaders of local civic life, his father being a prominent lawyer and scion of what some encyclopedias refer to as "one of the most distinguished families in Georgia." Joe Jr. was a skinny lad with a Roman nose, soft mouth, ears that stuck out, and aster-blue eyes. He had permission and a capacity to dream away the time on a pony or at the piano. His great inheritance was such stuff as dreams are made on, not privilege or wealth. In a spiritual sense, he joined American life, just missing World War II action but not the jazzy action that followed. He got his ears pinned back, got married, settled in Augusta, sired four children, then set out for Atlanta, like so many other small-town Southerners, to find his destiny.

That destiny turned out to be magazine journalism. William A. Emerson Jr., a friend who had worked on the Harvard *Advocate* and at *Colliers*, had set himself up as a one-person regional bureau in Atlanta for *Newsweek* in the early fifties. By 1957, after the year-long Montgomery bus boycott had grabbed the world's attention and before the Little Rock crisis erupted, Emerson realized he needed help. Riots were breaking out. Instead of getting an experienced news hand—someone like wire-service trouper Claude Sitton, who was about to open a *New York Times* bureau in Atlanta—he hired Joe Cumming, a sweet-natured gentleman with a poet's love of words. It was a risky, intuitive gamble.

Within four years, Emerson had moved on to higher realms at *Newsweek* in New York, leaving his younger colleague as bureau chief. Cumming was ambitious and scared, so he learned fast what New York expected. Throughout the sixties, the teletype clattered in the bureau offices. The old rotary phones ran up enormous long-distance tolls. Sunday papers from every major Southern city grew in columns against a wall like giant termite colonies. He hired and groomed reporters who would go on to run other *Newsweek* bureaus around the world or become legendary as reporters and writers: Gerald Lubenow, Karl Fleming, Andrew Jaffe, Hank Leiferman, William Cook, Marshall Frady, Eleanor Clift. He selected talented stringers in newsrooms throughout the South to keep watch on the action. The files he sent to New York, in which he rendered exhaustive reporting into sparkling prose, would end up as fragments—a quote or an anecdote here and there in someone else's sparkling prose. There were few by-lines at *Newsweek* in those days. The reporting was always re-written.

But the dreamer had his writing dreams, and like Joseph in Egypt, this Joe could interpret dreams. He had a feeling that he could bear witness to what was happening in the South in some higher form than his *Newsweek* files. Something told him there was a place for his literary imagination—the peculiar Southern music and the metaphoric flight pattern of his private writing. Now it just so happened that a new kind of journalism was gestating in the precincts of New York in the early sixties. At the *New York Herald-Tribune's* Sunday magazine and at *Esquire*, editors Clay Felker and Harold Hayes (both of them dapper Southern boys) were taking literary leaps with non-fiction writing, going a little wild and crazy to capture the maelstrom energy of this new thing, the sixties. Their magazine experiments would soon be called the New Journalism. Cumming was visiting New York, a guest of *Newsweek*, when he gained entry into Hayes's office to pitch a story idea, something like "So What Did You Do in the War, Daddy?" Hayes liked the idea, and told him to send it over. So he did. And that story, the first of the published freelance articles printed in this collection, appeared in the November 1963 issue of *Esquire* under the title "The Art of Not Being 37."

Two things about that article are worth noting here. One is that it is not about what this *Newsweek* bureau chief was covering in the South, but is about his own subjective experience as a 37-year-old American at this particular time and place in the history of civilization. The New Journalism opened up the space of subjective personal experience like a Moog synthesizer or an acid trip. It was perfect for Joe Cumming. And the second thing is this: His article appeared in the same issue with the very first "New Journalism" article by a new talent named Tom Wolfe. Wolfe's article was titled "There Goes [Varoom! Varoom!] That Kandy-Colored Tangerine-Flake Streamline Baby."

***

If some "news muse," as he puts it (or dumb luck) launched his freelance writing career, I feel blessed with a similar luck or muse for having grown up with Joe Cumming as a father. Falling asleep upstairs in the Cumming house was a cozy way to go. We children could drift off to the sounds of Daddy on the grand piano downstairs, stroking the rich chords and tripping down arpeggios of "Stardust" or "Moonglow." Or your last dot of consciousness might be the sound of loud storytelling and crowd laughter. Or when only Daddy was still up, under the last light on, I could faintly hear the sweet pattering of his big manual typewriter. He was working on another freelance piece.

But the best part for me came after leaving home for college. That's when he and I began writing letters back and forth, typewritten riffs of mutual encouragement, show-off literary allusions, and preposterous verbal experimentation. It was a private thing we had going, and I thought I would never find a legitimate description of it until I read this in Nabokov's *Speak, Memory*, about his White Russian father: "Our relationship was marked by that habitual exchange of homespun nonsense, comically garbled words, proposed imitations of supposed intonations, and all those private jokes which is the secret code of happy families." Within my first week as a college freshman, under the spell of courses in history and poetry, I was pecking out trippy letters home. He wrote back, "Your communiqués zip silver about the emptying space, enlivening the growing of light into September." Once, after he saw a performance of Dylan Thomas's "Under Milkwood," he let the fireworks fly in a letter to me. He got rolling on pure sounds of "flush and rush out all old dried up dreams and schemes and new hatched sky-stretched visions from seed to pumpkin, from acorn to solemn oak from molecule to the great globe itself and carefully from the atom to be strewn across the galaxy." (He still says blessings at family meals like this, too.) Not that anybody can say what it means but let me quote a paragraph from that letter of December 2, 1972:

And last night dreaming of being with mountain people, old Foxfire sorts, in stone crumbling chimneys, good dry-straw-smelling people as I knew were dwelling in my [mind] when hearing and breathing Under Milkwood. For I seem more and more to be drawn toward people I cover [like] Pentecostal preachers (see Newsweek, lead anecdote was mine, Nov. 27th, page 93), country music fans (page 62) in Wheeling, W.Va. . . And just now walking past Union Mission realizing my life's chance would be to listen with those derelicts and harvest their tales, each representing in human terms the malfunctioning of society. And this is somehow opposite of what I sense is the Political Radical glorification of The People. I feel very out with that impulse, for it is all external to heart and deals with people externally. Liberals and radicals are too often bright pastless people who are bored with human relating and who have no ear for music. It's cold and insect-like.

Perhaps it was as odd as Joe Cumming becoming a journalist, but in June of 1974 I drove from my graduation at a liberal arts college in Vermont, with no training or education in journalism, straight to my first real job as a summer intern in the newsroom of the *Raleigh Times.* I learned fast, and kept working for newspapers for the next twenty-six years, with a couple of interludes editing regional magazines and a couple of reverse sabbaticals on Ivy League campuses. We continued writing our glimmering letters, my father and I, and sharing poems we wrote. But my earnest career plan was to make it in the ink-stained profession on my own, not as Joe Cumming's son.

I think I did pretty well on my own feet, though in truth those last two decades of the Golden Age of American newspapers (a century from about 1890 to 1990) offered a gush of advertising dollars that made it fairly easy for a young reporter to flourish if he or she made half an effort. In Raleigh, I concluded that the excitement of writing up the civil rights movement was just about played out. (In the summer of 1975, the murder trial of a poor black woman named Joan Little, who had ice-picked her white jailor after he forced his porky self on her, drew some of the smart reporters who would go on endlessly seeking a dénouement to the great Homeric saga.) I was lucky to work next at the *Providence Journal-Bulletin* over a thirteen year period when it was admired as "a writer's paper." I thought my connection with my father then was private and precious, like his letters. But here and there, I would run into journalists who wondered if I might be related to . . .[in tones of awe] . . .Joe Cumming. I was not at all embarrassed to acknowledge it. Then they would offer some hushed confession or animated story, the gist of which was that Joe Cumming had changed their life. He had either hired them as a stringer, or taken the time to encourage their writing, or shown them how a journalist could have a sensitive or dreamy side, or made them snap out of their dreamy side, or he simply passed through their consciousness as that piano-playing, poetry-spouting *Newsweek* bureau chief in Atlanta. I had this experience at surprisingly remote spots, far off on a press junket to see the turbines of Hydro Quebec on the tundra of James Bay, on another junket to the oil patch around Monroe, Louisiana, and even when I dropped into a wire-service bureau in South Africa. Apparently, I was not the only one he had taught and inspired.

In fact, he had been a sort of ring-leader of literary journalism in Atlanta. He had organized various floating downtown lunches for the journalists who worked in the Atlanta bureaus of national news organizations, a weekly salon that for awhile he named "Tuesday Tables." Dinner parties at the Cumming house, or weekend house parties at our place in the mountains in North Georgia (see the exquisite essay on "Tate" on page 31) would often draw writer friends like Frady, Pat Conroy, Anne Rivers Siddons, and after his return to Atlanta, big Bill Emerson. Later, I would find Daddy's name exalted in the acknowledgements of their books or disguised in their novels as a character or an anecdote. Occasionally, a well-known writer visiting Atlanta for an article would wind up at our house over drinks or dinner, luminaries like Mary McCarthy and Garry Wills. My parents once took *Washington Post* publisher Kay Graham to a play.

***

The end of the seventies swerved, and flung Cumming into a new calling—higher education. He spent a year as a visiting instructor at the University of Georgia, and then earned a master's degree in liberal arts at Emory University. His master's thesis was a case study of civil rights journalism, based on the most independent knowledgeable reporter in Mississippi, Bill Minor. During the eighties, he taught in the department of mass communications and theater at what was then called West Georgia College in Carrollton. All the while, he continued to freelance, writing regular columns on the book page of the *Atlanta Journal-Constitution* about writers and readings. Then he cranked out opinion pieces in other venues, mostly about his well-lathed mental map he called "the new learning." These ideas are the refinements of a lifetime of wondering, thinking and writing, a lovely cat's cradle of connections between teaching and learning, news and history. Listen folks, he just wants to pass it on. Take it and use it, somebody, please.

But there was always a bigger project he had in mind. Even in his first letter to me when I went off to college, he referred to beginning work on his movie, tomorrow. "I have a deadline upcoming," he said, "when the director will be in town." A few years later, the idea had grown to be a book, a novel. "I take off next week for three weeks to begin the novel," he wrote me in April of '72. Later, it grew to be The Project, a little self-mockingly, even acquiring a secret code number. Something was always getting in the way. One more "utterly last statement about the South. . .for a crummy magazine. . .and it is damn good." Or reading the clips of another young kid fresh out of college who wanted to write for magazines. Or a family vacation, or family crisis. Or Tuesday Tables or another great house party. Or writing an anniversary poem, or another letter to me. Or directing a musical comedy, or writing one. Always something, distractions that piled on other distractions to make up, over the years, the whole of who he really was and is. Like "The Other Wise Man" in that Henry Van Dyke story, he was forever being pulled off his task of reaching Bethlehem by the needs of people along the way, and by his own delight in meeting those needs. Only after a lifetime of frustration in the pattern is it revealed that meeting such needs was, in truth, reaching Bethlehem. Still, he longed to see it in a book, something we can all pull down from the shelf and enjoy, and pass along.

So this, finally, is that book.

Doug Cumming, Ph.D.
Washington & Lee University
Lexington, Virginia

I. Articles

Esquire **magazine**
November 1963

The Art of Not Being 37

SINCE CHILDHOOD I HAVE HAD a poor opinion of 37. To be 37 years old, it seemed from my youthful perspective, was to be everything uninteresting and unimportant. People of that age were all but invisible, showing up only now and then as substitute Sunday-school teachers or assistant scoutmasters. They were never in the crowd that dropped by for drinks with my parents on the lawn at twilight—they were off somewhere in double-breasted suits, working, without the trace of a smile, on inventory audits. As a teenager, in my day, we knew instinctively that people of 37 would not have pretty daughters of an exciting age. And, to the post-college and young-married set, people of 37 were the lumpish users-of-space on Saturday nights at the country club, cluttering up the floor with the wrong kind of dancing, lingering interminably at the table where they had eaten. And, if you went over to speak to them (not knowing whether to call them mister), you would notice they flicked cigarette ashes in their coffee cups. You would sense from them a force of boredom, pulling them down in their chairs, dragging on their laughter. As you walked away you would be annoyed by the feeling that they had even less interest in you than you had in them.

Behold, I am now 37. It still seems an age without luster or image or proper label. Of course, the view from here is somewhat different from what it was further down the slope, which gives a certain sportsmanlike quality to my present opinion. But it remains the age symbolized by the dotted-line man shown on page two of the insurance brochure when page one had asked the question of a glowing family group: "Who's missing from this picture?" On the record, 37 does not mark any official coming-of-age as 16 does (you can get a driver's license), or 35 (qualify to become president), or 21 (marry without consent or buy liquor in public). Off the record, 37 is a weightless time suspended between the seven-year itch and the purple flash, when you have none of the excuses of being young, yet are hopelessly far away from that life that begins at top-hatted and debonair 40. You may well be at the peak of your powers: never so clear in your view of the system, or more canny in organizing your work, or resourceful in salesmanship. But somehow you seem stuck as the able assistant, the district manager, the old reliable workhorse. There seems no way or no time to break out, to dislodge Mr. Waddles, to nudge yourself to the attention of the penthouse or the White House or the majority stockholder. Some tuck in their chins, shoot their cuffs and try to bluff it through by pronouncing their i-n-g's. But the art lies elsewhere; for the sting of exuberance has gone and the sleepiness of wisdom has not yet arrived.

But I go too far here, generalize too broadly. Let us consider, rather, what it means to be 37 at this particular moment in time. What era or motif belongs to us: what jazz singer, poet, sport, movie star or car style can we call our own? Aye, there's the rub. We missed it all. We, who were born in 1926 or 1927, probably knew childhood in a brick or stucco bungalow, built after World War I that no doubt had stacks of hand-me-down *National Geographics* in the attic. Certainly we have no claim to the flapper and bathtub-gin business that was on its way out by the time we learned to say "Goo goo googly." No—as they say in the television documentaries, "The Roaring Twenties were coming to an end. Just around the corner was a man named Franklin D. Roosevelt and a car called the V-8 Ford."

So what about the Great Depression? Unless we ourselves went hungry we can hardly indulge in tough-luck stories of how difficult it was to get a job. It's difficult for a ten-year-old to get a job any time. We were old enough to catch some of the excitement of that fabulous blue eagle glued on everybody's window that said, "We Do Our Part." But something happened to that bird. In its place came a shovelful of jokes about the W.P.A.

The war? We were 15 when Pearl Harbor was bombed. And college—we had a little time before military service, but what we found was a few civilians with thick glasses and heart murmurs who languished in the soda shop while the proud ranks of the V-12 Naval Officers training unit marched in the sunlight down University Avenue, swinging along with their navigation books and singing, in manly unison, *I've Got Sixpence…and Bless 'em all, bless 'em all, the long and the short and the tall.* All the famous beer parties and Christmas dances were suspended for the duration. Gardens went to seed around the closed fraternity houses. So even college wasn't the old Parker Pen eyes-on-the-horizon, beer-swilling, trouble-making, poetry-spouting experience described in the Bill of Rights. As soon as possible we signed up to go to war and, in no time at all, we were marching in the sunlight down University Avenue, in the ranks of the V-12 Naval Officers training unit, singing *I've Got Sixpence.*

Those days are very much with me of late. My three sons have discovered World War II. They know all about Messerschmitts, Guadalcanal and Ernie Pyle. They feast on comic books lurid with grimacing Nazis, riddled by doggies with helmet chin straps hanging loose, cigarettes dangling from their lips. Their hero is a one-man army called "Rock of Easy" who can demolish a German tank with a single hand grenade and capture a company of Krauts with an empty Colt .45. They let supper grow cold watching television shows called *Combat* and *The Gallant Men*. Recently, they came home from seeing *The Longest Day* and asked me, for the fifth time:

"Daddy, now what was it you did in the war?"

"Well, I can remember . . .oh, this was exciting …I remember hearing an eyewitness account of the scuttling of the German pocket battleship *Graf Spee* off the coast of South America. An unheard-of thing . . .I actually heard it *as* it was happening …on the radio."

"The radio?" Their faces squinted up like when there's no dessert. "But what did *you* do?"

"Well, I played the saxophone at the Catholic U.S.O. Club on Saturday nights. Look, I was only fifteen when Pearl Harbor was bombed."

But the old answers weren't sticking. Not this time. Not after *The Longest Day.*

I tried associating myself with greatness: "I heard Winston Churchill make his famous speech after the Battle of Britain . . .*Never in the field of human conflict…*"

"On the radio?"

"But, Daddy," said second son. "Weren't you in the Navy?"

"Yes. Eventually."

"So what did you *do*?"

"Well, I went to Japan and helped sweep mines in these little wooden-hulled ships. . . Very dangerous work. If a mine explodes too close!"

"How many mines did you blow up?"

"How many? Yes. Well, you see we didn't actually ever blow any up. We didn't ever really see any. But it was dangerous anyway."

"Did you ever shoot anybody?"

"Well, no . . .you see . . ."

"Weren't you in any battles?"

"Actually, son, the war was just about over when I got overseas."

"Just about?"

"It'd been over just about three months."

We knew it would be like this. Back in V-12 we were drilling over dry brown grass of the football field while American soldiers swarmed ashore at Normandy. And for the next year, as we labored through the endless training cycle of pre-midshipmen school, midshipmen school, post-midshipmen school, we watched with mixed feelings the chipping away of the last of the Great Wars. And whenever the routine of training seemed particularly pointless we mocked ourselves with the classic question: "And what did you do in the Great War, Daddy?"

Let the record show that many who are now thirty-seven were in the thick of the war and, to them, we were the "lucky" ones. But at the time there was much impatience to get out of training and into fighting. Now and then a midshipman would drop out of the officer program and go to boot camp to hasten his way to the shooting war. Usually these men, being officer material, ended up in a series of specialist schools and, like a friend of mine, finished the war in storekeeper school in Poughkeepsie, New York.

In May of 1945 I was sent to Miami for my last school before overseas duty. The war in Europe was over, but in the Pacific it was getting down to the nut-cutting stage. The Kamikaze suicide planes, with their cavalier attitude, were raising hell with our carrier decks. At this school in Miami the curriculum included a special course on the techniques in fighting Kamikaze planes, taught by men fresh back from the battle of Okinawa. This was, curiously, a one-lecture course near the end of the school and we waited with particular interest for it.

"About Kamikaze," the Lieutenant Commander began the lecture. "There really isn't much you can do."

So, there it was. We were finally locked on our destiny. Nothing stood between us and the final holocaust it would take to win the war. The *coup de grace* belonged to us. Here, at last, we were to become part of history. The prospect was terrifying and Shakespearean:

> "He that shall live this day, and comes safe home
> Will stand a tiptoe when this day is named,
> And rouse him at the name of Crispian.
> He that shall live this day, and see old age,
> Will yearly on the vigil feast his neighbours
> And say, 'Tomorrow is St. Crispian':
> Then will he strip his sleeve and show his scars . . ."

But alas, alack, as the Bard would say, the great drama paled and fell apart the way a nightclub act would die if a window full of sharp sun suddenly blasted across the stage. As we steamed out of Biscayne Bay for a final week of training at sea, the news brushed about of some terrible bomb. And when we sailed back into port the streets were full of shouting.

Thus, all that mighty time was finished. And, what a war it was. All the strength and art and discipline of Western man, gathered for centuries, came together in one glorious synthesis. There was Shakespeare writing speeches for Churchill, Beethoven putting the Morse Code to victory music and Auguste Rodin coming from the last land to do the Marines raising the flag on Mt. Suribachi. The dead and the living, the old and the young children who collected scrap, ladies who served doughnuts, movie stars selling war bonds and draft-board members smoking pipes, the propagandists, the politicians, hoarders, the female welders, the war profiteers—all had their part in the last Crusade. But not all of us who are now thirty-seven. We who are now thirty-seven sailed into the lonely western seas to sweep up, like some janitor in a deserted theatre. I shall never forget standing on the deck of a waddling LST as we churned under the Golden Gate Bridge. The day was over, the war was over and even summer was coming to an end. A giant sign read: "Well Done—Welcome Home."

On this green and essentially congenial planet, in this period between ice ages, the human creature has done well with that exclusive feature, the opposing thumb. He has put civilization in business. But each individual who has used his thumb in the cause also has a private need to use his forefinger—to stab on the page of recorded history and say: That's where I was; that's what I helped to do; those were my times.

When we got back to civilian life we blended into the postwar world as "veterans." Everything was for the "returning G.I.," but we didn't feel G.I. This just wasn't our *in hoc signo*. In every barbershop and sporting-goods store were men with shrapnel scars who could tell about being pinned down by crossfire in some Italian village. All we could tell about was dropping a handy-billy overboard and goofing up the commissary records.

What we needed was some vivid, even theatrical idiom to call our own. Something like the Lost Generation of the Twenties where the sun also rises and it was good. And, about this time, at a house party in the mountains, someone put on an old Artie Shaw record. My date and I were listening, and—it must have been *Moonglow* (or the new talk of cool combos replacing the big bands)—we suddenly came together on the idea that we both belonged to the big-band era. (We also came together on the even more swinging idea that we belonged together.) A few years after we were married we went to see the movie *The Glenn Miller Story* and we noted with satisfaction other couples our same age, some with babies in their laps. The movie started right off with that sweet, reedy music of the Glenn Miller theme *Moonlight Serenade*. We all whistled and clapped and suddenly, there was that remembered sound when Perry Como used to come on the Chesterfield Supper Club broadcast. And, a few years ago, when Jo Stafford recorded *I'll Be Seeing You* in a nostalgic album, we sat very still and listened and once again we conjured up a fantasy past which involved us personally "in that small café, the park across the way, the children's carousel, the chestnut tree, the wishing well."

And so we were—or are—of the big-band era, more or less. But the truth is, I was just old enough to join the Boy Scouts when Goodman was King and started a riot with *Sing Sing Sing.* I was worrywart kid brother when my sister danced dreamily to *I'll Never Smile Again* and I was off in the cattails gigging frogs when Billy Butterfield's immortal trumpet solo on Artie Shaw's immortal recording of Hoagy Carmichael's immortal *Stardust* first came to echo over a thousand summer lakes and seaside pavilions.

By the time the beatnik came on the scene we were pretty much emotionally committed to P.T.A. paper sales.

But wait. I am not getting this right, this story of the brotherhood of being thirty-seven. It's our people who are in there programming computers, building bigger rockets and smaller transistors, writing textbooks on new math and treatises on Existentialism. Look, one of our boys orbited the earth.

It is not important, really, that we do remember another world when little boys wore Lindbergh-type caps to keep their ears warm, or collected big-little books or listened to Jack Armstrong or the Lux Radio Theatre or Major Bowes, and little girls sent off for Little Orphan Annie Ovaltine shakers and later wore broomstick skirts. It was quite a different world in that trains were pulled by steam engines, cities served by streetcars and a tourist court was not something you mentioned. It was a world when the *Beer Barrel Polka* captured a whole summer, when Wee Bonnie Baker sang *Oh, Johnny* and Ella Mae Morse sang the *Cow Cow Boogie*, Kay Kyser said, "Evenin' folks how y'all," and Helen O'Connell made a production out of "those cool and limpid green eyes." There is no significance whatever that we remember running boards and dusty country roads and men wearing skimmers in the bleachers at the ball game. And there is no glory in boasting that you remember only one President throughout your youth.

But there is something about being thirty-seven that is important and it is a secret and it is best summed up in the words of that immortal French general who said:

"My house payment is overdue, my children are hopeless, my job is driving me nuts. Situation excellent. *J'attaque!*"

So if on some Friday night in early October you are home from work, standing in the kitchen reading something aloud to your wife who is fixing supper, and the children, who have been put to bed somehow escape, pajama-clad, drawn by some invisible excitement in the air to the lawn to yell and chase with the dog through a pile of dry leaves in the light of the rising hunter's moon, and, perhaps, because of the refill you hold in your hand you are not fretted by this blatant disobedience; and if, later, after supper, when the children are finally asleep, you and your wife walk out and stroll around the deserted streets and happen on another couple who are old friends and who have, themselves, come to smell the nutty air and sense the fresh feel of a shiny new season coming up, and, if they tell you they have lit their first fire of the season and insist that you come in, and you sit before the fire, and cheese and wine glasses appear and you talk, or, as only old friends can do, sit silent and listen to the comical wheezing of the fire as gasses squeak out of a hole in the log; and if, later at home, as you go to bed and open the window and smell the air and hear a train whistle far off reminding you of something long ago, and you are glad to be exactly where you are—if this is the way it is, hold tight, man, you're in the secret kingdom of thirty-seven. And things like that don't last forever.

***

Atlanta **magazine**
October 1965

The Pinks and Jells

Once upon a time—adrift in time and free from care—there was a land of concupiscent innocence, ruled by an oligarchy of queens known as "pinks" and attended by males called "jells." It was a land of white orchids and racing convertibles and eager stag lines at fragrant formal dances (not to mention an endless crap game in the basement). There was lots of hanging around and small talk between the sexes, weightless, floating talk of great significance about nothing at all in particular. On Sunday night the "jells," who tended to travel in great damp clumps, would pay long, icebox-raiding visits on the "pinks" of their choice.

"Pink" and "jell" were terms applied—in mock scorn and secret envy—to the members of an in group of Atlanta high school students between the early 1930s and the late 1940s. The "pinks" were the girls, "jells" or "jellies" the boys, and no two people exactly agree on a definition. The origin of the terms is obscure, but the words themselves are almost self-defining, carrying an overtone that marks them as genuine folk expressions. The very word "pink" (forgetting the lumpish John Birch usage) implies a feminine softness, a blushing affluence, and a breathy Angora sweater. And "jelly" (foreshortened, some say, from "jelly bean") carries the faint implication of a non-football player, yet a lad with a sort of jitterbug, white-saddle-oxford springiness, a Coke-and-cookie ease.

The Atlantans today who belonged to that milieu will invariably deny that they themselves were "pinks" or "jells"—even those who still bear the nickname Jelly or who were written up in the school gossip column called "The Pink Parade" or were recorded in the high school manual as "Biggest Jelly." Yet when they are reminded of those yesteryears, their eyes will change focus length, and they will laugh in a half-private way. Then, as through a golden haze of lazy, lacy memory, they will speak of that time and evoke the feeling of a style, an essence, an approach to life, a set of values that really existed and yet were make-believe. It was, they will say, frivolous and marvelous. They will not deny it was snobbish and extravagant, and graceful, superficial, exuberant, and heartbreaking. Some try to say their own children don't have as much fun, and it was better back then. But, somehow, the comparison doesn't fit. The terms of life are different. Then, they all end up saying, in a tone hard to interpret: "Those days will never come again."

Technically, the world of "pinks" and "jells" was a sub-culture that existed within the high school fraternity and sorority system. All of life was choreographed into a highly polished informality—in a Great Dance so compelling it tended to make college and even debuts an anti-climax. It took school officials twelve years to stamp it out.

What made it different from Freckles and his Friends, or anybody else's rumble-seated, whoop-and-go, flirtatious, drug store high school days, was the excess:

Every weekend reached for the frenzy and splendor that today is only attempted on that once-a-year occasion of the Senior Prom.

Each Friday night of the winter and spring ("there were hardly enough weekends to go around") one of the score of fraternities and sororities would put on its big formal dance to which all were invited. This was invariably preceded by a seated dinner and capped off with a breakfast until 4 a.m. "And sometimes after that," a former "pink" confessed, "We'd all go out and climb Stone Mountain…" "Or," said a "jell," "we'd go out and race cars on the Marietta Highway until dawn."

"Each girl thought she should have a new evening dress for each weekly dance," said an Atlanta mother-of-four, remembering; and she remembered how every evening dress was all-bouffant—an airy puff of crinoline held out by hoops.

A girl could have three dates for the evening—one for the dinner, another for the dance, still another for the breakfast.

"That meant three orchids," said one of the old crew. "And if she were an officer of the sorority giving the dance, she could have as many as six. And not just purple orchids; they had to be white. And if there had been such a thing as lavender striped orchids they would have been lavender striped."

It was all a cloud kingdom, unrelated to the toiling earth. It flourished in the darkest years of the Depression and deep into World War II. An Atlanta matron who graduated from high school in 1934 said it was all in place when she came along. She was president of her sorority in that year. She admitted: "We didn't know what the Depression was. Orchids? Lord, honey, we had 'em all the way down the front."

Sociologists, who always seem uncomfortable in the presence of unexplained frivolity, could no doubt devise an explanation for this social phenomenon, documented with clipboard statistics. Atlanta, they might find, was just the right size between country town and big city, was Southern but not too Southern, was at just the right stage of new wealth maturing toward old aristocracy. Wealth, it must be stressed, was not at all a prerequisite for being a "jell" or even a "pink." Probably a majority of the whole crowd was not from what could be called really rich families. Attractiveness rated somewhat higher as a life-value than money. But the general tone was one of a well-situated, milk-fed, sleep-late, coupon-clipping self assurance. Private schools, particularly Washington Seminary, provided the controlling image.

One bitter critic of those times says flatly it was sick. "It was anti-life, anti-sex. The relationships were non-relationships. Nobody ever really did anything or said anything important." This charge could be answered—or agreed with—so on, into the night. But no one argues that the style, for better or worse, was a genuine original. Despite the hoop skirts and the fact that many "pinks" were Scarlet, it never surrendered into self-conscious imitation of ante-bellum South. When they danced at the Brookhaven Country Club, or East Lake, no one closed his eyes and thought he was at Wingate Hall. And, if the sound of revelry seemed an echo from the adjacent twenties, made glorious and notorious by F. Scott Fitzgerald, one can be sure no "pink" or "jell" thought of himself as this side of paradise. Instead of being like something else, they were only and exactly what they were. It fit. And no one's feet touched the ground.

Popularity was the thing, and the "pink" who didn't have a flock of "jells" hanging around her house every afternoon, or a pack of twenty or thirty who would come around Sunday night, might not get the rush from the stag line at the dances. But then, if a girl were seen to be popular at a dance she would have no trouble being visited in the afternoon. This was the wheel of life. A "pink" who had it spinning her way would be broken in on at a dance every few seconds.

"I remember watching one girl from the band stand," said George Leonard, who fronted his own band for some of the sorority dances in the early 1940s, "and I counted. During one slow chorus of *Moonglow*—that was our theme song, and we played it slowly—but during one chorus this one girl was broken on thirty times."

Of course, there were no-breaks, but even that took an extravagant turn. The girls would line up their no-breaks, sometimes, years in advance. One "jell" remembered that for two years he had a standing no-break with a "pink"—the third no-break.

Not every girl made it. "Jells" were ruthless cowards when it came to dancing with a girl who was not getting a rush. This was part of the game—and the heartbreak. Young girls would tremble with fear before their first dance, knowing of the deadly Go or No-Go cycle, and lives could be blighted in the turn of events of an evening. Or so it seemed.

"Being a 'pink,'" said a former "pink," smiling and tilting her head toward her shoulder in the old way, "meant smiling when someone broke in and saying, 'Thank you, enjoyed it, come back, hear?'" This would be said with a special squeeze of the hand and a warm "just you" look in the eye. Then, real pinkmanship meant she would come up with that same secret implication when she turned to the new dancing partner who had just broken and say: "Hey there, Tom; how're you?"

In a hundred-mile radius of Atlanta are many small towns full of people who hate Atlanta as much as they like to visit it. They knew about Atlanta "pinks" and regarded them as haughty and heartless creatures who thought they had the world on a string—the same string, no doubt, that they kept a dozen boys on. They pictured "pinks" as madcap sophisticates, as glamorous and naughty as the Broadway Baby who says goodnight early in the morning.

This provincial view was not too different from that held by some of the "jells" themselves. The definition of a "pink" was attempted in a short-lived high school publication called *The Collegiate*. It went like this:

"A gal who's got more strings on her than a ball of cord and who really wants to go to everything provided it's on someone else. A gal who jumps behind the screen door like you were going to bite her when you say 'goodnight'...A gal who makes five dates on the same night and has every one of them on their toes expecting a big time and then keeps it with the one who has a convertible. A gal who could show the real fish some new swimming strokes and then some. In general, a girl who plays dumb, strings everybody, and, to hear her tell it, has never ever kissed the boys."

But this was the narrow idea of a "pink," and it was obviously written in a great heat of personal feeling. It is true that some girls made a sport of seeing how many fraternity pins they could collect, but the tribal customs were somewhat different then. As one Atlanta lawyer observed of those days of his youth, "Being pinned meant taking the pin off when you had a date with the other guy. But, it was a game and everybody knew it."

And "jells" were by no means mere pawns in the game. "To be a jell," said an Atlanta housewife, pouring coffee for a visitor sitting in the kitchen, "meant you would hang around the girls and think about what party you were going to. They thought about how sharp they were in their springy shoes and their cashmere sweaters. Oh, I can still remember how sexy those fraternity pins looked on those cashmere sweaters and they knew it."

And from the same contemporary publication, *The Collegiate*, there is a definition of "jelly," as written by a girl. "A jelly is a high school lad who is out to paint the town red, have a swell time, and attend every important party...." And when girls were polled for the qualities they liked in a boy, the two that came up most were "wear good clothes" and "be a smooth dancer."

Those were the values: popularity, clothes, dancing, and a clean sweeping ride in a convertible. And school—well, that was where the fraternities and sororities were. There was North Fulton, Boys High, North Avenue Presbyterian School (called NAPS, the forerunner of today's Westminster Schools), Marist, and Druid Hills. And Washington Seminary.

Washington Seminary was a "white columns" on Peachtree just a block from WSB's present "white columns on Peachtree." It stood, incredibly enough, in stately isolation on the very knoll that is now spread with the sleek and glittery Riviera Motel. This sedate and proper institution had served the well-to-do young ladies of Atlanta since 1878, and many traditions had built up around it. One tradition from the era of "pinks" was that most of sixth period at Washington Seminary was devoted to girls' primping, fixing their hair and lipstick and fingernails in preparation for that climactic moment of the school day—walking out of school and down the driveway to the sidewalk. For, there at the street and clustering on the sidewalk were the "jells" who had leapt in cars and sped to Washington Seminary in time to watch the girls come out. The refinements of the ritual vary with the era and the person recalling it, but all agreed it was one of important moments of the day.

"Just before you stepped outside," recounted a handsome Atlanta wife and mother, "you would push the sleeves of your sweater up just below the elbow—just right. You know, casual. Then, the great thing was to step out the door and try to make a quick appraisal of what boys were there and where the one was you wanted a ride home with. Then you would walk down the driveway without seeming to know they were there. Until you knew you were in the right place then…'Oh, why, hey there.' And he'd take your books and put them in his car."

A Boys High lad remembered: "After school we would dash madly over to Washington Seminary just to watch the girls coming out. We would park and watch them. They did look good. They had that little pink way of walking—you know, you sort of put your toes in. It was very stupid. When that was over, we would dash up to North Fulton. Same thing. Nothing."

In front of North Fulton was an area ringed by a concrete walkway. It was called "the circle" and every day after school everybody would gather there. "That's where everybody was after school," said David Le Bey, Jr. "I don't know why, but you just had to be there." From there some would wander over to Wender & Roberts in Buckhead. Those who had cars would pile it with people and end up somewhere like the

Pig shop for a fudge cake. The Pig shop was a Pig 'n Whistle Drive-In located on the present site of John Escoe's restaurant. There were other hangouts: Peacock Alley (where Cross Roads Restaurant is), Minor and Carter (downtown and good for Saturday mornings). And, of course, the Varsity, which was very big at intermission of dances where there was just time for a "p.c. (plain chocolate) and a dog."

There were dozens of other touch points: like Snake-eyes the carhop who named some of his children after the "pink" and "jell" who were his customers or the one-armed pool hustler who hung around the Q-hall. There were some memorable fist fights, usually "outside" at a dance though one well-remembered time a prominent Atlantan was sent sailing through the French doors at the Druid Hills Country Club. And there were famous car races. Like the night The White Roach (a '39 Mercury convertible) pulled out of the pack, went zooming past the line in a challenge, while Bobby Gaston rose up out of the back window and shouted:

"Whether we rise or whether we fall
We race one, we race all."

Or the series of races out on Death Hill between Earnest Beaudry's '39 Mercury and Ogden Doremus' '35 Ford.

The whole era is a pepperpot of memories for those who were there: The night they taught Jane Jarvis' parrot a dirty word and shoved it in the ice box so it would squawk its profanity when someone opened the door; the Emory Aces, Bill Clark; the song Danny Zoll wrote for Jean Fraser, which he managed to get arranged and which he would sing in front of a big band, Sinatra-like, on request. Some of the old "pinks" and "jells" still remember how it went: "It was just infatuation/ It seemed so real, that fascination...."

But, as they say, those days will not come again. Life is far too earnest today and that philosophy was much too shallow. Some former "pinks" have confessed to feelings of great guilt in reaction. Others blame the breakup of their marriages on the icing-thin foundation of pinkhood. Yet the statistics are unconvincing that there is any connection. And it may well be that there were some qualities worthy of attention buried in the excesses of that society. Today one finds among those people who were part of that time a certain admirable ability to celebrate the surface of life, a blessed and restful talent for easy relationships, for casual grace. And while former "pinks" are not much on what the intellectual community refers to as "notions," they are today among the more comfortable people to be with. Ladies who were "pinks" don't flirt anymore, but they surely know how to be good company for a man. As the times grow deep-featured and doom-sculptured, humanity could do worse than learn from "pinks" and "jells."

Of course, it is unthinkable that teenagers of today would succumb to the general philosophy of life that sustained "pinks" and "jells." If young people of today are at all conscious, they can hardly miss the terror and excitement that lies all about them. They should be fretting about "growing up absurd," haunted by *Lord of the Flies* or feeling the existential need to encounter and confront. They exist in a time pavilioned by the over-arching nightshades of The Bomb, the Malthusian disaster, and the icy, eyeless rhetoric of cybernetics. Yet there may be something of that frivolous yesterday that could teach them the small arts of human society. And they should consider, for the time will come when they will need the release that is found in that swift beauty of spirit that can sally out like a Frisbee, canting on the wind, hanging aloft in playful suspension between the blundering earth and the thunders of heaven.

***

Atlanta **magazine**
January 1967

The Big Little World of Martin and Sibley

Celestine Sibley and Harold Martin are weathered and comfortable in what may be the world's most eclectic newspaper office—and possibly one of the smallest. But from it they manage to catch the music of the earth.

If, some idle afternoon, you should fall in behind one of Atlanta's more reputable derelicts, drunkenly slapping his feet against the pavement up Forsyth Street to push through the heavy glass doors of *The Atlanta Journal-Constitution* building, you could safely predict he'll end up on the fifth floor at an office with a sign on the door that says, "Stop! Gas! See Big Snake!"

And in that small office the watery one would not only see a snake (as ashtray), but an eagle (stuffed), a grinning jaguar (skinned), toe-dancing cypress knees, a life preserver from the *Daniel H. Lownsdale,* a photograph of a pygmy elephant (named "Plop"), and two work-stunned, amiable bears who look like people and write like angels.

"Write like an angel" is an old newspaperman's awkward way of giving praise. And in that stiff jury of their journalistic peers, Celestine Sibley and Harold Martin, the two woodsy old pros who occupy this creature-cluttered office, are judged among the top in the nation. "They are the real ones who catch the music of the earth," says Eugene Patterson, editor of *The Atlanta Constitution.*

It is more or less accident that these two share an office. Celestine Sibley is a tall, handsome, homespun widow of forty-nine with a long, strong-featured face which always seems half-lit with impending merriment. An enduring pioneer strength rings through her almost mockingly ladylike manners and beneath her charming quilting-bee chatter one is aware of a fine-grained human being who has known work and will prevail. She has been a reporter for twenty-five years and a daily columnist for twenty years for the *Constitution*, traveling over the state covering murder trials and politics. One of her three books, *Peachtree Street U.S.A.*, is setting a record in sales at Rich's, outselling every other book but the Bible. Her columns, syndicated in a score of newspapers around the country, regularly win her praise and prizes.

Harold Martin, at fifty-six, is a hulking, pipe-smoking ex-Marine whose massive head and blunt features would make him fierce as a wrestler except for the uncontrollable generosity of his mouth and the kind look in his eyes. For twenty years he has been writing feature articles for *The Saturday Evening Post.* As an editor-at-large for the *Post*, he has poked around most of the earth's surface and into most of the affairs of mankind, earning a reputation as a top magazine writer and one of the few great war journalists. His stories out of Korea in the early '50s are considered masterpieces. At one point in the '40s he worked on the staff of *The Atlanta Constitution*, and, half from habit, he now rents office space in the building and contributes three columns weekly which, as it happens, run on the same page with Celestine's columns.

While Harold and Celestine are friends and comrades of long years in the trade and respect each other's talents, they do not consider that their jobs are at all similar or that their work is in any way comparable. They both tend to labor in a cocoon of self-absorption and will sometimes go half a day with no more than a muttered greeting between them. Their paths rarely cross outside of office hours and when gangs of school kids on guided tours of the newspaper building clump up outside their opened door and stare in for one pointless, slack-jawed-awed moment they both seem faintly annoyed, as though their separate and fierce integrity were vaguely compromised. They would be a good deal more annoyed if they ever came to realize that the guides were telling the children that in this office "are the last vestigial remains of the colorful old newspaper days."

"We may be growing long in the tooth," Harold would probably say, drawing himself up and casting about him with the old fashioned country courtesy of a man checking for ladies before he curses, "but, by God, I damn sure don't consider myself any vestigial remain...."

But for all their individual uniqueness, Celestine and Harold must finally be judged together. "They draw from the same deep well," says Gene Patterson. "They both came out of the poor backwoods South. They have the same unerring feeling for the land and the people. They get right to overall values and never waver. They are our rocks in a weary land."

This similarity of background and talent makes the tone of their columns more nearly alike than any other two in the Atlanta papers. In their prose style they have neither the relentless craftsmanship of Patterson nor the Old Testament certitude of Ralph McGill. They write by ear with the felicity of natural yarn-spinners, and somehow their frame of reference is set more to the rhythms of the earth and the changing seasons than the fiscal year or the new administration; their real interest seems less in the issues of the day than in the daily life of Everyman who is born, grows, suffers, laughs, and dreams foolishly.

Their office is a refuge for foolish dreamers, for the lost and the seeking, the self-pitying and the boozy, and sometimes for an untroubled visitor, dropping by just to sit in the rocking chair and be caught up in the vast mythology of characters that inhabit Harold's and Celestine's columns (when deadlines are not pushing). It is a mythology worthy of Bulfinch; it seems to serve as a parable for mankind itself.

Bit by bit familiar names come forth if the mood is right: Mrs. Peevy, Parsival Cobb, J. Bugger Dowdy, Aunt Dilly, Muv. The characters from the tinsel circuit fly through the talk like something in a Chagall painting. There are wing-walkers and bareback riders, Zimmy the legless swimmer who could drink a Coca-Cola under water, and Daredevil Zeke Shumway who got chewed on by a fed-up old lion while flinging himself and the lion around the vertical walls of a carnival hippodrome; the retired snake charmer who lived on a $48-a-month welfare check, but, as Celestine wrote, "in her dreams she lived not in a slum where the weather was cold and the kerosene for her two-burner stove had just run out but in a warm and fragrant vineyard in Spain." Or Arizona Bell who once toured with Mary Pickford ("she died in my arms every night"), but lived out the last of her life selling *The Atlanta Constitution* on windy street corners. Celestine took Arizona to the Metropolitan

Opera one year, and it is said one could tell from the way she wore a fine borrowed gown that she had once been a figure of grace and glamour.

And Harold might tell of the time he took Francis Brunton to the Cathedral of St. Philip for Sunday service. Francis Brunton is the goat-bearded, boot-wearing eccentric who used to prance around the streets of Atlanta with globes of the world hung about him and his arms loaded with old encyclopedias, a copy of *Who's Who*, and a wad of out-of-date newspapers, all of which he would pretentiously read with a magnifying glass. One day Francis let it drop to Harold that he was an Episcopalian, so Harold took him to church. At the coffee hour afterward, as Harold describes it, "Francis handed all his paraphernalia to an astonished lady, drew himself up like a race horse and charged four times around the Hall of Bishops to demonstrate his theory on how to stimulate the circulation of the blood."

When Francis changed his address from the alley at the side entrance of the Fox Theatre to a spot under the Spring Street Viaduct he gave Celestine as a forwarding address. She duly received his mail and, eventually, a personal visit from a bill collector. Before Francis left town, headed vaguely west, he gave Celestine what was interpreted to be a deeply significant wink and nod and said, "I think we've got the Lutheran Church sewed up."

Then there's Harold's tale of the man drinking himself stupid from the shock of discovering his wife was having an affair with his brother. Harold tried to console him until it came out that it had all happened twenty-five years before. Or Celestine's friend, the convicted rapist, murderer, and robber who shrugged, "Ain't nobody perfect."

Both Celestine and Harold own cabins in the north Georgia mountains and their mythology inescapably includes some mountain folk. Celestine has a little old lady friend she calls Miss Pal who "has no use in this world for the easy way of doing anything." She lives miles back in the coves and will not have her cabin wired for electricity because it "draws lightning." Just recently she stopped dyeing her own cloth and went to store-bought fabrics, "goods for a meeting frock." She makes her dresses from patterns out of the 1922 *Atlanta Constitution* which, as it happens, are sort of back in style.

Harold tells of Dr. Perrow, a learned Harvard Ph.D. who chucked the academic life that was fretting him to a nervous breakdown and came to live by his own hand in the north Georgia hills. His unfamiliar accent and unfathomable motives caused the natives to view him suspiciously until one night he attended a prayer meeting at one of those primitive churches "where the spirit comes down and dwells in the hearts of the faithful and they speak in unknown tongues." In the midst of the meeting they called upon Dr. Perrow to testify. He got up and began to speak. He spoke a few sentences in English and then got off into Latin and quoted Virgil for about fifteen minutes. "That was about as unknown a tongue as ever was heard in that part of the country," wrote Harold. "And ever since then Dr. Perrow has been looked upon with great respect as a man whom the Spirit has truly possessed."

Their office is located right at the entrance of *The Atlanta Constitution* city room and across the hall from publisher Ralph McGill, and some afternoons the talk gets around to the folklore of the old days at the paper. Like the time Harold, then a young reporter, paid an itinerant Italian to bring his trained bear up the freight elevator to slip up behind Pop Hines, the city editor, who was sitting alone in the city room. The bear reached a paw around Pop. Pop looked up. Looked again and vaulted over three rows of desks.

And when the mood is really tuned like a fiddle, Harold will act out some of the characters from his childhood.

Harold was born in the town of Commerce, the county seat of Banks County, on September 17, 1910; his father was a colorful courtroom lawyer and later a judge. Harold spent summers working in the fields on his grandparents' farm. Those were hard times in Dixie, and when young Martin presented himself at the University of Georgia in the fall of 1929 to begin what was to be his third year of college he was wearing his grandmother's linen duster and had only $10 in his pocket.

"Son, that's just not enough to enroll you," said the admissions official. Dejected, Harold walked along Prince Avenue, fell in step with his cousin, Jack Harber, who had just been kicked out of school for less honorable reasons, and presently they found themselves hitching a ride south. For the next two years it was one of those golden, slaphappy, existential times when a young man goes on-the-road and lives in that land on the backside of the rainbow. It was a time of second-hand Harley-Davidson motorcycles, epic smashups, miraculous makeshift repairs, and highways and beaches without end; a time of being broke and living on bananas and milk and working at odd jobs like dish washer or selling magazines or being doorman in a shady Miami night club (and fleeing in the night when raided by the law); of sleeping in haystacks or taking up residence in Depression-abandoned houses. It was a time when vagabond companions of a like heart drifted together, made their way as spirit or circumstance prompted, through cities and towns, from Florida to Texas, and memory made record of it all: the gladness and the close calls, the girls named Marvelyn and the Negroes named Barrelhead and getting arrested and waking up with a mule poking his head in the jail window.

When he finally came home, back to Commerce, his father looked up from reading his evening paper, eyed the mustache his son had grown and said, "Go shave that thing off." And not until Harold came back downstairs clean shaven did they settle into the fatted-calf greeting.

Harold went back to the University of Georgia, wrote a column for *The Red and Black* called "Leroy's Letters Home," which strongly foreshadowed his style to come. After graduation he worked as sports writer and then as general reporter for what is always referred to as "the old Georgian," a Hearst-owned Atlanta paper that folded in 1939, the night of the *Gone With the Wind* movie premiere (which Harold wrote up). Before leaving for the war he worked a while for *The Constitution* and as manager of the Fox Theatre.

In 1935 he married Boyce Lokey from Atlanta, the dark-eyed, beautiful sister of his college chum, Hamilton Lokey. They have four children: the two oldest, Marion and Skippy (Harold Jr.) are married and living in St. Joseph, Missouri, and London, respectively; Johnny is just back from a tough year in Vietnam, and Nancy, the youngest, is getting an M.A. in sociology at the University of Georgia.

Harold began his wartime career in the Marines, trapped on Hawaii, "Writing tributes to the Hawaiian sunset and sending them to *The Constitution* for columns." A Marine captain figured this gift should be used to project the image of Marine aviation. He fixed up a set of wildest-dream-come-true orders that gave Harold carte blanche to island hop, follow the action (he even made it to Peking), and write about Marine aviation. When he came home he found his stories had been sold to many of the leading magazines—*Collier's, Harper's, Reader's Digest, Liberty*, and *The Saturday Evening Post*—and a fat check of more than $2,000 waiting for him. He and Boyce went to New York to celebrate, and he ended up with a job at *The Saturday Evening Post.*

Since that time he has written more than two hundred articles for the *Post* on just about every subject of interest or importance from NATO to the KKK, from gold outflow to the megalopolis. His series on General Matthew Ridgeway became the basis of the General's biography *Soldier* which he and Harold co-authored. He has bar-hopped with Brendan Behan around Dublin, spent time with Julie Christie "on location" for the filming of *Dr. Zhivago* in Spain, sipped vodka with Khrushchev's old home-town buddies in Khrushchev's old home town, and he has known, with varying degrees of amity and enmity, Fidel Castro, Billy James Hargis, George Wallace, Happy Chandler, and Alf Landon.

At work Harold Martin is a solemn, heavy-breathing man who pushes up his sleeve as his concentration deepens. He is one of the few journalists who do not use a typewriter. He writes with ball point pen or pencil on yellow legal pad, which may contribute to his being an incurable doodler who will draw a mustache on every printed face in reach. He tends to be awkward with cocktail party small talk, declines to make speeches, and is judged shy or standoffish by those who have never seen him with an anthology of verse and a sympathetic crowd. He enjoys reading poems that unroll with a contented smack, poems with lines like "strong gongs groaning in the hills half heard" or "I was prince of apple towns." The only thing that keeps him from being the greatest storyteller in the world is a tendency to break down and quake with laughter until tears fill his eyes as he contemplates the approaching punch line. He has a special gift for breaking the stiff silence in a crowded elevator.

"I guess you wonder," he said recently as an elevator full of people started down, "why I have asked you all to gather here today." And the other day he addressed himself to an elevator packed with shy secretaries: "Would any of you girls like to wrassle?"

Celestine Sibley was born in Holly, Florida, in 1917, but soon moved to Creola, Alabama, eighteen miles north of Mobile where her father ran a saw mill and naval stores complex. "I always thought it was the nicest place in the world," she says in a tone that assembles a scene of Currier & Ives' clean simplicity. "There was a mill pond for swimming and a horse to ride. My job was to refill the lamps, clean the lamp chimneys, and refill the water pitcher in the bedroom.

"I walked three miles to a country two-room school—wading creeks and picking violets when the barefoot season started in the spring and shimmying up trees looking for persimmons after the first frost in the fall...."

She arranged to go to high school in Mobile where one of her teachers was Miss Anita Wagner who, as a student at Wesleyan College in Macon, Georgia, had been a correspondent for *The Atlanta Constitution*. "She made me think newspapers were a holy cause." Celestine still feels that way today. After attending Spring Hill College, a Jesuit school for boys which admitted a few girls as day students, Celestine went on to what she considers her more significant education in the newspaper business. She got a job with *The Mobile Press Register* working on Saturday "for experience," and finally made the payroll—$5.00 for a week's work. "The boys on the paper taught me many things," she recalls, "to appreciate Dreiser, to get along with people, to cover shipwrecks and hurricanes, and to see dead people without getting ladyfied and vaporish."

She married James W. Little, Jr., a fellow reporter in Mobile, and, after some years of moving about during the war, they ended up in Atlanta where Jim was copy editor for *The Atlanta Journal*. He died in 1953 leaving her with the full burden of raising the three children—Jimmy, Mary, and Susan.

"I think being a reporter is the world's highest calling," says Celestine. But then she adds, "And I think being a mother is a tad higher than that." She has brought both affections into her column; the result is an everlasting quality that makes each domestic crisis she describes not just her singular, amusing misadventure but a sort of universal experience, articulated for all people everywhere to share in and recognize as part of themselves.

This universal quality comes to Celestine's work unself-consciously. When she was first approached by Jack Tarver, president of Atlanta Newspapers, Inc., about syndicating her column she demurred. "I can't write for all kinds of people. My column is just written for one little old lady in Hogansville."

"Well, just write for a lot of little old ladies in Hogansville," he answered.

Celestine has worked hard at her trade. She used to make extra money freelancing stories for detective and romance magazines, based on episodes she had covered as a reporter. She would interview the subjects and convert their recounting into tight and passionate first-person prose with such titles as "I Was a Carnival Junkie" or "I Want to Die." One story called, "I Sold My Baby for $300" was based on a mountain girl who had so disposed of her out-of-wedlock child, and Celestine could only get the family's approval to do the story on a contingent basis. She would have to read it to them, and if they approved, she could send it in and get paid.

"I went to their cabin up in the mountains and began to read this thing to them. I kept reading when I came to the seduction scene, and the girl flung herself across the bed weeping and the mother flipped her apron up over her head. Doggedly, I read on, sure they would never approve. When I finished there was a long pause—the mother took her apron down from her face and finally said, 'Now I know in my soul that's as pretty a story as I've ever heard told.'"

One of the experiences that turned Celestine away from this freelancing was the day she had to go with a poor mother of twelve children to break the news to the children that their father had been killed. When Celestine came back to her own children that night she told them about her experience and read them "Lament" by Edna St. Vincent Millay, which begins, "Listen, children, your father is dead" and ends this way:

"Life must go on, though good men die
Life must go on…I forget just why."

Celestine has worked even harder at being a mother and keeper of the hearth. She lives today in a log cabin built in 1842 that hums with warmth and life. Four years ago it was a bone grey huddle of timbers and shingles, all but buried in a jungle of vines and weeds and trees, settled in to wait for death of decay. Celestine bought the land and its wreck and with the help of friends (who swear she can outwork any three men in hard, beam-lifting) reconstituted it into a snug home filled lovingly with things old and true. And quaint—like the pump organ with an ancient pirate's chest for a bench. The yard with its new well-house and brick patio and borders of wholesome shrubs and flowers and the little cabin out back for isolation when she wants to write another book. All go to make Sweet Apple, as it is called, so fetching a landmark that the ladies of nearby Roswell asked Celestine if it could be included on the springtime tour of homes. She politely declined.

"Celestine has a personal war on against chrome and plastic," said a close friend. "Her taste runs true to things natural and things old. She dislikes froth in conversation and personality."

But she does like good conversation, even with difficult personalities. She once said to her friend and fellow-novelist Margaret Long, "Maggie, you're so unholy fierce. I let people kick me around just for the feel of a human foot."

"Her hands seem to love everything they touch," said another friend who has seen Celestine in the kitchen, pulling pies from the oven, sending clouds of flour into the morning sunlight that comes through her eastern window over the sink.

In 1951 Celestine won a cash prize of $2,000 and a bronze medallion as a Christopher Award for a simple little column she did about a child in a restaurant asking the blessing before the meal. She won a Pall Mall Big Story Award for her work that led to a pardon for convicted murderer Floyd Woodward.

In her novel *The Malignant Heart* Celestine has the heroine Katy Kincaid (a female columnist on a daily newspaper) say, "I make them smile when they call me a sob sister." And this is her own sentiment entirely.

She is not a sob sister, and Harold Martin is not a garden club columnist on cute-squirrels-I-have-known. It is true that many of their columns seem to be about matters that are excruciatingly unimportant: on hand painted hat pins or leaf raking, on how to get rid of bulb-eating moles, or how to roast chestnuts over the open fire. But look again, for here is the stuff of Frost and Mark Twain, of Steinbeck and Hemingway, of Jan Struther and Thoreau, of Kipling and Thornton Wilder.

"You go to far places and you see strange things, and you think, now that is a great wonder. That is something to remember and tell about when I am home again. [This is Harold, writing after being away for three months, traveling 19,000 miles to three continents and half a dozen countries.] But when you get home, somehow, it does not work out that way. You start to talk about the horse race, out on the plains of Argentina with the gaucho riders, stripped to the waist, riding like centaurs, yelling, and what an exciting thing it was, there under the great sky, with the clatter of spoken Spanish all around you, and the horses running. Or you remember the way the road curves, down the jungled hills, from Sao Paulo to the sea, and the wild traffic on the road, the racing cars flying with their tires screaming on the curves. Or you think of a rainy night in a Dublin pub, and the old piano hammering, and a weird old woman singing, in Gaelic, the old songs of Ireland. But when you talk about these things people begin to yawn a little behind their hands and their eyes glaze, and you know you are boring them.

"For the only things that interest people, actually, are the experiences that they themselves have shared."

Or Celestine, hurrying home to her cabin at Sweet Apple on an April evening: "And even if the light is gone when we turn off the paved road on to the dirt road leading to Sweet Apple, I can smell the sweet shrub and some delicate, indefinable fragrance from the hollow where the muscadines grow . . ."

It could be said that they are not hip; they do not cluster with the liberals and intellectuals who burn with the excitement of a new language and brave bright plans. Harold and Celestine are not really at home with abstractions. They don't write on the Great Ideas of Western Man (although Harold was so intrigued with the anthology of think-essays *The Adventures of the Mind* he sent copies to his friends).

But they perform an alchemy that converts these important abstractions into human terms. And thus they celebrate out of an instinct for joy and mischief, all the ceremonies of life: life itself and birth and marriage and names and seasons, storms and sunsets and old men who come home from thousands of miles to say farewell to clocks that strike with a deep, remembered bong.

Celestine can go on for paragraphs caressingly listing names—of wild spring weeds, of Georgia towns, or wares in booths at a county fair until one sees the ghost of Emily Webb in the last act of *Our Town* saying farewell to earth. Harold can describe a storm so sharply you will huddle your shoulders a little reading it:

"The first big thunderstorm of the summer is roaring and banging and crashing through the hills. There have been rains before but nothing like this. The little house seems isolated in the midst of all this flashing light and noise, rocking under the blows, leaking from a dozen cracks, with the rain blown in by the wind at the windows. It is a cold and icy rain from the highest sky and it falls in great windblown sheets, shutting off all sight of the surrounding hills. Sitting here, trying to write, is like sitting in a great metal cauldron on which somebody is banging with iron hammers."

They are not clever phrase-makers, fashioning brittle vowel juxtapositions. But the richness of images they draw from their own memories or country-store instincts would make them company with Mark Twain or Augustus Baldwin Longstreet. Thus, Harold describes a little bar on Bourbon Street as being "so small there's not room enough to swing a cat in, even if a man was foolish enough to show up on Bourbon Street with a cat he wanted to swing." Celestine speaks of getting "the down yonders" and anybody who has experienced Sunday afternoon knows what she means. A snake-bit dog Harold described as having a head swollen "big as a dollar watermelon," or something as "soft as the inside of a hound's ear."

They are not moralists. Once in a great while they may write a column in irritation (Celestine against commercial courtesy, for example) or crusade (for longer lasting light bulbs, against capital punishment), but they never write in hate and they rarely judge. They never psychoanalyze the people they write about or fall into the temptation of looking wise by explaining other people's motives.

They could be seen as tender shepherds, at once innocent and redeeming, who seem to be saying of themselves and their fellow human beings, "Well, here we are, frail, troubled creatures, marching hither and thither but capable now and then of goose bumps and belly laughs." But what they are in fact are chroniclers who know man's half-sorry story is rimmed with a glow that they must catch and tell.

***

Atlanta **magazine**
May 1968

Vacation: The Mountains

VACATION: THE WORD MEANS MOUNTAINS, means tires singing the monotony of a flat highway, to turn up into blue, folded hills, surging against curves and to come, finally, believing into a new light and a green time. And there, in some enclave of billowing conviviality, a man might restore himself. Vacation.

In North Georgia there are sweetwater lakes among the mountains that shimmer the sun and echo the sound of voices into sheer innocence. Fishermen will spend the livelong day making drowsy scraping sounds in sympathetic old green boats and at dusk fling dry flies to the still pools of water near the alder bushes around the edge of the lake.

We go to a place that is blessed with meadows (which some call a once and future golf course). In early June, small, wild strawberries that taste immodestly sweet, grow close to the ground, and, above them, thousands of white daisies bow in childlike agreement when a wind crosses the slope.

As June ripens the daisies die and the hot grasses stickle and hum with stinging sounds. In early morning crows call across the rinsed air, gather flapping and close down on the tops of trees. I am told their cawing is a warning to lesser creatures that a predatory owl is near.

July opens like a split watermelon; the afternoons are orange. The shadows thicken. A swimmer will stand on the grey boards of the dock at hot noon, contemplate the sunrods that plunge up through the wavering depths, then dive in and let the coolness cover his body like a new skin. He will turn slowly, weightless in purpose. Somewhere on a porch there is good talk and the slinksound of ice in gin and tonic.

Sometimes, on the far slope of the summer solstice, strange things can happen in a mid-summer night's waking. Several years ago we seemed visited by witchcraft; the light of a full moon poured over the hillsides and houses, filling the bedrooms and sending children out all night long, laughing on the old golf course and through familiar paths. Sleep was banished. It was the Night of Nights. Adults lit up the houses and broke out the ice. Midnight came early as groups took to the road and visited about in the dry, warm air. Dogs barked, distance disappeared, the generation gap was no more. All were at their best—singing and shouting and taking giant strides, and seemed mutually possessed with a paradoxical clarity of vision, as though, in the moonlight, you could see more. I remember noting, as 3 o'clock passed, how everyone was engaged in some caricature project, mocking the day: teenagers dumped each other from the hammock, boys played army, cousins played tennis in the straw-pile light, and a visiting insurance man went skinny dipping with his wife.

"Ah, the laws of physics are reversed on such a night," said my esteemed friend of the good cigar, giving a twitch of wisdom to his thick, avuncular eyebrows.

When summer steepens into August one feels the pull to the higher mountains of western North Carolina where the rhododendron is thick and the paths among the giant white pines and hemlocks are springy and padded as though to keep holy the silence of the forest.

I like to drive through Highlands, North Carolina to blink up a teenage memory of a nestled white village of brisk, transparent air and tall, calling blue twilights when my cousin and I would set forth. The town is muffled in elegance now, with cashmere sweaters across the shoulders of ladies strolling about woodsy shoppes and casually inviting the right person for a martini at the golden hour.

We often end up for a day or two at Kanuga, a beloved Episcopal hide-away, and wander among such murmuring sounds as a bishop's deep voice talking with a Charleston lady of ancient kinsmen.

Then, one day after a thunder storm, the late August air will sparkle new and you know summer is over.

Sometimes in October we like to pack a picnic and go up to our North Georgia place for the day for some of that old lonely autumn look: the dock deserted, leaves falling, sky new-shelled in blue, the tennis court peppered with acorns. Once I picked up a Dixie cup the wind was blowing in a little semi-circle on the ground. I plopped in four or five acorns, hard brown and shiny. They made a great rich, tight sound when I jiggled them around in the cup. I remember standing there with the leaves falling, my wife packing up the lunch, the sun warm, the air cool, and I raised my cup in a sort of mute, private toast. I don't know why.

***

Atlanta **magazine**
September 1969

The American Idea in the South

SEPTEMBER SLANTS TO DRY GRASS: pony days and summer sounds begin the long withdrawal. The sugarberry leaf, inconsequential, takes to the curb and I would summon remembrance of Septembers past. This is the fifteenth year since the U.S. Supreme Court broke into the collective private vision of the white South with the dictum that separate is not equal, that public schools must desegregate. As a reporter for *Newsweek* during most of those years I have spent many hot September days standing before school houses across the South, watching other people's water-fresh kids swing lunch boxes past the flagpole sound of ticking halyards and snapping American flags.

To me these years have been filled with a special singing and anger, historic marches, brutalities and triumphs; it has been the most fearsome and frothy time since the Civil War. Martin Luther King, Jr. and the Civil Rights movement came into history, new laws and voting rights activity came to bear on the life and the politics of the South, Charles Evers was elected mayor of Fayette, Mississippi, and the black man moved subtly out of the category of being understood and loved with a household-pet kindness and closer to being a human and a citizen, difficult and demanding. During this time the South experienced its own privacy of invasion as troubadour priests and mulish Marxists, students, saints, crackpots, sociologists and French photographers poured into the region, fevering its ghetto back-streets, plotting beneath chinaberry trees and comprehending what few white Southerners had the opportunity to know: that something significant was happening in the land; that America was moving deeper into an understanding of itself.

"I'll admit," said conservative editor Grover G. Hall, coming out of a Negro mass meeting in the early days of the movement, "they have all the clichés of Western man on their side."

For a while the South took on the role as the prick to the nation's conscience, the national enchanted forest in which were acted out all the American allegories of good and evil, decadence and redemption. This tended to put the white South on the defensive and generated a notable bitterness among white Southerners. As one who was sympathetic to the Negro struggle I had to work my way through all the arguments that made men grow pale with outrage, their lips drawn to the color of clay. The race issue went far deeper than reason, generating unacceptable images of a black sweaty fieldhand at the wedding reception, of a glistening roadgang hand in the boudoir. It cleaved friendships between Southerners and disrupted families at Sunday dinner with chairs slammed back from the table, napkins hurled at the center piece.

Today, it happens that the school desegregation issue is still running a temperature. And the sense of crouched danger lurks in every street demonstration. Yet, something remarkable has happened in the South in those fifteen years. The American Idea worked. Careful now, I did not say the racial problem was solved or that prejudice was banished. Problems of human society are not "solved;" they are whittled down to workable size. The founding fathers calculated quite explicitly on the flawed nature of man, and what we have seen in the South is an important example of how their plan works, how ingeniously the machinery can function to bring us a little closer to the ideal. It has been a long slow process over the years of America, but history has produced enough response for people to believe that it can work. And this is the magic ingredient: that enough people believe it will work. The Civil War was a great test; Teddy Roosevelt busting up the corrupting accumulation of power of big business was another. Legal recognition of the rights of labor unions in the 30s was another. None of these victories brought perfection. America is not Disneyland; it is a nation in the act of becoming, an Idea being tested. The silver thread must hold; continuity is a gift only time can give. Each crisis that ends with America coming closer to the ideal instead of further away adds strength to the Idea. The impatient radicals today do not believe in the long, slow correcting process. They have a point: for this country to have suffered the existence of slavery in the face of the declared belief that all men are created equal and endowed by their creator with certain unalienable rights…it seems to them prima facie hypocrisy. But these zealots are steeped in the sweet Rousseauesque notion that human nature is not so imperfect and destruction of the clumsy machinery of government that now exists would produce a twilight garden of gentle simplicity. They have not talked to the hunter or the Cadillac dealer. The destruction of the American Idea would mean the death of freedom with no guarantee that all the flaws would be made straight.

It is fitting for a patriotic American to be impatient with the slight changes that have been made in the South. And understandable that a black would feel frustration. On the golf courses, in church, at board meetings and on the popping motorcycles interweaving themselves in the Shrine parade, the change of a segregated pattern of life is almost invisible. Some suggest the South has answered the classic riddle of what happens when an irresistible force meets an immovable object: it goes through without leaving a hole.

But it is wrong to leave out the invisible. For that judgment must be reckoned against the South when in 1954, John W. Davis, attorney against school desegregation, said blood will flow in the streets and reporter John Bartlow Martin, after lengthy and deep research, wrote his book *The Deep South Says Never*. Those were the days when governors whipped the air with cries of tyranny and interposition and cab drivers would turn off the meter to finish their lecture to a northern reporter on the doctrine of *stare decisis* or the proven cranium capacity of the Negroid race.

"Integration means slavery," said T. Eugene "Bull" Connor, the totalitarian demagogue of Birmingham. "Integration means slavery to your children and your children's children. We cannot have it. We will not have it."

Today, in the South, no one argues the basic rights established by the Civil Rights Act of 1964 or the Voting Rights Act of 1965. Segregation, preferred still by most white Southerners, redefined by the implications of black power, has been decommissioned. It is no longer a state religion. And this is what happened in these fifteen years and it is important. The thread held. The American Idea grew just a tad stronger when President Eisenhower sent troops to Little Rock (on fragile legal authority) to enforce the court order to integrate the high school. And it was important that John. F. Kennedy sent 14,000 troops into Oxford, Mississippi—their tents haunting the countryside like a Civil War photo by Brady—to make clear the right of one Negro, James Meredith, to attend the tax-supported university of his native state. A few years before, another Mississippi Negro had been committed to the state mental hospital for applying to Ole Miss. In a hundred other encounters in the South, from Rosa Parks' refusal to get up for a white bus customer to the Selma march, each time the national will prevailed against regional prejudice the American Idea grew a little stronger. Some say God was on our side. But really, it was just politics.

The political traditions as practiced and as underlined by the Constitution have been the genius of our system—what gets us into trouble, and out of it. It was politics that institutionalized racism in the South in the first place. Before Negroes were registered to vote in the South, office seekers carefully and diabolically nurtured our fear of the dark. They insinuated that only they could divine the full danger that lurked in the unfulfilled revenge of the black man. The game was to elect the candidate who could describe the most demonic threats from Negroes. He was the man most qualified to protect the voters from these evil forces. Then, as Negroes migrated in great number to Northern cities and registered to vote, congressmen and senators and candidates for president began to recall those privileges and immunities guaranteed to Negroes in the thirteenth, fourteenth and fifteenth amendments. This began the national pressure on the South and when the Supreme Court handed down its historic ruling in 1954, the Reconstruction which had been stopped by a slick trade in the election of Hays in 1877, was back in business.

The cry of defiance of Southern politicians was never intended to be taken literally. When Governor Orval E. Faubus blocked integration of Central High School, forcing the Federal troops, he was not interested in overturning the Federal government or, really, in preventing the integration of the high school. What he wanted to do was be able to say, "Now begins the crucifixion," and be elected for three more terms. He did. He was. When George Wallace called a federal judge an "integrating, scalawagging, carpet-bagging, bald-faced liar," he just wanted to be governor.

Sheriff James Clark of Dallas County, Alabama, a man of brisk ambitions, won exactly the reputation he was seeking when his mounted posse waded into Negro marchers in Selma, bashing heads in front of television cameras. He simply miscalculated; the horror scene led to the passing of the voting rights act which brought enough Negro registration to Dallas County to defeat Clark in his race for re-election.

This is the way the system works, eventually. It is rigged so that the deep drive for personal power must somehow reckon with the well-being of a majority of the voters (". . .derive their just powers from the consent of the governed.") As simple as that. Not perfect, but millions have understood it and believe it can work. It has worked to give former slaves some hope of participating in the decisions of their country. White Southerners, of course, still hold a lingering obedience to their century-long conditioning by demagogic politicians. George Wallace can still sweep the region with code words and that, too, is the way the system works. But the frantic cry for chastity in segregation ("no, not one!") has passed out of the consciousness; the metaphor about a little pregnancy with all its sexual overtones is no longer heard. It could be truthfully said that it was an apt metaphor, for we are no longer virginal. But, then, whites have not suffered any real inconvenience to their daily lives or their inner visions from this shift in doctrine. Such integration that has come to Dixie has scarcely caused any identity crisis in the white Southerner who can still hear the maiden aunt intone "we know who we are." To the power elite, life goes on bigger than ever in the suds of arriving prosperity: football weekends, African safari, Beech Mountain, Hilton Head. Sherry dry old ladies hum in their summer gardens, snipping cut flowers for the silver bowl in the cool ancestral hall. Suburban Republicans give their children dynastic middle names and meet together at cocktails for tight laughter and loose talk beneath new portraits. Rumpled roll-top-desk old Democrat-liberals, raised in the love of large old-fashioned rooms, musty with books and pipe smoke and sewing baskets, still romanticize about the old Populist movement. The bread routeman with name on shirt pocket saves money for his kid to go to the university while he and the wife swing to the pine bark and bar-b-cue twang of country music and the rich gut sound of Cale Yarbrough's car in the stock car races.

Looking back, it does not seem that these fifteen years have been such a blinding moment of redemption for the South. In terms of what lies ahead it has been a very simple achievement. The challenges shaping up are far more fundamental, dealing with value systems, with the distribution of wealth, with haves versus have-nots. The new dynamics will produce far more perilous times for America and the South: a black demagoguery armed with concentrations of city power, intent on a turn at exploitation; a WASP elite attitude reinforced by the vast system of private schools that could snap the last vestige of a democratic tone inherited from the South's century of underdogism. We may yet feel the impact of a civil rights-labor coalition; or the input of a new college generation which is both conservative and liberal but essentially free from old racial attitudes. We may encounter, as I have several times, a maddening, studied and insistent irrationality that seems to be saying "all your anal value, your rational, logical and lineal lives is only a trick bag to keep me oppressed."

These new forces are shaping up to be far more formidable than accepting Negroes as citizens and human beings. And the credibility gap is dangerously wide. A spark could jump and the whole thing go up in flames. For example, I see the possibility of fateful danger in such a thing as the voting rights act. If it were not renewed, the way would be opened for county officials to purge the rolls and re-instate all the old tricks for keeping down Negro registration. This could encourage a neo-demagoguery. But I don't think we would be allowed the luxury of going through the whole process again. For any such serious failure of the working of the system would confirm the tense hysteria today that decries the system as finished and dead anyway.

Because of what has happened in the South, I tend to be hopeful that this nation has the vitality to respond and strengthen the working system. Yet I must admit sometimes on the back roads in the land of despair I imagine how it might be to hear the chilling eternal swoosh, feel the cellar-cool breath of the closing of a great book.

"Oh well," God sighs, "it was just an idea . . . ."

***

Georgia **magazine**
June 1972

A Final Farewell

This has got to stop—these endless farewells. The South seems to have an incurable impulse for bittersweet goodbyes to itself—sad, low murmurings into mauve twilights, adieux to gold dust glories and lost green afternoons. It is a posturing usually followed by a few boasting, boosterish "hi there's" to some brand-name New South. The hail-and-farewell tradition began even before the *sanglot* sob of taps at Appomattox and swept forward in the post bellum by good Father Ryan, Confederate priest who sang, "Furl that Banner, softly, slowly… unfurl it never." I wonder if we, in the South, have not furled it too softly, too slowly.

Twice already this year I have attended symposiums in the South, on the South, that resonated with "this is the last" and "this is the first." Now I, your student of lingering departures, come to tell you this: it is over this time. Finished and done. The Old South *and* the New South. That is to say, the South as a separate, self-conscious concept is simply no longer fascinating. What use are farewells and welcomes when no one cares? *Gone with the Wind* may still be read in 62 languages and did, indeed, open a musical in London recently, but the final, extravagant morality play that made the South of the past 15 years into a universal allegory is over. The curtain has come down; the world has gone home. And if I, myself, seem ambiguously caught up in prolonging the epilogue by this very article, perhaps it is the reporter in me. Maybe I want you, good reader, scanning this fine magazine in your den or dentist waiting room, to share some of what I discovered in covering those news events in the South in those years of our time. For I sense it slipping away into two flat dimensions as a text book heading called Civil Rights Movement in the South. How can that hold the event that was as irrepressible as the War Between the States, as traumatic as Prohibition, as morally clear-cut as World War II, an epic moment that can give us peace with our past and bring an end to this restless threnody.

Or, perhaps I am not speaking as reporter, but as a son of the old South in a private quest for a benediction that will stick. For my tympani tones still come of an ancient past. I am all too familiar with the speech my great grandfather made in Charleston in 1893 in response to the toast "New South, New Departures" with its melancholy and eloquent "salve et vale." Even my royal, loyal self some years back, spare and white linen-suited among tombs of Magnolia Cemetery in the leaf-light of April, delivered long-armed gestures to the ladies of the UDC on Confederate Memorial Day, saying, "It is over. Let the dead past bury its dead." Or some such.

But the South was not over then. It was just beginning. For that was the year a weary seamstress over here in Montgomery, Alabama, named Rosa Parks declined to get up and give her seat on the city bus to a white person as was required by law and custom. This led to her arrest and to a young Rev. Martin Luther King Jr. being called on to organize a boycott of the buses. The boycott worked, and grew and became a Movement which entered history as an Idea whose time had come. And it developed a new weapon for warfare: love. Strange times were afoot in the South. And, at this time, for reasons unrelated to these events, I stepped from ancestral shadows and entered the world of journalism. It was a hefty educational experience for a son of the old South; to see paratroopers sweep into Little Rock, Arkansas, in a wet fall dusk and occupy the town so that nine Negro students could attend Central High School pursuant to a court order.

Those of you, friendly readers, who are young now or those older with faulty memory may not exactly recognize that racial segregation in the South was a *sacred*, not a *secular*, "way of life." Segregation held doctrinal status with Christianity and Americanism. *The Deep South Says Never* was the title of a book of accurate reporting on the prevailing white attitude throughout Dixie in 1955. And "never" meant "no, not one"—not one Negro shall enter a white school with whites, drink from the wrong fountain, shall be called Mr. or Mrs., certainly not eat on the white side of the café or stay in a regular hotel. This was a theological absolute. Thus, when the temple was rent and segregation was violated by nine Negro students in Little Rock, it had symbolic significance akin to the loss of virginity. It little seemed to matter after that first staining of innocence. Such was a kind of Pooh Bah logic from liberals that said "since segregation is technically over, then it might as well be said to *be* over. And if it is *said* to be over, might as well t'say it *is* over."

And this laid the basis for a new wave of goodbyes, written by liberals, the first of which was Harry Ashmore's book, *An Epitaph for Dixie.* Others of the genre were *A Republic of Equals* by Leslie Dunbar, one-time executive director of Southern Regional Council, or Pat Watter's *The South and the Nation.* There were others and the theme was basically that once segregation was lifted from the South as a burdensome dogma, then the South, for better or worse, would become Americanized.

It is self apparent that the thesis is both right and wrong: we do have national branch operations and Republicans but we also talk a special way and dig certain cooking. Furthermore, we have now discovered that a certain racism is pervasive throughout the nation, which was the attitudinal basis for our institutional segregation. This has given a gossip's smack of satisfaction to those folk around here who always rather liked the institution of segregation.

But Ashmore's book was premature. It could not be the final epitaph. It was written before the really Chaucerian episodes in the civil rights struggle took place. It scarcely hinted at what was to come. For segregation did not fall of its own weight, it was rooted out by the mass participation of black (and some white) Southerners, coming alive to their own selfhood and straightening up against the incredibly interlocking web of resistance—finding somehow a platform to stand on to move the world. I suppose that platform was the news media, especially television; but I am bound to say the media was not, as some insisted, manipulated into giving false importance to events. This was a major piece of history happening: black people summoning a courage against all instincts of self-preservation, singing and clapping and building their faith in hot little country churches, marching right up in town to the courthouse, in town after town, numbering in the hundreds, spread over lonely rolling farm lands in deep South states, stirring from a century of zombie somnolence and intolerable poverty, marching and being arrested and put off the land, enduring, coming to some kind of inner change, some kind of knowledge that a new time was at hand, catching the imagination of the nation, the world. And me. Pat Watters had to come back and write another book to capture this fleeting wisp of glory.

I think it was to finally set all this separate, to keep it un-commingled with later disaffections, that I was drawn to these two symposiums, hoping for a ritualized summing up and finis. The first was held in January at the University of South Florida in Tampa. It was put together by Dr. James W. Silver, that weary, wary mocking old prof who was a benchmark of sanity at Ole Miss during the James Meredith crisis of 1962 and who later was harried out of Mississippi after 27 years for assembling too much painful truth in one book, *Mississippi: The Closed Society*. The participants and panelists were historians, journalists, intellectuals, writers, politicians, editors, educators, many of whom had done front line duty during the 1960s and had moved on to back rooms in civil rights agencies or to high offices in large eastern foundations.

"Silver has arranged a nice winter vacation for all us liberals emeritus," said one, and this was the tone. Like White Russian émigrés in Berlin, they gathered in an almost Nabokovian sherry-dry tone of irony as if mutually determined to avoid the garrulous, whooping Wa'Eagle sounds of typical old veterans in reunion. Instead there was a tone of faint self-mocking, lying in the soft sun at the Clearwater Hilton, tapping croquet balls over the court as graceful seabirds landed nearby and Harold Fleming raised his eyebrows quietly at the birds, saying, "Each player must have his tern."

When Pat Watters ended the opening talk on the first day's panel with an attack on those who attack white moderates and a generally despairing outlook, Leslie Dunbar, the moderator, a brilliant droll old party with the long-faced diffidence of a displaced Oxford don, said:

"Thank you, Pat. That got us off on a properly gloomy note."

Then, in the same tone of unangry cynicism, he introduced the next speaker:

"Ten years ago the white liberal leadership in Mississippi consisted of Hodding Carter and one or two others. Today it is Hodding Carter and one or two others."

No, this meeting would not be the ultimate internment. There was too much cool analysis, too determined a scholar's caution as though any crowing over things accomplished would look like Jim Crowing.

"I must say, I am rejoicing in the pessimism I find here," said Dr. George H. Mayer, professor of history at the University of South Florida. "I thought this would be a celebration of the New South and I would be the one to come and throw cold water on it."

The New York Times led off its story with faithful irony:

> If a gathering here this week was any indication, Southern intellectuals have almost abandoned the North as a fit model for imitation in any field, from human rights to the building of cities.

Of course, there were some affirmations, especially by politicians. "To those who say there is no new politics in the South, what is the lieutenant governor of Mississippi doing at a meeting like this?" asked the lieutenant governor of Mississippi, William Winter.

And Eugene Patterson, master of affirmation, former editor of *The Atlanta Constitution* (on his way to *The St. Petersburg Times*), who is really more the spiritual descendant than his beloved predecessor Ralph McGill, gave a powerful and tempting vision of the present day potential in the South.

"What a powerful chapter it would be in American life if the white Southern people led their politicians into a final surrender of the struggle against our better selves and, in a kind of counter-Appomattox, stood free at last of the racial ball and chain that has chain-ganged the South long enough."

Slyly seeking to inspire self-confidence—the old Henry Grady trick, "the closed doors of racial separation we inherited have been cracked and can be opened to the clean air of a new day. . ."

But mostly the speakers at this five-day affair enjoyed embracing the paradoxes and contradictions of Southern history, counseling "the tragic view," as Paul Gaston phrased it, to keep it from all seeming useless. "The South," someone quoted, "is a history without a country."

John Egerton wrote a piece about the Tampa symposium entitled *Notes from a Christening/Wake/Revival Celebrating the Birth/Death/ Resurrection of the Old/Contemporary/New South.*

Still, it was not the last word in farewells.

And neither was the second symposium, this one two weeks long, held on the campus of the University of North Carolina at Chapel Hill at the end of March, put on by a group of incredibly attractive, uncluttered, intelligent students. Yet, this symposium seemed to be saying something broader than the first. It displayed a South beyond the self-consciousness of the Old and New, beyond the definitions imposed by the race question.

The first week, called "The Soul of the South," brought in a wide and lively variety of cultural events: a black theatre group from Texas, the Olympia Brass Band from New Orleans, bluegrass music and cloggers, fiddlers and old Doc Watson, a mystical blind folk-country singer from the real hills. Craft demonstrations featured quilting, dulcimer-making, pottery; then the Anne Jones Gospel Singers were so everlasting and joyful that the crowd stayed for hours after the regular show and sang along with the performers. There was even a stock car event, a pit stop tire changing contest, to give recognition to that exciting and expanding Southern cultural original. In the evenings old movies about the South were shown, like, "To Kill a Mockingbird," "All the King's Men" and "Sweet Bird of Youth."

And the North Carolina School of Arts performed its original ballet of William Faulkner's gothic tale, "A Rose for Miss Emily."

The second week led off with a growl of grizzled old guzzlers sitting on stage, moistened with Jack Daniels, telling with a certain familiar style and appreciation for the higher, anecdotal Truth, twice-told tales of red-eyed and rascally Southern governors from the immediate past. These raconteurs had all been reporters or editors in the South in the 50s and 60s. There was William A. Emerson, Jr., once with *Newsweek* in the South, then editor of the late *Saturday Evening Post* and now bearded and writing books on Jesus and sin; John Popham, garrulous and eloquent ex-Marine, Ex-*New York Times* reporter, now with *Chattanooga Times*; Harry Ashmore, Pulitzer Prize winner who battled for the Lord against Governor Orval Faubus in the famous days of Little Rock; Claude Sitton, who covered the Movement in the South for *The New*

York Times with as much raw talent and dogged energy as anyone ever did. And, I was invited to be on this panel as a last minute substitute. Eugene Patterson was responsible for getting it together and naming it "Old Times There Are Not Forgotten." He was moderator.

They told stories that are firming up into classics. Like Patterson's narrative of a badly hung over Big Jim Folsom watching a jet fighter plane accidently crash in the ocean on what was billed as a "show" for dignitaries. "Now," blinked Big Jim, "if that ain't a show, I'll kiss yo' foot."

Or Emerson on the late former governor of North Carolina, Robert Gregg Cherry. "Old Gov. Cherry was a wonderful man," roared Emerson. "He hated people."

And Claude Sitton recounted again his favorite on Marse Ross Barnett, former governor of Mississippi who expressed dismay that a prison trusty had not returned from a trip to Texas where he had been sent with the expectation of returning with a stud for breeding purposes at Parchman Prison. Said Barnett wistfully, "If you can't trust a trusty, who can you trust?"

The second week was called "Mind of the South" and brought to the campus, swollen with spring, a solid representation of civil rights figures, old and new—Julian Bond, Jesse Jackson, John Lewis; politicians—Governor Linwood Holton, Senators Ernest Hollings and Sam Ervin, presidential candidate and Duke University president Terry Sanford (George Wallace was scheduled, but had to change at the last minute to intensify his campaigning in Wisconsin); radicals—Charles Morgan, the Rev. Will D. Campbell, Sister Anne Catherine.

But beyond race and politics were such figures as Albert Murray, black intellectual; Robert Coles, psychiatrist, ubiquitous in highbrow journals nowadays; William Styron, novelist; and then the scandalous, splendiferous poet James Dickey, who held 1,500 students spellbound reading his poems with his hulking and hunched animal cunning, his soft-padded charm and dangerous smile. He ended reading a passage from *Deliverance*—his book, becoming a movie—that made the rapt silence glisten with suspense.

And the whole thing ended, as it is ordained by appropriateness, as the Tampa meeting ended, with an address by the granddaddy of all present day Southern observers and interpreters, the much respected historian C. Vann Woodward.

But it was not at all a farewell.

Yet, there was something about these two symposiums and their relationship to each other, something about their placement in time, in the year 1972, that nagged at me. Let's see: One was in winter, was dominated by aging old warriors who had given the best of their energies to battle the racial burden of the South. The second was astraddle the breaking forth of spring, was put on by young people already free of that ancient burden and interested in all kinds of forgotten and unattended things in their native South. Between the first and second meeting, it was as though something had happened; as if history had switched to another calibration grid. For one thing, on March 16th—in the period between the two meetings—President Richard Nixon went on national television to declare himself opposed to busing to achieve racial balance in schools (something, by the way, the rural South had been doing for two years). Remembering this, I think I realized we were now really part of America; or, America was a part of us and there was no more time for, or need for, any further valedictions.

But, because of another television feature in April and something my 15-year-old daughter said, I know there is something left to be said. We were watching the three-hour special on the life of Martin Luther King on the anniversary of his assassination, April 4th. The old news footage showed all the scenes I remembered covering: police dogs and fire hoses in Birmingham, the Selma march, the packed churches, the sweet preaching.

"Why didn't you tell me about all this?" my daughter complained.

She had a point. For, as time flows forward, the South has something now to look back to besides the War Between the States. In those eleven years between Little Rock and the death of King, the South really accomplished something of great importance. And if you, dear reader, happened to have resisted with heart and mind the achievement of basic black rights, you are all the more important in what was achieved. It could not have been important without you. And you, like everyone from George Wallace to Reubin Askew, are larger for acknowledging that there were great wrongs and great oppressions along with certain rare relationships between the races that the media and intellectuals are only now coming to acknowledge.

If there are angers and fears today, it does not take from the honor of what was cleanly and well done. For the civil rights movement in the South was a dramatic whole. It had a beginning, a middle and while its best spirit flourishes still in the South today in small towns that have not passed through their "redeeming" experience, it had an end. It may have been the last great crusade, the best example of the American Idea working, the clearest triumph of the human spirit.

And I would like to take some youth by the shoulders, as King Arthur did to young Tom Mallory in the last act of Camelot, and say "Don't let it be forgot." And I would lay it out, those brief years, in three acts of classic sequence as if inviting some future Shakespeare, prowling history for a majestic theme for his dramatic art.

It would be outlined this way:

Prologue: The Supreme Court decision of May 17, 1954, declares that separate is not equal in Southern schools and the laws segregating the races are unconstitutional.

Act I: Begins in 1957 when the first massive resistance by the ruling whites gave way to federal troops sent in by President Dwight Eisenhower, a man, by the way, with a caste-system military upbringing who never really fancied the egalitarian strain of our national heritage and who had chuckled at the silliness of the idea two months before when a reporter asked him if he would send in troops if necessary.

And then comes, oh, such a cry of outrage, of arguments and polemics about rights and fears and the marrying of sisters and *stare decisis*.

Just before the end of Act I would be a foreshadowing mention of some new thing that got started in Greensboro, North Carolina, in February, 1960: sit-ins.

Act II: Starts in the middle of the sit-in movement, arrests, fists and blood and seats removed from counters, young blacks getting organized, King prevailing with his doctrine of non-violence, of wearing down the enemy with love, but more and more being challenged.

This act would go through Birmingham, the march on Washington (1963) with a hint at the early forming of radical-minded leftists condemning the mild approach of King, calling for destruction of the system, calling the March on Washington and King's "dream" a colossal sell-out to the middle-class establishment mentality. But the main theme grows with the passage of the 1964 Civil Rights Act which outlawed all segregation in restaurants, hotels, buses, etc. Comic relief could be provided by someone who cries after each gain of rights, "That's enough, don't push too far. You can't legislate conduct. It's gotta take time to undo a hundred years . . ."

The end of Act II would come with the Selma march, the series of murders of preachers and blacks and Mrs. Viola Liuzzo along the route and, finally, the passage of the Voting Rights Act of 1965.

Act III would move into deeper times, stronger feeling of disaster to come and the disintegration of a cohesive movement. Radicals begin to come in stronger, inspiring with acts of bravery, dividing with acts of violence. By 1966 and 1967 things begin to fall apart. King has lost support for his involvement in the peace movement. City riots spread. White backlash begins.

The end would be King's assassination. By this time black anger in the nation was virulent. Many felt that the killing of King was the end of all chance of reconciliation. I had the curious feeling that, in the South, there was an opposite effect; that, somehow, after King's death, a slow repairing of relations between the races was beginning to take place. I know many whites who were shocked by King's death into an active participation in race relations activity, people who had managed to resist the appeals for help before.

That is only the public outline of the drama. The true human interest would come in the telling of a thousand tales of courage and fear and cruelty and pathos and humor that took place in the daily lives of people involved.

So, I herewith make my own personal farewell and I will resist the cynicism so popular among my old comrades of saying that nothing, really, has been accomplished. Lord knows, as radicals constantly point out, none of us have achieved virtue. We are sinners, still, and the Idea we struggle with is still hiding its power to perfect.

Yet we do stand in the grey ghost light of some dusk-dawn, half confusing weariness and excitement. I don't know which way we are likely to go. There is much talk of avoiding the mistakes of the North. I don't know. But I know that now we have a country and are free to start a new history. It could be something special. But it could be that the film could run backward, back in time by some slick disenfranchisement of our black brothers, or back to separation, into a neo-institutional segregation. If that should happen, I only say it will be a cold, dark day and all the airports will be deserted.

***

***Georgia* magazine**
November 1972

Augusta, Georgia: The Burum Company

I WENT HOME FOR A family wedding recently and learned that Burum Company had gone out of business. I worked for Burum Company for eight years after World War II. It was a small but venerable building supply company, started by my great grandfather on my mother's side in 1866 and handed down through the generations to my Uncle Harry Burum.

One name—one firm—one family
There must be a reason

We stamped this slogan in green ink on the monthly statements. Burum Company was not a fancy-looking place. The old warehouse seemed to lean out of the weeds across the Georgia Railroad yard tracks in downtown Augusta as you drove from the main business district out 9th Street. The side of the building was adorned with signs advertising brands of cement and wall board that had been discontinued since the Depression. The office was gritty with a few well-worn wood surfaces that revealed the areas of daily routine: the order desk, the high-legged mahogany bookkeeping desk, the captain's chair by the window. The display merchandise tended to be chipped, bent, and slightly damaged. It was a small office but there was room for dark corners stoutly defended by shin-bruising abandoned billing machines, spikes overflowing with dried and dusty invoices, broken electric heaters. There was an old cigar box kept handy on the order desk for odd sizes of nuts, pencils, rubber bands, washers and the tiny lead caps off lighter fluid cans which Uncle Harry saved against the day the world would suddenly be caught in an acute lead shortage and his lighter fluid caps would fetch a stunning price.

I quit Burum Company in 1955 and moved to Atlanta with my family; went forth, as they say, to seek my fortune. I lucked into the absorbing work of being a reporter covering the civil rights movement. Yet, all during those years I had, and still have, a recurring dream that I am back working at Burum Company. Sometimes these dreams seemed symbolic. In one, for example, William Faulkner, the patron saint of Southern writers, was the boss of Burum Company, and hard as nails. I said to myself in the dream, "I'm just not mean enough to be a merchant." The obvious message is that I'm not mean enough to be a writer.

The fact of these dreams seems curious to me. Recurring dreams should be from childhood. Burum Company was never part of my growing up. But I have come to realize it was an essential part of my going forth. It served as a fine finishing flourish to my education, a salting down after the Christian gentleman training of the University of the South at Sewanee; it was a counterpoint (or rabbit punch) to my upbringing. I was raised in innocence and honor, imbued with the proper sense of how one should conduct oneself and, by subtle extension, of how the world ought to be. At Burum Company, located there on the edge of the black and Irish ghetto, I learned something of how it is.

My family on my father's side was not rich in money but we were rolling in that commodity that has such inflated value in the South: background. An unending line of worthies stretched like a long shadow back to Thomas Cumming, the first Intendent (mayor) of Augusta in 1798. His son, Henry H. Cumming, distinguished himself by pushing through a major civic project: the digging of the Augusta Canal in the 1840s as a source of power to bring in industry. It saved the town which had been slowly drying up from the loss of river barge traffic to the growing railroads.

Ancestral portraits of these men hang in the family library. It was pretty overwhelming to me as a young man starting out. Then, in my first years at Burum Company, I became aware that on summer mornings about 9 o'clock, there was always heard a sudden, loud, mysterious sound, almost musical but clearly a crashing, breaking sound. It came from the direction of Jerry Scully's tavern. I finally investigated and discovered it was Scully's man dumping a box full of empty liquor bottles from the previous night's business into my great, great grandfather's all-but-dried-up canal. I was learning.

Each age is a dream that is dying
Or one that is coming to birth.

Even before I learned of its demise, Burum Company insinuated itself into the festivities during this recent visit home for my niece's wedding. It was still full daylight when we left the Good Shepherd Church at 8:30 Saturday evening after the church ceremony. This was in June. The air had cooled and most of us in the family—including cousins visiting from New Jersey—decided to walk home through the ruined gardens once owned by a Chicago millionaire who made his money in Quaker puffed oats. From my parents' house a group of us loaded into three cars and started downtown to the wedding reception. We took a back way, down Fenwick Street, that went past Burum Company. Not realizing it was defunct I was a little surprised at how overgrown it appeared. Two blocks down from Burum Company we were cut off by a long, slow freight train. Car motors were turned off, everyone descended into the deserted street.

"I'll never be hungry again," emoted my sister Nancy theatrically, in honor of the swirling red sunset that did, indeed, exactly reproduce the sunset in "Gone with the Wind," just before intermission when Vivian Leigh delivered those lines.

"Get MGM on the phone," said my wife Emily. A special mood was gathering on us, the men in white dinner jackets, ladies in elegantly cool long dresses; a kind of luminous, easy formality that cleansed the dusk and made it not like Saturday at all. We milled about, some danced, humming their private Viennese waltzes, others told stories inspired by this special moment handed us like a gift.

Watching the slow freight I recalled a Burum Company story about the day when Zebedee Montgomery and Clyde D'Antignac were sitting in the warehouse door naming the railroad box cars from the initials on the side.

"L & N . . .that's Louisville and Nashville," Clyde pronounced.

"CG . . .Central of Georgia. And here's the Chesapeake and Ohio," said Zeb.

"What you reckon is the CB&Q?" Clyde wondered.

"The CB&Q," replied Zeb with hardly a falter, "is the Cerebellum and the Queen Astor."

That's what you call folk genius. Cerebellum and the Queen Astor. To this day we refer to something huffin' and puffin' (extending a box car into a whole old-timey coal burning mainline engine) as sounding like the Cerebellum and the Queen Astor.

I heard from Uncle Harry a few years ago that Zebedee Montgomery is a "chef cook" in a Baltimore Hospital and Clyde D'Antignac is living in an old folks home, confined to a wheel chair because he had to have his leg amputated.

When I say Burum Company—and dream of it—it includes not only the people who worked there and the customers and salesmen and passers-by but the neighbors up and around 9th and Fenwick Streets. Across the canal from Burum Company, of course, was Jerry Scully who ran the tavern with his wife Maude. They sold liquor to the blacks and Irish who lived in the neighborhood and sometimes took a drink themselves. Jerry Scully was a large, sly man with a W.C. Fields nose. He wore a derby hat to enhance his posture as a friendly Irish politician, which he was, being on the city council of Augusta, representing the nearly all-black third ward even though he lived across the Savannah River in South Carolina. It was one of those arrangements.

Up from Scully's was a Chinese store, then The Fish House, which was always failing and changing hands, a "mdse" store run by Russo, a half-mad Italian who would chase young Negroes away from his magazine rack with a long barrel .38 pistol if he thought they were more interested in looking than buying. Next up 9th Street was Mr. Schneider, a very low-key old white-haired Jewish man who would roll several racks of cheap dresses out on the sidewalk along with cardboard boxes of shoes, sit amongst them all day and somehow make a living. Across the street was Buffalo Thunder Cloud Medicine (Buffalo claimed to be an Indian but most people thought he was a Negro), Piggy's Wood Yard and Kelly's Tombstone carving establishment. And, further up the block was Nick Galafanakas, a fine cabinetmaker and carver of church altars. He once told me a home remedy they used for the common cold in the Greek Island where he was raised.

"No one in my village ever got pneumonia," he boasted. The cure involved putting suction cups on the patient's back to "draw out the cold." I tried it once and, sure enough, I didn't get pneumonia.

Willie Green and Jesse Taylor were the main two truck drivers during my years at Burum Company. I learned a lot from them. For one thing, I learned that not all black people are lazy. When there was a boxcar of cement to be uploaded they would set about plopping 94 pound sacks of cement on the hand truck, banging across the clattery iron catwalk into the warehouse and stirring up such a cloud of cement dust they would end the job wringing wet and white as ghosts.

Jesse Taylor had a lot of flare and an impressive sense of his own dignity. He lived at a Negro funeral home and drove the ambulance and helped conduct funerals. He would come to work wearing the cutaway coat and striped pants of this other profession. And if he felt he was not being duly recognized for this trade he would let drop how many red lights he went through in a race with death the night before, or he would describe the condition of the "body" he had been sent to pickup.

Willie Green was a tragic figure—almost a metaphor of the struggling but hopelessly dispossessed Southern black. He was a small man with a sweet disposition who could turn out the work load of a forklift truck. But he could never gain on his troubles. He made very little salary and was always being dunned by collectors. He drank whenever he got the chance and seemed to get beat up by his large wife more than he deserved. Once he borrowed a mason's trowel and level from me, hoping to make a little money on a jackleg brick-laying job. After several months I pressed him to return the tools and he kept "forgetting" to bring them from home. Finally, I located the tools at Mr. Joe's Pawn Shop on Broad Street. My reaction was to curse the arrangement of things that made Willie lie to me.

Uncle Harry used to let Willie hide his furniture in the back of the warehouse when it was in danger of being re-possessed by the finance company.

Uncle Harry had a clear understanding of the profit motive. In himself and others. And, I have to agree it was (and is) a simple key for predicting how most things are going to come out. I'm sure Unk must have found it hard to understand how I, a recent graduate from an expensive liberal arts college, could have so much trouble with the concept. He did not grasp that I had a perspective of how the world should be. And the profit-motive seemed (and still seems) one of the least ennobling of human drives. Yet, I learned every day at Burum Company it is real. Like sex or food. And to reject this reality would be like trying to live without paradox, like not having a sense of humor. And it might have kept me from appreciating, for example, the sensual attention that Jerry Scully gave to counting out one dollar bills when I would go over to get a twenty changed. He made each dollar bill rustle like a taffeta petticoat as he laid them gently one on top of the other.

And I might have missed the Elizabethan daring of those hard-breathing, heavy-striding men, energized with greedy vitality, who sought to make the leap from being a carpenter or a house painter to being a contractor. Burum Company seemed to attract the most marginal of these men seeking to leap across the socio-economic abyss.

"Nothing but a damn burglar," Unk muttered once when he had extended a line of credit to some concrete-splattered, wild-dreaming cracker who had a scheme for building cheap houses for ex-GIs with government loans. But Unk and these entrepreneurs understood each other without confusion. Unk would never have asked one, as I did, why he kept putting screen doors with the hardware cloth on the front doors when it would look better to use the screen door with the brass grille.

This man looked at me sideways to see if I was kidding, "My friend, you're not very sophisticated, are you?"

There were old dreamers, too, like old man H.L. Lunday who would stagger up the front steps of Burum Company in one of those protracted, hawking, wheezing death-rattle coughs that one hears of bleary-eyed old men on court house steps. But as he would stand at the order counter, scattering cigarette ashes, dandruff and strands of white hair from his convulsing, it was apparent that he saw himself in his highest possible role. He wore a black Homburg hat, pressed down at a slight tilt over his flowing white hair and featured black silk coats. He was never really a United States Senator but he had once served as mayor of South Nellieville.

I was always bedeviled by comparing literature and life and I would try to perceive among the salesmen who called on us which was a Willy Loman, the defeated man of Arthur Miller's play *Death of a Salesman*. But I never managed to separate them from their considerable, anecdote-telling charm, the symbolic spot on the hat that began Loman's decline.

Most of them called on us regularly, with products we would reorder as needed. They did more visiting than selling.

But now and then we would be treated to the awe-inspiring talents of a one-visit salesman.

One man came in selling check writers. He said very little. He merely asked Unk to write his name on a piece of paper. Then, he turned the signature upside down and perfectly reproduced the signature, tracing the lines backwards, from right to left on a piece of paper the shape and size of a check. Then he sealed the paper in an envelope and extracted it easily with a pair of special tweezers, presumably available to check-stealers. We instituted a check-writing system that day.

Then, there was the dome damper salesman working his way to Florida who left his blonde waiting outside in his Cadillac while he sold us a dome damper. He really knew his product, "Listen, my friend, I'm from Detroit and that is dome damper country." We had never bought a dome damper before from some one who actually came from dome damper country.

When I think back on the useful things I learned at Burum Company I have a special thought for Mr. ("I'm not really 'Dr.'") Corley. He was chubby, happy little man who used to sell Packard automobiles to my grandfather. He was an irresistible salesman. He started a company that sold an acne medicine based on a secret Indian formula. He believed in the medicine with all his heart. It had cured him of his acne. He operated out of a room in the Plaza Hotel around the corner from Burum Company and I still hold a stock certificate showing that I own $100 worth of The Corley Medicine Company. The certificate was one of those that is bought in pads from stationery stores with blanks for filling in the name of the company. It is perforated at the top for easy tearing. I have developed an investment strategy as a result of this transaction: avoid stocks with certificates that have perforations along the side.

My best years at Burum Company were those shared by my cousin, Henri McGowan, who worked them with me. Hank and I often tried to talk Unk into expanding the business, taking on a new line like mill work or lumber. But there were other things in which Unk and Hank would be together on the other side from me. Like when the fish house caught on fire and I rushed over, broke out the little glass window in the fire call box (a life long fantasy), pulled the handle and set the fire engines screaming from all corners of downtown converging on our neighborhood. The first engine to arrive put out the beginning fire easily with a fire extinguisher but there was a lot of excitement and I had a sort of secret hero feeling about my role in the affair. But I walked back to Burum Company and Hank and Unk were sitting on the steps with a look of something less than admiration.

"Well, you sure ruined what would have been a damn good fire," they said.

In 1955 it was the time of the tide in the affairs of men. Burum Company had taught me much of what I needed to know. I left for Atlanta and a few years later Hank quit and went with the First National Bank in Augusta. Shortly after that Unk sold the company and moved to California. Hank got a job for Robert Davis, a truck driver, at the First National. A couple of times Robert has come in and said he has a message for Mr. Harry, and Hank will call in the stenographer to take dictation. Robert has a little trouble understanding the concept of dictation. He stands firmly in the room as if in the presence of the party being addressed. And he begins to talk to the space before him as to an unseen presence.

"Mr. Harry," Robert began his letter once. "Old Coot is dead. His buddy says for you to send some money for a floral."

Several times Unk has received such an appeal as the old friends from earlier days die off. Unk has declined to contribute to the florals, suspecting a rake-off.

It was Hank, I think, who told me that Burum Company had gone out of business. He told me at the wedding reception.

I thought, perhaps this news would put an end to the recurring dream that I am back there working. But just the other night I dreamed I was back there and Burum Company had taken on a line of pornographic magazines. I have no idea what that signifies.

***

Southern Voices
March/April 1974

Greene County, Ala.: The Hope of the Future

To THE WHITE PEOPLE OF Greene County, Alabama – where blacks outnumber whites three to one – the idea of blacks taking over the county government was simply an idea that could not be taken seriously. It was a non-idea. In 1965 when a white businessman named Eugene Johnston warned white leaders that the Supreme Court would one day order complete integration of the Greene County public schools he was considered a bit hooky or at least out of line with a tasteless joke. And Eugene Johnston got little support for his plan to start a private school for whites. For anyone to have further suggested that one day blacks might vote themselves into dominant political power would have been to murder sleep, to stir the slumbering rape fantasy and the waking nightmare of social chaos and political anarchy. It was unthinkable.

Five years later the unthinkable had happened. Today black men occupy all five positions on the school board, all four seats on the county commission. The school superintendent is a black educator named Robert Brown and about 97 percent of the public school students are black. (Whites eventually gave full, frantic support to the private school started by Eugene Johnston.) More important, the probate judge, the most powerful elected official in the county, is a 56-year-old black preacher and one-time teacher in the county school system, William McKinley Branch. And one of Branch's former pupils is the sheriff. His name is Thomas Earl Gilmore. He is tall, cool, dapper and, at age 33, often singled out by those who follow civil rights in the nation as a model of the best of the kind of black man who came out of the movement and ended up in politics. Sheriff Gilmore is a native of Greene County.

Years earlier he had been pushed by his anger to California and into the black militant organization SNCC.

As a Southern reporter for *Newsweek* magazine for 17 years, I have covered the major events of the civil rights struggle in the South from the federal bayonets at Little Rock in 1957 through the assassination of Martin Luther King in 1968. I was in Birmingham in 1963 when Police Commissioner Eugene "Bull" Connor used police dogs and fire hoses against demonstrating blacks. I followed the series of killings of civil rights workers in Alabama in 1965 (Jimmie Lee Jackson in Marion, the Rev. James Reeb in Selma) and beatings (Sheriff Jim Clark's mounted posse at the Edmund Pettus Bridge) that culminated in the Selma march which I was on. There were two more civil rights killings in that general area of Alabama that year: Mrs. Viola Liuzzo, Detroit housewife, and Jonathan M. Daniels, Episcopal seminary student from New Hampshire – both in the South to work for black civil rights.

All of these events took place in what is called the black belt of Alabama. Greene County is at the northwest end of the black belt and had the vague reputation among us reporters of being rough. By the time I made my first – and very brief – visit there in 1965 there were stories of how the sheriff, Big Bill Lee, a former All-American football player, had brought his heavy cattle stick down on the head of young black "agitator" Tom Gilmore. But, as a native Southerner, I am also plugged into that white South that is one big small town and I discovered I had gone to college with a couple of the scions of the Banks family, the leading dynasty in Greene County. It was my old college chum Ralph Banks who later told me the story of how Sheriff Bill Lee had broken up a Klan rally one night by kicking over the cross and otherwise making the hooded ones feel unwelcomed. I also realized from Ralph Banks that there is a spirit of noblesse oblige in Greene County left over from the cotton plantation culture that existed there in the 1840s and 1850s. The Ku Klux Klan mentality never set the tone in Greene County. For one thing, the Banks family would never allow it.

Even so, the black ascendency was an outright political miracle. It took five years of exhausting, complex and bitter struggle. Even now both blacks and whites seem too stunned from the historic event to quite know what to do with it. A few whites, like the former probate judge, Dennis Herndon, left town to make their careers elsewhere. But most still seem too exhausted from the years of struggle to take decisive action toward the future. I went down from Atlanta to live in Greene County in the early spring of 1973. For a month I stayed, as an outsider, and saw what few who live there can see: There is a hushed quality of possibility in the air. Something important seems to be taking place in Greene County. In small, slow ways a few people are beginning to stir with life in the context of a new, enlarged reality. In the end it may be too few, too small, and too slow. But, for the moment, there is the fascinating chance that something important could take place in Greene County in the next five years that America could do well to notice.

To some it is miracle enough that there is surface peace between the races. Judge William Branch and Sheriff Thomas Gilmore, the two top political leaders of the blacks as well as the highest elected county officials, are both preachers and disciples of Martin Luther King's teachings of love. After their victory in November, 1970, they made it a point to meet hostile glowers with unangry neutrality if not overtures of friendship. They wanted to show that they were as interested in cooperating with whites as they were in helping the impoverished blacks who put them in office. Since that time whites have generally settled into a noncommittal attitude with public appearances of calm and courtesy.

"We're getting along just fine," they studiously say to outsiders, which is something, even if it said more for the sake of decorum than deep decency.

But, of course, it is not enough. Already a faction of more militant blacks is challenging the lack of substance in this strained, brittle politeness. Soon, in the city of Eutaw, black voters may outnumber whites, as they now do in the county, through annexation of black housing projects on the city limits. This could bring to an end the white control of the city of Eutaw, and the last enclave of white dominance. The idea of coalition politics would be the only hope for whites. People like Judge Branch and Tom Gilmore are always open to coalition with whites but they are also under pressure from black militants who seem to be rallying around the emerging leadership of School Superintendent Robert Brown. In the next five years the initiative will be with the whites. Their own self-interest will demand something very interesting and unaccustomed of them: that they enlarge the frame of reference in which they live and perceive their values. Because of a century of rigid defensiveness it will take many whites some effort to understand and help define the larger psychic horizon for coalition politics to work. They will not have to change so much, but they will have to grow considerably. In a way, the people of Greene County seem to stand at the classic dividing point between decadence and renewal, at that provocative Toynbeesque moment in their history when a culture either responds to the new challenge or is trapped forever in the backwaters. From what I saw in the after-image of my visit there, Greene County stands fair to round out an epoch of its history by producing a miracle: a situation of self-confidence and creative stability. However, this is a fragile image. Things could almost as easily go the other way. If not enough people – white and black – expand their perspective, Greene County could be doomed to a sour, mean and altogether typical small-town obscurity.

The first five years of this epoch of the miracle belonged to the blacks. From 1965 to 1970 they were in resonance with the civil rights movement as it swept across rural Alabama like a gust, like a ghost cloud filled with the sounds of battle, like an Old Testament epic. In the early days of this movement the very act of registering to vote was a personal act of courage for blacks in the movement.

And, with the election of black officials the black citizens of Greene County took on that restlessness called hope. In the phrase of Jack Burden in *All the King's Men* they moved out of history, into history and the awful responsibility of time.

The next five years whites will have to make their own existential choice. "We are proud of our Greek revival and our white survival," an elegant lady whispered playfully. (The hilltops of the county brood with ante-bellum homes with classic-columned porticoes.) But the expansive spirit that built and dwelt in those mansions seems to have shriveled in the descendents. And whites will not "survive" if survival is the limit of their striving.

When I checked into the old white brick Hotel Eutaw on the corner of the courthouse square for my month-long visit many people received me warmly and were friendly and helpful. But I was fairly overwhelmed by the tightness and fear I found among a great many others. It was much more suffocating than the caution and restraint I have learned to expect of people in small towns toward reporters.

"I heard you were in town," said a throaty female voice to me in an anonymous call to the hotel one night near midnight. "I've heard people say they're not going to tell you the truth. They tell you everybody's getting along fine but they're really suffering on the inside. You'll never know."

The caller was willing to talk further if I signed a paper swearing I would not use her name. That was hardly necessary. I had already been refused interviews by four people, including the chairman of the membership committee of the Chamber of Commerce. There were others who met me with wintry monosyllables. The effect was that of people caught behind that thick and heatless bullet-proof glass used in drive-in windows in suburban banks. One leading white citizen who knows the town well put it this way: "This town is paranoid."

That's a fun thing to say, of course, but it has no real meaning. More specifically it could be said that Greene County needs new industry. It needs political stability. And its citizens are in search of a richer meaning to their lives. (A sense of pervasive boredom emanates from the therapy sessions recently begun by the State Mental Health Department, held twice a week at the county health building in Eutaw. A notable number of white middle class folk consume too much alcohol desperately, as if life held no other serious choices. The suicide rate in Greene County is the highest in the state.) These three specific needs – new industry, political stability, a deeper meaning to life – are closely inter-related. And they stand unfulfilled from nothing more substantial than a lack of imagination. There is a strange, lingering fear – not of members of one race or the other – but a fear of seeming to be too helpful and cooperative across racial lines. Whites, for example, have never taken the least interest in Tom Gilmore's noble dream of a boys' ranch for the underprivileged or his Junior Deputy Program to inspire and teach the idle and mischievous-inclined black youth. On the other hand, Sheriff Gilmore can be a bit cautious, too. He once declined an invitation to attend a white church service when his presence on the occasion might have been helpful.

But who knows? I mean, it could happen on the golf course. Back in 1968 when whites controlled the county they began construction of a nine-hole golf course two miles outside of Eutaw. Then, under the black regime, the golf course was completed. It is now owned and operated by the black county government, but it is used much more by whites. Indeed, it is an important amenity in the lives of many whites: housewives, retired executives and military folk who have found Greene County a good home. Former Sheriff Bill Lee plays every day in a foursome. My friend Ralph Banks gets away from his law office three or four times a week to play. Listening to the way people talked about that golf course, the devotion and interest they had for the course and the game, made me realize it is an overwhelming symbol of the hope of Greene County.

While it has been a white man's game, blacks are coming to use the course more and are showing a competence that demands respect. A kind of suspension of disbelief takes place on the links that makes golf a working metaphor for the larger games. It is possible that the Greene County Golf Course will provide a stage on which blacks and whites can act out their relationships under the forgiving spaciousness of the sky, within the wider horizons of the land. For all the overtones of elitist power structure deals made among the neat, stick-clicking cliques out there on the fairway, there is a ruthless accountability in the game that humbles and, for an instant, tends to make folk equal.

Greene County lies 40 miles west of the steel-mill smoke of Birmingham, 32 miles south of Tuscaloosa, home of the University of Alabama, and past two brick silos painted like Schlitz beer cans. Some call it the middle of nowhere. The Greene County Chamber of Commerce, back when it had self-confidence, called it "the cross roads to everywhere."

Driving south out of the neon-gaudy highways around Tuscaloosa into lonely and uncluttered Greene County is like going from Technicolor into black and white. The town of Eutaw, with its Victorian and antebellum houses, has the effect of faded dignity like some grainy newsreel of visiting European royalty before World War I. Before the Civil War the county was rich with thriving fields of cotton and planters living in hilltop mansions. Today, most of the land has an idle look as it grows up in timber, or its hilly fields graze cattle. Little towns like Forkland and Boligee lie in weeds, half blind with memories, their empty brick stores baked in a Hopper light in the late day's sun. The flaking mansions that loom in silhouette are mostly unoccupied now. They are preserved as grand architectural examples of the culture that existed over a century ago when cotton was king. With names like Rosemount, Thornhill, Kirkwood, they are still honored by local ladies' societies and their Carrara marble mantels and walnut balustrades still bring soft in-takes of breath from tourists on the spring Pilgrimage of Homes.

Since the beginning of the 20th century Greene County has lived with a sense of slow doom, of time running out. In 1900 the population of the county was 20,000. It decreased every census and today is stable at 10,000. In slavery times it was the largest county in Alabama in population. Today it is the smallest in population and land area (it was divided up) and the second poorest in per capita income. A few industries have come in successfully in the past decade but others have failed. A group of Midwest farm entrepreneurs went broke in the 1960s trying to turn the gumbo soil of Greene County into a major soybean producer.

Yet, for those who read signs, there were also hints that Greene County might be preparing for some new destiny. One of these came out of a great personal tragedy in the early 1960s when Jamie O. Banks lost his wife in a fire that also destroyed their home. For a while there was talk that Jamie Banks might leave the county. If he did the county would suffer from the neglect of absentee ownership because Jamie Banks, now in his early 40s, owns more land and has more economic power than any other one individual in the county. He is head of Banks and Co., the family business established in 1889, and he is chairman of the board of the Merchants and Farmers Bank, the only bank in town. Jamie Banks is a hearty, bluff, likable man who works hard, dresses sharp and likes to travel about the world when he takes time off. As a child he showed a sharp trading instinct to the delight of his grandfather J. O. Banks Jr., after whom he is named. Jamie Banks decided not to move and, eventually, he married again and built a new home.

"I know a lot of people around here were reassured when Jamie built his house back," said an older man who moved to Greene County in the 1920s in search of opportunity. "They felt like if Jamie Banks stays it means he is committed to the future of the county."

But, it happens, there are a number of men in the community who feel Jamie is also very unprogressive. "He can always figure out why not to do something," one of them said.

Jamie is the key man people look to for leadership in getting new industry. He insists he tries but he seems to come up way short on imagination.

"We just don't know what else to do," he shrugs.

Once he and Judge Branch made a trip to Birmingham on an industry-seeking trip which, like others, turned out to be too little too late. Driving home along the miles of unproductive land, Judge Branch asked casually:

"Who you reckon owns this land along here?"

"This?" replied Jamie. "This along here . . . I own it."

They drove a few miles and Branch again wondered aloud who owned the land they were now passing.

"Well, that's some of mine too," said Jamie. "Yessir . . ."

And, once more, after a long silence and many miles of unused land Branch inquired and Jamie nodded it was his.

"Jamie," said Judge Branch, his voice rising in that singy, disarming way he uses with whites (criticized by some blacks as Uncle Tomish), "you better change your ways or you gonna burn in hell. When you die the Lord's gonna say 'I was hungry and you fed me not. I needed shelter and you left me out!' " Judge Branch was not dismayed by the amount of land owned by one man; it was that the land was idle when he knew there were thousands of unemployed blacks who might work the land.

To some young business-minded men in town Jamie is only one of a whole class of old family people who are holding back progress. "They've got their land and they've got their money and they've got their way of life and they're not interested in anything else."

For the handful of families at the top of the caste system, names like the Banks or the Rogers, this way of life would appear to be remarkably agreeable. They dwell in cool, tasteful and fiercely symmetrical homes set back in pine shade and well-tended gardens. The social ceremonials have not been touched by the new black political order. These people stay enormously busy with business, committee meetings, suppers, Heart Fund drives, bridge games, Army Reserve drills. The men come home in mid-day for "dinner" with their wives. ("Supper" is the evening meal.) The ladies take to heart what they learn in church study groups and are equally attentive to their appointments at the beauty parlor and dates for golf. In due season the men take off to hunt and fish. Trips to Tuscaloosa or Birmingham to shop or for a movie and a meal at a good restaurant come more frequently than the special vacation trips to New Orleans or New York or Europe. Football weekends and lavish expeditions to watch Bear Bryant's Crimson Tide play the inevitable bowl games are high points on the calendar. Christmas holidays are shiny with sacred services and the secular clinking of cocktails.

Now-a-days, a quiet tension runs through much of the social ceremonial. That old sense of the slow tolling of a bell marking the last days has given way to a confusion with the arrival of a new order that cannot be absorbed. The most diligent attention to social ritual cannot always obliterate the anguish. Indeed, at times it almost seems that some insist on celebrating the negative.

At 9 o'clock every weekday morning, promptly and unfailingly, Jamie Banks and his brother Phil, a quiet, decent, perpetually vexed man, walk down the wooden floored aisle of Banks and Co., their footsteps muffled by the thick racks of soft-goods merchandise, out the front door and down the square to Jimmy's Restaurant where they are joined for coffee by friends varying in number up to eight. Bradly Brown, manager of the Cotton Patch Restaurant—a famous evening eating place outside town—is usually there. And Peter McLean, a huge, shrewd-eyed dairy farmer. McLean has a regular thing of his own, too, a Thursday afternoon dice game out at his farm. It was robbed two years ago by masked bandits who went off with several thousand dollars.

The main function of this 9 o'clock coffee session seems to be for these white men to reassure each other that things *are* going to the dogs. Out of the specific topics such as land prices, beef market, government programs, and sorry labor come generalizations on the decline of values, the breakdown of discipline and the work ethic and, in general, despair over forces seeking to corrupt the cherished way. "Nigras" or, sometimes "niggers" come out to be a major cause and symbol of their woes.

Ralph Banks never joins his two younger brothers at Jimmy's Restaurant for 9 o'clock coffee. At that hour he is checking the morning mail at his cluttered office across the street from the courthouse, or whipping across the street to the sheriff's office, or lining up appointments with county committees, talking to Judge Branch. Ralph Banks, it turns out, is county attorney and deputy circuit solicitor which means he has constant business with Judge Branch and Sheriff Gilmore. Around 10 o'clock Ralph usually goes across the hall from the sheriff's office on the ground floor of the courthouse and gets his friend the county tax assessor, Breck Rogers, to join him for a cup of coffee, usually over in Ralph's office. Breckenridge A. B. Rogers is 37, white, and, like Ralph, a certified aristocrat from one of the top county families. He has a wife and kids, a clean college face and a sense of whimsy which he hides behind serious-rimmed glasses and an unconvincing, arms-length, innocent politeness. That Breck and Ralph have daily coffee together, usually alone, and have become friends has a symbolic significance neither of them would like to admit. For, as fellow conservative white Southerners, they would not like the idea that they are carriers of the hope of some kind of coalition politics between white and black in Greene County.

They both came to this uneasy position accidentally. Breck Rogers was securely ensconced as tax assessor during the time blacks were developing their political power and their political party—called National Democratic Party of Alabama. Then, in 1972, after blacks had clearly shown their power at the polls, it came time for Breck to run for re-election. Blacks came to him and asked him to run on their NDPA ticket. Breck agreed to do so, knowing they would run a candidate against him if he did not, but also knowing that he risked scorn from his fellow whites if he did. NDPA was still—and is still—anathema to most whites. There really wasn't much choice since Breck wanted the job. But there was *some* choice and the decision he made could end up being significant when the history of these times is written. The only thing that would keep it from being very significant is the fact that Ralph Banks had already opened up that territory to tolerance two years before.

Ralph Roundtree Banks Jr. is the oldest son of Miss Sarah (Mrs. Ralph) Banks, the grand dame of the Banks family and of Eutaw. (Her husband, father of Ralph, Phil and Jamie, died in 1959.) Ralph, now 49, is a high-strung, chain-smoking, spare man with a quick wit and a quick temper. He is an intellectual and an aristocrat and, in the tradition of both these types, has the dowdy sartorial instincts of a ferry boat captain or a police reporter. He is a hurrying, scurrying, restless man who is totally at peace with his chosen profession, the law. He is a loner, but one who loves the comradeship of a friend with a bottle after hours. He has a mean streak, but is also a compassionate man and as relentlessly fair-minded as a Roman when it comes to the law.

"It's the Law," he will insist in an argument, his voice rising on the word "law" like an exegete trying to convince the world of the ultimate answer.

If Ralph Banks had been called to the stage instead of the bar he could have won parts playing the role of President Andrew Jackson, a man Ralph hates because of Jackson's inhumane treatment of the Indians. Ralph has the same long jaw, high forehead, ruddy cheeks and intensity of expression with its flickering hints of storm. He talks with rapid-fire logic, his mind clicking like pool balls searching for pockets after the break. His eyes dart to the side as if to check something that just flashed across his peripheral vision. He moves about the county offices, seeming to pass through walls and closed doors. His advice is needed at all times and in all places in the county government and he gives it, quickly and surely, out of a profound knowledge of the law and the lore of the county.

Blacks in general do not trust Ralph Banks. He does not go out of his way to inspire their confidence. Neither his pronunciations nor his inflection in pronouncing "Negro" nor his sparing use of courtesy titles reflect any change in attitude toward blacks from days before the civil rights movement. But then, he is a bit like Henry Higgins. He treats everybody alike. He has the same harsh exactitude toward whites, especially in matters of law.

But there is a special significance about Ralph Banks that no one in Greene County seems to realize. Including Ralph Banks. For years he was the chief strategist of resistance to black political ascendency. It was his high dedication to prevent William Branch and Tom Gilmore from winning power over whites. Through those years of conflict he developed a genuine hostility toward them and felt the same from them toward him. Then, after the final black victory in November, 1970, Judge Branch asked Ralph to become county attorney, a position he had held off and on over the years. Ralph blinked in astonishment.

"Are you out of your mind?" he scowled at the new black judge. "I have fought you tooth and nail for five years . . ."

"Indeed so," said Judge Branch who is also a preacher and a man who can cast a conflict in large, forgiving tones. "But I would like you to consider staying as part of the county government . . ."

Ralph tried the idea out with a number of key whites whose opinion he respected and they almost all agreed it would be a helpful thing, not only to the inexperienced blacks but helpful for whites to have one of their own in there watching after their interests. So Ralph stayed with the county—both as county attorney and deputy circuit solicitor.

It was not particularly heroic of Ralph to accept these county jobs. He would draw a healthy salary from the positions—around $600 a month—with a generous retirement from the state for a few more years of county service. He would be doing what he loved and did well. He was independent enough and socially secure enough to ignore the criticisms that did come from some whites who preferred the strategy of "let 'em mess up and we'll take back over." But because Ralph Banks stayed and worked with the black administration, the possibility was opened for future cooperation by other whites, making it somehow acceptable. Breck Rogers' decision to run on the NDPA ticket was much easier to make because of Ralph Banks. And when white-black political coalitions begin, it will be because Ralph Banks was there, keeping the lines open.

(As a matter of fact, Ralph Banks recognized the need for coalition politics even when fighting Branch and Gilmore. He helped invent the Spotted Horse Party in 1970 so blacks could vote for white candidates without having to pull the regular Democratic Party handle that had George Wallace, then running for governor, at the head of the ticket.)

Now, after more than two years as county attorney under Probate Judge Branch, Ralph Banks says, "Judge Branch is the least vindictive man I have ever known."

His feelings about Tom Gilmore go deeper than that. Through many long hours of association with the sheriff, working together on county cases, in court, and in many long, after-hours bull sessions, Ralph has come to admire Gilmore as a man of honor and imagination. They have a relationship that approaches a man-to-man friendship, transcending the traditional, structured racial friendships in the South.

When Gilmore asked Ralph if he would support him when he ran for re-election as sheriff, Ralph said, "Hell, Tom, I'll be your campaign manager."

Ralph has not really had to "change" to come to this relationship. He is still a conservative, an orthodox member of the social structure, husband and father of two (both off at college, one married). And it might sound equally static and circumscribed that the institution that means the most to Ralph Banks is the Episcopal Church. But therein is one of the surprises I found.

St. Stephen's Episcopal Church is a modest stone structure two blocks from the square, spaciously surrounded by some of the loveliest of the old white wood homes. Its congregation is a remarkable concentration of secular power. Most of the members have claim to prominence, wealth or influence. The leading families in the county—the Banks, the Rogers—are the controlling voices of St. Stephen's.

On Dec. 9, 1970, a month after the traumatic election of Gilmore and Branch which completed the black takeover, an historic meeting was held in the parish house of the church. The 20-member vestry—the ruling body—was there along with a representative teenager, Lucile Banks, the lively daughter of Phil Banks who was himself present. The main point of the meeting was to discuss the kind of new minister they would like to replace their beloved Rev. Ralph Kendall who was retiring the next spring. To help direct the discussion, the bishop in Birmingham had sent over a young clergyman named Bob Ross who was experienced in group dynamics and sensitivity techniques.

"I didn't want to go," Ross recalled later. "I figured it would be a conservative group that wouldn't want to change anything. But when I walked in that meeting I caught something. And they caught something."

It became apparent immediately, to the surprise of everyone, that they were all hungry for new, dynamic leadership and ideas. They were led by Ross to speak openly of their feelings of fear from the black take-over and, in general, the sense of decline and dying in the county. As Ross later wrote in his report to the bishop, he found "a general feeling of malaise connected with dwindling population, lack of vigorous people in their 20s and 30s, and boredom." He discerned "a general wish for excitement and hope."

With great skill Ross was able to summon up the hope, deep-buried though it was, and marshal it as antidote to the fear. He invited them to fantasize the kind of parish they would most want, and when "Cile" Banks brought up the idea of having a folk mass and said, "But y'all won't let us do that," Bob Ross, who had been listening to the unspoken mood, addressed "Cile": "Honey, it sounds to me like they're saying they will let you . . . if you'll listen."

And, in ways some of the members still remember and remark, they did listen to each other that afternoon. From that meeting they agreed on the kind of new minister they wanted. And, to a stunning degree, they got exactly such a man in David Veal, a plump, pleasant, brilliant, 35-year-old man who was just finishing up theological seminary at Sewanee, Tenn.

David Veal gives a first impression of a man mild and smiling. But he is also deep and his smile is seen as what Sir Kenneth Clark called on Voltaire "the smile of reason." Except David Veal's heart is less with the 18th century enlightenment than it is with the cavalier spirit of the Stuart kings in 17th century England. He still hates Cromwell. He loves that Divine Right tradition of the Episcopal Church and fights to recover some of its grandeur from the dry and pinching puritanism that has come to dominate in the South. For something more important than shock value, David Veal will make a strong case for pornography in the company of important and highly shockable parishioners. He does it jokingly, of course. Yet they thought he must be joking when he said he voted for McGovern.

From the start everyone loved David. They didn't mind his being an admitted integrationist because he obviously did not have that bony sainthood, feverish quality that is the giveaway of an activist. In his plump and sure-footed way he broke through one sacred barrier after another. A few months after arriving he was host to Bishop Alphaeus Hamilton Zulu, a black, English-educated, conservative cleric from South Africa. It was almost exclusively members of St. Stephen's who made up the 20 or so whites in the audience for Bishop Zulu's public address at the courthouse.

Three months later, at ordination services when David Veal officially became a priest, he directly disobeyed the wishes of his senior warden by inviting the Rev. Branch and the Rev. Gilmore to participate. Only

Branch showed up, looking impressive in his scarlet-trimmed robes. The senior warden made a special point of welcoming Judge Branch and kneeling next to him during communion.

Somehow, because he is at once firm and unthreatening, David Veal came to be a source of strength for a number of people in Eutaw who felt the need to break out of the tight and orthodox expectancies. One young white family with enough money to send their children to the private school elected to send them to the public school and David Veal, in a quiet way, gave crucial, if silent, support to them in this lonely decision. And, because David Veal was there, I think, it gave courage to Eugene Johnston to push forward on his perilous course of being a Christian. (Veal left for a church in Texas in 1973. After months of searching, the vestry found a new man in January 1974.)

Eugene Johnston is the man who was so disturbed about the possibility of integration in 1965 that he started the move that led to the establishment of the Warrior Academy, the all-white private school. I noticed him my first night in Eutaw. He and his wife came to the hotel restaurant to try the boiled shrimp that was the Tuesday night special. I noticed them because, of the hundreds of married couples I see in restaurants as I have traveled about the South, they were one of those few who seemed to be truly alive to each other. There was also a vulnerable quality about them: she with her fragile, wispy sincerity, he with boyish blue eyes, chubby, sun-tanned face. I got to know Eugene best out of all the people in Greene County. He was least afraid of what I was about. But his openness came more from the fact that he was probably the only man there with any real, existential courage. He is the manager of the Greene County Golf Course and always seems involved in some elaborate scheme, the ultimate point of which is to "increase communications between people." Some regard him as a wacky sort of busybody. He doesn't mind.

"I have a gimmick," he explained, looking out of his wide-set eyes with a curiously innocent intensity. "I have been without a job. Do you understand?"

He was out of a job for two-and-a-half years and received a lot of criticism. He also went through a conversion experience and, as he puts it, "made the decision to take the Lord's Prayer seriously."

Eugene Johnston, 42, was raised in Selma, Ala., in the upper-middle class, enjoyed the typical warm but hierarchical relationship with Negroes. He went to the U. S. Naval Academy, married Mary Lou Off, a graduate of Goucher, received a medical discharge from the Navy and ended up back in Alabama in 1960. He showed himself to be a kind of natural engineering genius by designing and supervising the building of a soybean and fertilizer plant for a farm cooperative called Centrala in the south part of Greene County. The growing civil rights movement stirred labor troubles at his plant and, for a while, Eugene kept a pistol on the seat of his car. He was plant manager of Centrala when the question came up of whether Negro farmers should be allowed to be members of the co-op. At first Eugene was neutral on the question. The co-op president pointed out to Eugene that a Negro in the membership could, at least theoretically, mean his having a black boss. With that news, Eugene firmly opposed black membership. The idea of a black boss was unacceptable. Eugene became concerned about the threat of blacks to all areas of life. That's when he organized the effort to start a private school.

Then he lost his job. During the next few years he attended several communications conferences put on by the Episcopal Church where full-scale sensitivity training techniques were used - the touching and shouting and weeping and growing.

"They were strong medicine," he says. He began to open up in ways he had never dared to before.

He began to rethink his traditional attitude on race. When the job of golf course manager opened, he had reached the point where he could go to Judge Branch and the black county commission and ask them for the job. Black men would be his bosses.

"All at once the roles were reversed," he explained. "All my life I had looked down on the black man. Now I had to consider him at least an equal. You can't look down on somebody you're asking for a job."

He remembers well the day he started walking from his home toward the town square to ask for the job. A friend pulled up in a car.

"Where are you going?" the friend called out.

"Well, would you believe I'm going up here and ask Judge Branch to give me that job out at the golf course?"

"Eugene! You're kidding."

"I am not. I need the job. How about giving me a ride."

"Hell no," said the friend in genuine anger. "And I hope you don't get the job."

Eugene got the job; he learned to play the game, and he set about to get blacks and whites involved and in communication. He is still trying. He feels his job depends on it, for one thing. Whites make up nearly 90 percent of the habitual users of the golf course, but blacks, in effect, own and operate it. More important is the rightness of enlarging communications. He put together a greens committee, a semiformal advisory body to help him in setting up programs and running the golf course. This is perilous work and it has been very tricky just getting whites and blacks to agree to serve on the committee. (The percentage of each race, for example, required elaborate diplomacy and negotiation.)

On the night of Feb. 27, 1973, the greens committee met in the brightly lit, sterile conference room in city hall. Six whites, three blacks. Eugene sat at the head of the long table with a yellow pad full of notes. The friendly informality was a bit restrained. As the meeting went on, phrases like "we seem to be divided" and occasional brief flare-ups kept a quality of animosity in the air.

Eugene, going down his list, told of taking a group of high school golfers from Warrior Academy up to Tuscaloosa to meet the golf coaches at the university to work up a summer golf clinic for students.

"That's very nice," said E. W. Underwood, a fretful, reserved black man at the far end of the table. "But it sounds like you're kind of one-sided. How come you just took the white up there? Why didn't you take some black?"

"Because they didn't ask!" the sharp voice came from J. E. Gay, retired manager of the local Alabama Power office.

"I'd like him to answer the question," Underwood replied and the air bristled.

Eugene came forward in his chair, his face calm, alert. He planted his elbow far out on the table, pointed an open palm at the whole group, fingers extended like a hypnotist. Slowly the atmosphere calmed and the attention swung to Eugene.

He couldn't have asked for a better opening to describe his elaborate plans for a golf program in the public schools as well as the white private academy. And it also gave him a chance to air his own frustration in dealing with the black school superintendent, Robert Brown. Eugene revealed his annoyance at not being able to get an appointment with Brown inside of a week, with the failure of Brown to get the school coaches together as he had promised. Gay was not really listening. He was still smarting from what he considered a rudeness by Underwood.

The blacks on the greens committee, especially Underwood, approved of Eugene's efforts to start a program in the public schools. And, no doubt, they understood more of the political dynamics motivating Robert Brown than Eugene did. For it had been coming clear for some time to blacks that Superintendent Brown was emerging as a political force that might, in time, challenge Sheriff Gilmore and Branch by developing black vs. white strategies.

Brown had already shown himself willing to use his power as school superintendent in traditional political ways, like ordering the milk contract to be switched to a company represented by a political crony, or asking teachers for contributions for political campaigns and keeping a list of who gives and who does not.

Gay, uninterested in all this, brooded for days over Underwood's remark at the meeting. "I'm just not going to put up with that kind of thing," he told his golf buddies out at the pro shop.

Eugene may not have understood Robert Brown. But Brown was a challenge to Eugene. From his encounters with the superintendent, Eugene saw Brown as a man uptight. This was something Eugene did understand. He made a special appointment to talk to Brown with the idea of offering to help with some advice about management techniques. Eugene has a master's degree in industrial management. He wanted to show Brown how helpful it is in management to deal more openly with problems. Eugene finally got his interview with Brown but he received only a polite, passive listening.

Robert Brown is clearly interested in politics. Politics and sensitivity training don't mix. They are involved with different goals. Political power requires an intense concentration and carefulness. Sensitivity work encourages a spontaneity and an honesty of feeling that are exceedingly dangerous in politics. There are times when Robert Brown's political strategies appear to damage examples of rare and beautiful biracial harmony.

The PTA of the Middle Grade School in Eutaw, for example, has produced a model of biracial cooperation. Yet because the president of the PTA, a mild-mannered black man named David Spencer, appears to be a potential political threat, groups of blacks who are political associates of Robert Brown's began showing up at the PTA meetings, challenging Spencer's authority, creating divisions and factionalism.

There is a new, hopeful element present in that PTA that is likely to survive. It is a fresh, strong, unselfconscious spirit altogether outside the ken of Ralph Banks or Breck Rogers or even Eugene Johnston. It is the open and feisty involvement of a few working-class whites, traditionally the bitterest foes of blacks, with the black parents at Middle Grade. Greene County does not have many working-class whites and most of those managed to get their kids into the Warrior Academy. So those four or five poor white families who have their kids at the predominantly black school are not typical. But neither are they passive, forlorn victims. They are vigorous, scrappy participants, wholly inspired by the native leadership of one of their group named Betty Jones, a truck driver's wife with three beautiful children at Middle Grade. At first she and her husband Sparky tried to get their kids in Warrior Academy. They didn't have the money so they tried for a scholarship which is usually available to keep working-class whites from breaking caste. But, in the process Sparky and Betty Jones felt they were being snooted.

"He jes' turned away and wouldn't sign the paper," Betty related of the time they tried to get the final signature for the scholarship. "So we jes' said, well, to hell with you, and we come over here and put 'em in Middle Grade."

Betty Jones is a salty, angular, country-twangy, hotdiggity-dog kind of woman with endless energy and a Chaucerian breadth of spirit. Her eyes glitter in tight new moons of merriment when she tells the saga of "them lockers."

"Well, we seen there weren't no way for them kids to leave their books and coats and things at school. They'd have to drag 'em all home ever' day. So we said, OK, we going to get us some lockers. . ."

And for 18 months, white and black parents assaulted the problem of raising money for lockers. They put on cake bakes and attic sales and advertised each event as widely as possible.

"I even went to Birmingham to get Country Boy Eddie to talk about our cake bake on his radio program. Well, this man heard Country Boy Eddie talking about us needing lockers and he called up and offered us some second-hand. They'd been used in the dressing room of coal miners."

Even this good luck presented problems which led to Steinbeckian trips to Birmingham in battered, blue-smoking cars to tie the huge metal lockers precariously into the car trunks.

The final and successful conclusion of this project took place while I was in the county. And my last full day in town coincided with the PTA meeting at which Betty Jones and her committee were to proudly present the lockers. There was some uneasiness that something could happen to spoil the occasion. Only a few days before, Superintendent Brown had tossed in some arbitrary ruling that, if allowed to stand, would have delayed the presentation. That was worked out but there were fears the group challenging David Spencer might show up and disrupt the triumphant moment.

This last full day for me in Greene County was Ash Wednesday. It was one of God's most beautiful days. The sky was open and soft blue and everywhere were blooming golden jonquils, redbud, flowering quince and narcissus with hints of azalea and dogwood to come soon. The golf greens winked like jewels. Eugene Johnston, on this day, was able to persuade Sheriff Gilmore to come out to the golf course for the first time. The sheriff swore he had never before swung at a golf ball as he stepped up and clicked off a fine drive after brief instructions from Eugene. Unfortunately, the moment was marred when Eugene used his traditional pronunciation of "nigra" and the sheriff called him down about it and Eugene insisted on his right to his natural pronunciation instead of an awkward "Kneegrow." They agreed "black" would suffice but the two men did not make progress toward the larger perspective.

I had a brief, pleasant interview with Mrs. Sarah Banks over tea and cheese wafers in her cool, elegant living room with its large portraits, Williamsburg hurricane lamp and delicate porcelain figurines.

"Yes, people were afraid," she said of those times before the unthinkable had come to pass. "They thought the bottom was going to drop out, that it would be like living through Reconstruction again."

But we did not talk much of the present or the future. Conversation flowed more easily on talk of travel and family history.

That evening I attended a meeting of the Greene County Chamber of Commerce. It had not met for four months and was coming together to decide if the organization should continue. The industrial development picture was still dismal. But there was the feeling that the effort had to continue.

"I just don't understand where we're missing," Breck Rogers exploded after half an hour of the group spitting out the butt ends of many industrial prospects that had come to nothing. "We've got the transportation, and water. We have an industrial park, an airport. Interstate 59 connects us to everything. We must be doing something wrong. You drive up through Tennessee and every little town has industry with grounds just manicured to a tee. . . . I just don't understand."

"What we need," said Haynie Williams, present manager of the Alabama Power Co., "is some new ideas."

"Why don't we find somebody who can tell us the kind of things we need to do," offered Oscar Williams, a black man with long sideburns. There was a silence. If Jamie Banks had, at that moment, remembered the experience of St. Stephen's when Bob Ross came in and helped them understand their needs and express them, it might have saved Greene County years of unnecessary struggle. There are men only 32 miles away in Tuscaloosa at the University of Alabama who could do for the Chamber of Commerce what Bob Ross did for St. Stephen's. But Jamie Banks, the key leader in any such effort, was not thinking in those terms. Instead, he thought it might be time for his old joke about Levi Morrow's one-time bootlegging. Morrow is black, an elected member of the county commissioners, and he was present as a member of the chamber.

"Maybe we can find some way to legalize old Levi," said Jamie, chuckling.

"Ah, now . . ." Levi muttered, having long since wearied of the joke about this part of his past.

While this meeting was going on, so was the one of the PTA at Middle Grade school. To the relief of those present, the faction of dissidents, for some reason, did not show up. So, in flowing good will, the group congratulated themselves on the successful conclusion of the monumental locker project—they had some of the lockers on display in the meeting room - and talked of holding a dance or a tea. O. B. Harris, a round and pleasant black businessman who had come to the rescue at the last minute with some needed money to finish the locker payment, asked for the floor. (Harris, years ago, had instituted a voter-registration drive among blacks before the movement ever existed, and he was dubbed an Uncle Tom by the movement when he opposed its coming into Greene. He says he is going to write a book someday called *Uncle Tom Speaks Out*.) At the PTA meeting he rose to make his contribution to the interpretation of the problem in Greene County and its possible solution by reading a poem by Edwin Markham:

> He drew a circle that shut me out
> Heretic, rebel, a thing to flout.
> But love and I had the wit to win:
> We drew a circle that took him in.

When the meeting was over, O. B. Harris drove by the concrete-block church where the movement had begun in 1965. The lights were on and the sounds of a meeting came out as Harris parked and went in. Here were the people who had not come to challenge the PTA meeting. They were meeting in the church to organize a new local chapter of SCLC. Harris spoke to the meeting, trying to cool the idea of such a new organization, feeling that it meant a new effort to stir the spirit of antipathy between black and white.

"I was too late," he said later. "They were already talking about boycotts and legal defense funds."

Greene County, and especially its center, the town of Eutaw, is facing one of the most interesting futures in America. The myth of the small town as a place for the good life has never been wholly true. Provincial attitudes have always inhibited the larger scope of thought and action, whether in New England, the Midwest or the Texas Panhandle. But in Greene County, unlike most other places in the South where blacks have taken political power (Hancock County, Ga.; Fayette, Miss., etc.), the blacks have made it possible for whites to cooperate, and whites have not officially withdrawn behind a line of perpetual hostility. The forces of self-interest seem to be working toward a broader view.

Tom Gilmore left Alabama when he was a young man and went to California where he found racism as bad if not worse than he had known in Alabama. He told his wife, "If it's this way all over we just as well go home. A man's got to have a home and, hell, we know what it's like there."

Another time he said, half to himself, half to me, "People are always in search of some mystical place . . . ."

His tone suggested that the mystical place does not exist. But it was also saying maybe . . . And Tom Gilmore has done his part to make Greene County some such land. He waits, and hopes.

The Rev. Bob Ross, a man who has a grasp of how the inner force in people can shape the outer space, said recently, "If racial accord ever occurs in the United States, Greene County will be the first place . . . ."

***

Esquire **magazine**
February 1977

To Love One Woman

GEESE ARE MONOGAMOUS; DUCKS ARE not. Humans—well. Used to be women *were*; men were *not*. Along came Jong and N.O.W. and today neither men nor women are considered designed by nature for one mate only.

Which may be so. But if it is, I come to tell you this: there are some people out here practicing unnatural acts. I don't mean married couples who are "faithful," who "do not play around" and who must rank with such specimens of the yawn as the Christian athlete and the volunteer community worker. Say the words "happily married" and the mind goes blank. Speak of "a loyal husband and wife" and you see an upright piano, complete with shawl and sheet music, a man with a parson's part in his hair who calls his trowel-puttering wife "dear." Sex is not hiding. It has been borne away by boredom.

No, I come to spill what goes on with a small, secret minority right in the toothpaste suburbs in the middle of the middle-aged middle class. Amid that cocktail chatter, clatter and alimony, there is a dark magic being practiced by certain married folk that needs a new verb. I herewith propose: *to monog.* Monogging is no kin to merely being faithful. And playing around is one of the things it mainly is.

I am a monogger. Monogging is basically subversive and antisocial. In Victorian times it cut at the very foundations of the family structure, threatening the doctrine of the separation of wife and mistress. But attitudes have broadened and today monogging is no real threat to society or to the G.N.P.; it is only a strange and quaint anachronism. Actually, I *believe* in monogging. If I could forget a basic truth—that monoggers are born, not made—I would be tempted to *promote* it. There is much to be said in its favor.

Monogging could be called the last frontier of American sex, the one kinky aberration still to be experimented with by the sexually chic. It is the basis of a style that is this country's equivalent to being continental—the farthest outpost of irony, the logical conclusion of savoir faire. The patron saint of monoggers is Fred Astaire.

Monoggers may be as rare as White Russians, but they are not elitists. I know from many conversations with admitted monoggers that they would love to convert others, would even write how-to books or articles if it would do any good. It wouldn't. Being a monogger is an accident of birth, fixed in the stars, beyond praise or blame. And the number of practicing monoggers in this country is far too small for them to consider imitating other minorities. It would never do for monoggers to come out of the closet, use political pressure, proclaim special days, picket, march and try to turn the country around. Economically, monoggers are about as weighty as cheese salesmen; politically, they couldn't outvote a block of oboe players.

Poet Robert Graves has a five-stanza poem that nails monoggers. It begins:

To love one woman, or to sit
Always beneath the same tall tree,
Argues a certain lack of wit
Two steps from imbecility.

I should say that most monoggers are sympathetic to divorce and often feel closer to divorceés in search of true love than to married couples who have died alive, sighing at utility bills. Of course, monoggers, being basically two-by-two people, are less attuned to divorce in search of the Real Me. Some of the liveliest monoggers I know are people in their second marriage.

One such couple, friends of ours—second marriage for both—played host for a small dinner party the other night for the naughty and clever Barbara Howar, who was in town promoting her book.

"Nobody I know in Washington is happily married," she declared at the end of the main course. Since she knows everybody who's anybody, well...The silence that followed had a quality that suddenly made me know at least two of the five couples present were monoggers. But, again, what could one say? *Qui s'excuse s'accuse.* The host and others began clearing off plates and by the time all but the host were back at the table Barbara was expounding further on marriage, which, despite her much celebrated bad one, she was not necessarily against.

"Sure, I would like to have someone in my corner," she said, as the sound from the pantry of the host scraping plates detonated her quick wit. "Or in the pantry scraping plates."

But we all felt she was speaking theoretically, that she felt the happy marriage (viz. monogging) existed only as romantic myth. Graves calls it miracle in the third verse:

Yet if, miraculously enough,
(And why set miracles apart?)
Woman and tree prove of a stuff
Wholly to glamour his wild heart?

Myth or miracle? I enter now the heart of this confession and the question becomes crucial. Is this a true confession, or one invented to make a point of higher truth? Are the details from my private life I am about to flash before you to be taken literally, or as the working out of a symbolic fantasy? I must proceed with the question open; this will give me at least a frail defense for my apparent violation of the stern law of monogging: Thou shalt not tell.

Let us say, then, that I am writing this in the mountains of north Georgia, in the cold, bright days of December, spending the month with Emily, my wife of twenty-seven years, in our summer place, built for a thousand Julys. Say that I am on a sabbatical from *Newsweek* magazine, where I have worked for nineteen years in the Atlanta bureau; and say that two of our four children are with us for part of this special time: Walter, twenty-two, whose life at present is roaming in Wyoming, and Anne, nineteen, who is on Christmas break from college.

Would you believe that we rise, these days, with the first ginger light, build a fire in the living room to begin the battle against the cold (helped later when the noon sun streams through windows); that Emily sets the smells of coffee and bacon going in the kitchen where we eat and I write at a large table, while I build a fire in the spunky little cast-iron stove called FATSO (on the lid) that we installed for this special time; that sometimes we tune the radio to a little early-morning gospel or country music; that more often we put on a record of Bach's *Magnificat*—or The Swingle Singers doing Bach—to accompany breakfast and the glassy winter sunrise, or The Beatles' *Abbey Road*, side two that begins with *Here Comes the Sun*, leaving the Duke, Ella and Artie Shaw for later in the day; that yesterday we made an expedition into the sleety woods to cut a Christmas tree that is now giving a spicy scent to the chill air of the living room; that it was twelve degrees this morning; that I heard a pipe pop?

And if you accept this setting will you let me describe Emily as I see her: a broad-browed and smiling brunette with short, often unmanageable hair, as lithe and light of step as when I first met her in World War II (I won't ask you to believe under the Biltmore clock, but it's true), cool as a schoolgirl lit with mischief, yet warm in the womanly ways of a world-famed mistress. I could go on and mention qualities from the likes of Julie Andrews, Erma Bombeck and Annie Dillard, but it would embarrass her and make you suspicious. So I will simply record here what she is saying as I type at the kitchen table while she is over there kneading dough.

"Lord, I love this . . .," she is talking idly half to herself, as she presses and shapes the fleshy lump. "It's so sensual. There's something eternal about it." She does not realize I am typing what she is saying—a direct quote, as we say in the news business. "It pulls at your womb...makes you feel at one with all the mothers who ever lived...Russian peasants... Jewish mothers...the mother of Jesus."

This—this unselfconscious hum of humor and poetry that flows from her when we are private—is part of the stuff that wholly glamours my heart. It comes out irrepressibly—the other day listening to music she began to laugh at the cellos that sounded like "old men at their club, smoking their cigars, deep in their dewlap [here she acts the part], harrumphing profundities"; or hearing a soprano so awful she said it was "like someone at an audition where even her mother is squirming....You see the judge holding his sinuses [pince-nez gesture, eyes closed in grave discomfort]: That'll be all, Miss Bowlump...don't call us."

She has a gift that only I receive: it brings from the day's doings, the supermarket and city sidewalk, Chaucerian tales of characters so vivid they remain in my head for years. In some stray dog or neighborhood waif she might see the comic grace of Jesus the clown; a whiskery panhandler is thought of as "old shipmate"; a skinflint bachelor acquaintance has lips that "look as if they were sewed together by the undertaker." And just this week she brought home from a trip to the village a gothic tale that only this mountain landscape could produce or she have the instinct to perceive.

...there was a wreck on the mountain road, the yellow flashing light, "that burnt electric smell of emergency that tightens the pores." A doleful crowd was peering over the steep embankment watching a totally wrecked car being winched up the rocky stubble. She noticed a pale, blond mountain youth standing along; he had been the driver and had escaped miraculously unscathed.

"I went over and stood beside him for a minute. I had this strange feeling he was a ghost, lingering to see the recovery of his mortal remains. He was one of those transparent mountain blonds with that pale unhealthy look that comes from eating white bread and being inbred...."

And if such visions from the void
As shone in fever there, or there,
Assemble, hold and are enjoyed
On climbing one familiar stair...?

The visions hold. They would for any man living with a woman who shouts at dried-up little towns driven through at midnight ("Pendergrass has gone to grass. Wake up, Pendergrass. Armageddon is coming!"); who may be saddened by Muzak, thinking of the anonymous musician, his cheap toupee, his fourth-story walk-up apartment, the metal edges on the rubber stair treads, the smell of gas in the dim hallway; who senses the lake freezing at night, "tightening its skin."

This, yes, is part of what glamours my heart, this gift of see and tell. But there is so much more. When *Newsweek* was doing a story on swinging singles, I had an exchange with a disciple of the *Playboy* philosophy who spoke of his commitment to "live life to the fullest," by which he meant sex in endless nightly encounters. "I knew a guy once who remembered one of the girls' names and he married her."

I tried to challenge him. "Would you admit that in even the most fleeting sexual encounter there is some ceremonial murmur of affection, some parody of love in your foreplay?"

"Well, sure," he shrugged. "If she likes that kind of thing. What's that prove?" Then he asked me his question. "With you, is there ever some fantasizing, some game playing of strangers in the night?"

I don't know what it proves, but *oh, wow*, if he only knew.

Now, if you are to believe any of this, I must say we have our problems, our fusses, our quick angers that sometimes leave low-grade sulking of silence and body English for a few days. There are even some deep doctrinal differences that rise on occasion, threatening the countryside. But I think mostly we figure we're pretty much on the same side against the beasts of the forests and need to help each other through the night.

Also you should know that one essential part of good monogging is to assume your partner is attractive enough to tempt a tempter or temptress. We enjoy talking about this, about the problems our would-be lovers will have catching on to our private literature. Emily knows I have an average American male's problem about blonds. Sometimes she says she wishes she were blond for me, with long, golden locks to lie in a tangle on the pillow. She can perfectly imitate the head toss and hooking of tresses behind the ears of a blond. But she also warns: "When you look deep into those blue eyes, look again. She is not staring into your soul; she is looking at her own reflection in your glasses."

Christmas has come and gone since I started writing this. Walter has gone now to climb the Grand Teton on New Year's Day. Anne left for New England to visit her other two brothers and friends. But they were here for Christmas morning. It was a real monoggers' affair. Before breakfast we had a sort of mock enactment of the children's stockings. Anne and Walter duly showed Betty Boop surprise at the tiny gifts and nuts and fruit candies Emily had assembled and tucked in stockings the night before. Then Emily remembered she had a bottle of champagne on ice. Why not have it now, before breakfast?! We love ceremonies, especially "traditional—once only" first and last annual affairs. We popped the cork and drank toasts—or were they blessings—to ourselves, our missing sons, to Santa Claus, the baby Jesus and all the blessed fallen and redeemed. Old FATSO was warming up the kitchen where we went light-footed and heady to breakfast. As we left the living room a young fire crackled healthily in the fireplace. I looked out of the window and saw, as I have done many times before, the reflection of the fire on the rhododendron outside. "Look," I said, "it's the burning bush." Emily looked and from where she stood the reflection hit the top of the distant hill. "It's a fire on the mountain!" she said.

Give Graves the last word:
To change and chance he took a vow,
As he thought fitting. None the less,
What of a phoenix on the bough,
Or a sole woman's fatefulness?

***

The Quill
The Magazine for ΣΔΧ
May 1977

What the News Muse Knows

WHAT DOES THE HANGMAN SAY to his daughter, the poet asks.

And you, reader and watcher of the news, might wish to ask me, a reporter, how it feels to be sitting, say, in the Plains Baptist Church when a strange black man—the Rev. Clennon King—comes forward for membership and a white man, a member of the church, stalks out with his two children shouting with understandable indignation at the TV cameras and the pack of reporters and photographers, "Why don't you leave us alone?"

I'll tell you how I felt; I wished I were up there singing in the choir, obscure, contributing, otherwise involved than as sneak-peek outsider.

And yet, I wouldn't have missed it for the world. I am in the news business. I work for "the Newsweek," as George Wallace used to call us, and in 20 years of covering my native South I have come to realize that those are the moments that count. The news is not a business. It is a household god that has dominion over the basic human need to know what's happening, and it functions—happenstantially—to keep people, churches, regions, towns, countries and institutions from getting too isolated, becoming too self-absorbed. As a minor muse News will never rank with the elegant Nine. News tends to die each day and, like the paper it's printed on, be blown about alleyways, be rumpled by idle old men in the lobbies of seedy hotels, buried in dark musty reference rooms, smoldering, fermenting, growing venerable. When it emerges, is born again as a book, ah, then it is well-behaved enough to belong to Clio, the Muse of History. But, in its living form News the Muse is a hobo, a disruptive, insensitive, impudent deity, basically amoral for all its righteous pretensions, its pompous underdogisms.

But it is essential and what it does, without meaning to, is connect all people of the world so that they are never total strangers. The interest of the millions plays across the action of the few. And whether that interest be lurid, prurient or noble, in the long run it is a cleansing thing. For an average citizen to suddenly be part of the news—like that father in Plains, like Patty Hearst—must be like swimming in the ocean—the sensation of knowing that all the salty seas of the world are in direct contact with you, are aware of, care about but don't really care about you. Send not to know for whom the bell tolls…

As Mr. Bumble in Dickens says "the law, sir, is a ass," you might say "the news, sir, is a agitator," and I would reply "yer right." It doesn't mean to be—it's not supposed to be. But it is, and that's where it is finally: health-giving. And as essential to the body politic as oxygen or white corpuscles are to the human body. I perceive news as part of the life cycle, one small function in the process wherein societies live, grow, decay, die, or are renewed. Some days my elusive Muse is like a bee, spreading pollen as it is sucking honey (or seeking flesh to sting). Other days it comes like a cloven hoof, breaking up the crust that forms on dried-out cultures; or lightning that jolts new blood into hardened arteries in an old order grown bored and moribund. On the other hand: there is a white pine I know that grows beside a wide meadow. Day and night, summer and winter winds buffet the tree—cold, icy winds, dry, hot winds. That tree is thick and green and richly healthy. So, at times, News-the-Disrupter will bring about a reassertion of good tradition; will cause the strengthening of some ancient set of values that only needed to be blown about a bit. Of course, I have seen the news destroy good things and people. And this tears me up. But white corpuscles are not less vital even though they are the unbalance in leukemia.

News. I mean Big News. Big Bad News generally—encounter, conflict, achievement or behavior that stirs the gossip interest of the nation, the world. News that sweeps into town with major TV network logos, semi-famous newsmen, the names of national news services, magazines, the big-city dailies. Priests and acolytes of the News Muse. They bring in an air of danger and excitement like an army of friendlies whose presence is a threat to the established tempo of the town and to the virtue of restless daughters. The News in this form is a gruff Music Man conning the susceptible locals with the implication that there's a world out there beyond Yonkers.

Such an invasion took place in my home town, Augusta, Ga., in 1952 when Dwight Eisenhower was elected president and came to play golf and rest at the Augusta National Golf Club. There I was, peacefully selling cement and flue lining in my uncle's building supply business. Suddenly my old hangout, the Bon Air Hotel, was alive with these strange, shaggy, intense people—the White House press corps. They seemed gnarled and battered, rootless and restless, yet burning and crankily companionable like condemned men trying desperately to realize all the details of the world; or have one last drunken laugh with friends.

Now, I didn't respond like some excitable little cripple, some flushed Amahl saying "take me along." The News Muse works slowly. But there was a connection between that first impression I had and the chain of events that led me into my career in news a few years later. My brother-in-law, on the other hand, was a promising young reporter for the Augusta Chronicle at the time. He spent some time with the cream of the nation's press corps. At a party in Augusta on Christmas day, when Marvin Arrowsmith told how, yes, he had managed to see his family two days before, my brother-in-law got his own chain of events going that led him out of news into a respected career in business.

But the extraordinary time when the News came among us in the South was during the civil rights movement. And, in the privacy of our invasion, we encountered not only the world's press but armies of the righteous—students, priests, radicals, politicians. The movement was homegrown to start with and then a lot of Southerners got caught up in events and found their lives changed dramatically from that time forward. I know many a white lawyer, black preachers, redneck and college girl who found they had to respond to the moral questions raised by the movement and do some serious thinking about themselves, their lives, the United States Constitution, the meaning of Christianity. Many today are walking around carrying in their hearts permanent wounds or trophies because of their response to the conflict and challenge of those times.

But the larger effect of that news time was less dramatic. The effect, as inadvertent as it was inevitable, was to soften among Southerners the hostile sense of "outsider," to enlarge the circle that sets off "us" from "them." Major changes happen slowly, quietly. For years segregation in the South was a sacred doctrine, upheld not only be law but by Belief (and confirmed by demagogic politicians). Now it is hard to remember it ever existed. Not that all racial troubles are over. But they are not being fought out in that old context.

The News Muse is not a reformer. It only knows that most people are not really interested in manning barricades as long as they can keep up with what's going on.

That may not seem much. But it is.

***

Atlanta **magazine**
September 1979

So Long, Downtown

NEWCOMERS MIGHT NOT APPRECIATE HOW lucky they are just to move here without becoming a symbol like poor Mr. Million. Mr. Million was a man transferred by his company from Ohio to Atlanta. Then Fate and the Atlanta Chamber of Commerce picked him to represent the one millionth citizen in the Metro Atlanta area.

It was a demographic disaster. The man was showered with a game-show vulgarity of gifts and sent forth on a year-long tour of personal appearances. The spotlight was too much for him; before the year was up he had lost his job, his wife and his perspective. He left town pronouncing anathemas on Atlanta and the famous "Atlanta way."

My family and I moved to town without fanfare in 1957. We bought a house in Buckhead, near the bus line.

Sometimes I would catch the very early bus to town when daylight was just beginning. I could stand in the middle of the street and see downtown five miles away. In that velvety half-dark, the towers of Atlanta glittered like crown jewels, like the Emerald City in the Land of Oz.

I rode later buses, too: the standing-room only rush-hour bus with working girls all bingo bright and young lawyers dressed like Princeton grads. And sometimes I would catch the late morning bus of old folk—white-haired ladies going down to check out J.P. Allen's and Davison's; retired executives going to lunch at the Commerce Club for a life-giving whiff of the old battle smoke.

But those early bus rides through cold winter dawns were the most vivid. The bus would come winking 'round the bend up by St. Phillip's lullabying its sleepy cargo of night watchmen and nurses, all bundled up and going home. And there would be early birds like me, seeking the city at the fresh hour.

The city around seven is fresh, yes, but there is also a slam-bank sort of wildness too—delivery trucks bucking up to loading ramps, construction gangs shouting and cranking up monster machines. In the tattering night, before light slides down the glass towers, there is a brute stagehand efficiency at work getting the scene ready for the play acting of the day: man in watch cap, cigarette dangling from mouth, stashing the boxes with the morning street edition of *The Atlanta Constitution*; 'Little Orphan Clara' hefting up roll-front to the concession stand in the marble lobby; waxy-weary uniformed guard hauling in time clock and night table to freight elevator.

Lights first flutter on at the S&W around six. Aromas of coffee and bacon follow, as breakfasts begin at Woolworth's and on down the hill: Leroy's, Tasty Town, the Healey Building cafeteria. I used to sit with old man Tom Linder, former Secretary of Agriculture, at breakfast in the Healey Building. Once he took me to his office in the Flatiron Building to see his 14-year work covering the walls—his charts of the Book of Revelation complete with Armageddon, the Beast with Seven Heads and the Opening of the Seventh Seal.

The late bus rides home are both vivid and dreamlike in my memory. Often, I caught the bus after the street-sweeper crews had opened the fire hydrants so that water washed the day's litter down the storm sewers and sweetened the streets with the smell of rain. The bus, on the other hand, was still sticky with the day's accumulation of trash and grit. Coke bottles would be rolling around under the seats.

Somehow the bus on that late ride would become possessed by a will of its own, hurtling itself through the tunnel of darkness out West Peachtree, wind whistling at the windows, hitting bumps that would bounce the numbed passengers and the skin of dirt on the floor three or four inches in the air, lifting an abandoned section of the blue streak *Journal* off the floor to float like a lazy ghost in the middle air above the aisle.

I will miss those wild rides.

In those years the *Newsweek* office moved six times, following the march of progress. At first we were near the Fulton National Bank Building, the red brick building on Marietta Street by the statue of

Henry Grady. It was the tallest building in town from 1955 to 1961. Henry Grady Square seemed the center of things then. A sharp geometry of sunlight, the rush of pigeons rising across a crowd hurrying to make the light while the Fulton bell tower warbled down an electronic medley of old time gospel and Cole Porter tunes.

We moved eastward toward Five Points; then north, following the skyline up the hill, ending up at John Portman's acropolis, Peachtree Center.

In the still-Wintry earlier months of this year—when my own decision to make a change was fraught with uncertainties and peril—the city, too, seemed to be in a crisis of confidence in its midlife passage.

Reporter Robert Scheer's article in *The Los Angeles Times* appeared locally. It called Atlanta's downtown "a holding cell for society's rejects," except for the middle-class tourists and workers who were likened to gerbils, scurrying through their plastic tubes over streets, between buildings. Georgia-Pacific Corporation threatened to reconsider its plan to build a skyscraper for its headquarters in the heart of Downtown.

I found myself walking around looking at the city as if I were one of those nametagged conventioneers or camera-bearing tourists who looks us over with such bland curiosity.

And, as a stranger, separated from past knowledge and future hope, what I saw was a bombed-out city, a bleak landscape of cracked sidewalks and dead asphalt-paved parking lots. The ragged butt ends of small buildings lacked zest or connection with the isolated glamorous towers, which seemed drawn up defensively against the green space of Central City Park instead of proud possessors and protectors of it.

In the narrow cross streets, I kept encountering dead doorways, the smell of urine, alleys of broken wine bottles and old derelicts. The litter blowing about the cold streets seemed almost the result of a conscious effort of a citizen volunteer group out to keep our streets littered. This thought occurred when I saw the swift efficiency with which a man delivered his crumpled cigarette package to the pavement.

I felt Downtown drop below my security index of 26 percent. Security index is my private formula for the percent of sympathetic-looking people it takes to feel secure in a public crowd. The percent is about half your age and should not—but usually does—work around to be a racial thing.

I shifted perspective then and began to walk around not as a stranger but as one who has lived here for years.

That was even more depressing.

A whole civilization seemed to have vanished. I remembered the recent fire and demolition of the DeGive's Opera house. And I had photographed out of my Equitable office window the wrecking ball crumbling the Bank of Gibraltar to dust. I hummed Cole Porter (" . . . in time Gibraltar my crumble . . . ") as I clicked pictures of the firehouse plumes of water damping down the roiling nebula of dust.

But what had happened to the Dinkler Plaza with all its ambiance of political excitement? It had become a parking lot as blank of memory as a brickbat. It was hard to conjure up the old Town and Country restaurant with its winking owls and three-martini lunches which had occupied the same level of ground that was now flat asphalt behind a fence. Gone, too, was my old barber shop, named The Gay Nineties without fear of misinterpretation. It had a copy of that famous picture of a modest nude, *September Morn*. I did love it so. And Tanner's orange juice place on Pryor Street that had drawings of World War I airplane dogfights around the walls. The orange juice tasted of additives.

Street characters are always disappearing and materializing. But I did think of Fancis Brunton in my reminiscences. He went about the streets with globes of our world hung about him, lugging old newspapers and thick encyclopedias. When he left Atlanta—headed vaguely west—he gave Celestine Sibley a significant wink and said, "I think we've got the Lutherans sewed up."

Where the First National Bank is was a two-story, glass-roofed mall called the Peachtree Arcade. It was chic and cheery as the Crystal Palace, except by the early Sixties its smart millinery shops and fine jewelry stores had given way to home loans and hearing aid service centers.

But was there really a Piedmont Hotel of faded grandeur, with crystal chandeliers and marble lions' heads? And was there not—or did I dream—a clock shop somewhere nearby where dozens of fine wall clocks with pendulums ticked busily away like a German folk tale? And when the hour came, they all struck with their bings and plings and bongs until the room seemed like a pet shop of mechanical birds in rebellion.

The Piedmont Hotel occupied the block where the Equitable Building is now. In my walkabout, there was a chain link fence MARTA had put up in front of the Equitable Building that all but blocked the entrance to Thomas Cook Travel.

"Welcome to Stalag 17," said Barbara, who works at Thomas Cook. She sounded bitter.

There was a clattering explosion underground.

The days grew less Wintry and my career situation began to take shape. As I tended to errands around downtown, I would remember funny little things.

Like my friend who tried to open a checking account at the Federal Reserve Bank. When uniformed guards pointed shotguns at him, he considered that a serious breakdown in the Bank's understanding of customer relations had occurred.

Or the night of the presidential election in 1960. Bill Emerson, then-bureau chief for *Newsweek*, and I were calling in returns from our office in the C&S Bank Building when an explosion rattled the windows.

"I don't know what that was," said Bill after a few seconds of silence and wild surmise. "But I bet it exceeded somebody's expectation."

It did. The explosion was from a small brass cannon which Henry Grady, famed one-time editor of *The Atlanta Constitution*, had had made to be fired whenever the Democrats retook the White House. So, *Constitution* Publisher Ralph McGill and Editor Eugene Patterson took up the tradition with zeal. Such zeal in fact that the recoil of the thing banged McGill's shins, and the flare from the explosion singed his eyebrows.

Windows rattled in those days because windows opened in those days—opened to get the breeze in the spring; to toss down confetti on Richard Nixon in 1960; to toss paper airplanes out of; or, like my friend advertising executive E. Clayton Scofield, to see if it is possible to bounce a ball of art gum eraser on Cone Street from the eighth floor of the Walton Building so that it would clear the two-story house on the other side of Cone Street. Senior Partner Bill Neal in the same ad agency used the open window to shout at the Cone Street Garage attendant that, by damn, he'd better move Neal's red Oldsmobile off the roof and park it inside where he was paying them to park it.

And windows closed against sudden storms, the scream of the Grady ambulance, the raucous shouts I always took to be railroad men getting off the midnight shift, heading for the all-night Krystal on Marietta Street.

In memory the trivial and the important possess equal weight. I think of Lester Maddox inserting himself, red-faced, into a KKK confrontation with black picketers at Forsyth and Luckie streets, shouting nose-to-nose with a black over the relative merits of "Negro" vs. "nigra" as the pronunciation of the black race. This was before the word "black" obviated the issue.

And I think of how prankster banker Mills B. Lane Jr. could generally be reached by reporters at his office at six or seven o'clock in the morning. My image is of him sitting there (wearing his necktie with his slogan, "It's a wonderful world," written on it), his hands flat on the desk on either side of an opened, chilled bottle of Coca-Cola sitting on a blotter. Mills Lane got up earlier than anybody so he could think and plot ahead.

One April morning Mills left his office at eight and walked over to Ivan Allen's office and tossed a double-faced mailer on Allen's desk. It was a mailer asking people if they would like Allen to run for mayor. Ivan Allen describes the scene in his book, *Mayor: Notes on the Sixties.*

"Have you already printed these things?" Allen asked.

"Sure have," Mills answered.

"When did you think about it?"

"About four o'clock this morning."

"When did you print them?"

"About eight o'clock this morning."

"When will you mail them out?"

"They've already gone out."

Allen was first shocked to learn Mills had spent $11,000 on the mailing; then, as a C&S stockholder, Allen was relieved to learn Mills paid for it out of his own pocket.

Allen ran, was elected, and was one of Atlanta's great mayors for two terms. Maybe Atlanta's Pericles. With Mills' urging him on and putting up much of the front-end money, Ivan pushed the construction of the Atlanta stadium when the city had no major sport franchise signed up or lined up.

Atlanta always seems to elect the best mayor for the times. William Hartsfield was a giant, leading the city out of the Depression and through the first phase of racial politics. Ivan Allen was perfect for integrating public accommodations. The social elite couldn't ostracize him—he was the Grand Marshal of the Atlanta Debutante Club's Bal de Salut, the central social event of the year.

Sam Massell was young enough and hip enough as mayor to come down on the crazies around the 10th Street Strip area back in the stoned age in 1971. Bikers and dope heads had taken to shooting each other and generally making it difficult for conventioneers to drive by and gawk in peace.

Maynard Jackson will certainly be judged as the best man to be the first black mayor.

Spring became June. Good things began to happen about the future. For one thing, I signed on to do a weekly column for the Atlanta newspapers which would give me a once-a-week reason to go Downtown.

And I went Downtown in early June and happened to hit one of those clear, crisp, blue days, cool as a clarinet adlibbing in G. A school's-out-shout kind of day.

I walked about Downtown, suddenly taken with the theme of rebirth, Atlanta's phoenix symbol: new life out of the ashes. I had not noticed—in my winter ramblings—how many trees there now are Downtown. On this day their leaves were shaking themselves in light. Fountains plumed white in the sun exactly where the Bank of Gibraltar had crumbled. Central City Park at noon, by some miracle, seemed free of litter and full of pretty girls. My security index was well over 26 percent. But not too much over to be boring. There was jive and variety enough to keep the feeling of being alive. It was not quite like Rome as described by Juvenal, which was full of "audacious hucksters…hoarse-throated beggars…(where) one man digs an elbow into me, another a hard sedan-pole, one bangs a beam, another a wine cask against my head." Yet exciting enough to cry with Cicero of Rome: "The city, the city—residence elsewhere is mere eclipse."

How bootless to mope over things departed in a renewing world. If Tanner's has gone there is fresh, no-additive orange juice at Jus' Juice at a small window on the street in the Flatiron Building. Old man Tom

Linder is dead, now, and all his walls of Revelation are gone. But the Flatiron Building has been steam cleaned and spruced up with green awnings. I bought a cookie from The Cookie Works in the prow of the building.

Everywhere I went that day things seemed alive, attractive. The tall skyscrapers seemed part of the park space and struck a lively, playful relationship with the whimsically painted "city walls," the art on old buildings. The chain link fence was gone from the Equitable Building, and beds of marigolds were planted over the MARTA scar. Muse's window display had stylish accessories around a bale of hay in a let's-go-country theme. The brass hunting horn in Brooks Brothers was burnished to match the spic-and-span shine of the ornate brass doors of the elevators in the lobby of the Rhodes-Haverty Building.

And any marble lions I might lament from the Piedmont Hotel were more than matched by the veritable circus of sculpture that adorns the Candler Building, where gryphons, dolphins, dragons, lions, cherubs, seraphim and any number of members of the Candler family are all preserved in marble. And down in the basement of the Candler Building is my old barber shop, now called The Brass Chair, but featuring still my lady of *September Morn*.

It was such a magical day even Hosea Williams was polite leading his picketers in front of Church's Fried Chicken. "We appreciate your kindness very much…" he was saying through his bullhorn as I passed by.

Outside the Atlanta Newspaper Building, blacks were picketing for an end to "exploitation of black workers," which struck me as a sign of a sort of progress. In the Sixties they were marching just to get jobs.

Also, on the sidewalk outside the building was a white man with his head tilted way back, his eyes closed and clutching a Bible. He was wearing a shirt on which was printed in random patterns: "John One Ten." And he was whistling a shrill, lyrical bird song. And I thought, by God, Francis Brunton may be right. We may, indeed, have the Lutherans sewed up.

The lift and mood of this luminous day in early June led me to some new-old thoughts about a city and the necessity for it to have a center, a downtown. I have friends who say," Downtown is drying, taken over by tourists, government workers and blacks." And they retreat to the suburbs in search of that small town, neighborly communion, where you see friends and people in associated fields on the street, going to the bank, to lunch.

Trouble is, the office park where you go to get this might not turn out to be where it's happening. It might be ten miles further along the Perimeter or on the other side of town.

A town, a city, will have a center because that's almost what a city is; certainly it's where it starts. Sure, Atlanta's center could shift to Decatur, to Buckhead, to College Park. I have heard all these places argued as "the new center" of Atlanta.

My money is that downtown Atlanta will be the center. That's where the powers and the towers are. And in those towers are not only offices of marvelous grace, tastefully enriched with works of art, with antiques of great value, libraries and conference rooms that hum with big decisions, but there are also plans and models for new building, great parks, renovations of most of the sections of Downtown. There is even a plan for something called Peachtree Arcade. I believe this is put forward by developers from Ohio, and one wonders if they realize there was a Peachtree Arcade at almost the same place of their proposal.

I am only giving the poetry here. Certainly, there are problems: money, crime, litter. Shortly after my great June day, I was again in town and found the city muggy and trashy again, way below the mark of my security index.

But I am convinced that—for the long haul—downtown Atlanta will be the place as the song says, ". . . where all the lights are bright. . . everything'll be all right. . . downtown."

I don't know what exciting is going on in the suburbs and shopping centers these days, but I sense that in Downtown the fun is just beginning.

I suppose there is a message in all this after all: The beauty of a city is in the day of the beholder.

***

Atlanta **magazine**
September 1982

Shelter as Self-Expression

WHO SPEAKS FOR THE SOUTH? How about houses? I think houses have a lot to say about the people who build and live in them. And yet, if houses in the South truly speak for us, then we are not what we say we are.

For the past six months, my wife and I have been looking for a house to buy—or a piece of land to build on—in the medium small Southern town where we now live. Half a dozen real estate ladies have shown us scores of houses and lots. The more we tried to explain what we wanted, the less they produced.

"We want a generous-spirited house," we would say. The ladies, being practical-minded, wanted that in specifics. Okay, say, high ceilings. We were shown high ceilings in small, square rooms that inspired feelings of trapped loneliness and terror. It was, you might say, the guillotine effect.

"We would like a house suited to the ceremonials of friendship and family gatherings . . . smilax on the banisters at Christmas, a fireplace . . . that sort of thing." Oh, fireplace. We were taken to view fake fireplaces with pipe-vented gas logs or coal-grate fireplaces hardly big enough to qualify as a niche. A stingy joy for Ebenezer; a grim insult to Santa.

We had even less luck asking to be shown land on which we might build a house.

"We need it oriented so the morning light will come in the kitchen," we began, reciting a priority list formulated from 35 years of on-site testing. "We want the winter sunshine to flood the living room. You know, the passive solar principle—a roof overhang that cuts out the summer sun but lets in the winter light. This room, of course, must face south, and, with all that glass, needs privacy from the road."

We also tried to express our desire for a deep screened porch, something like we had in our last house, where we could sit half-hidden behind magnolia leaves yet, looking down, could see and call out greetings to neighbors strolling by in the twilight. We loved reading the Sunday morning papers on that porch, especially in a spring rain. And often on summer evenings, we would dine there by candlelight. It felt as if we were on some great ship.

In other words, we want a house that sensibly reflects the climate we live in and provides for those qualities of character and lifestyle that are often thought of as Southern.

It was not the fault of the real estate ladies that we couldn't find our heart's vision in the house market. But I do think it showed that we Southerners, as a people, never had enough confidence in our uniqueness to develop a style—or several styles...a feeling—of architecture drawn from our special qualities.

For years, we Southerners have declared our robust individuality. We are, we say, a people with a sense of the past, a love of family and a hospitality toward neighbors and, for that matter, strangers who aren't manifestly hostile or paranoid. We claim to have a mystical feeling toward the land and the order of nature and declare a great appetite for sitting on porches and telling stories.

I like to think these boasts are true. And yet the houses we have built in the past three decades reflect almost none of these qualities. Since World War II, we have planted thousands of acres of suburbs in the old cotton fields, but as far as the eye can see, these houses decline to assert any regional uniqueness. They follow the same national fads that inspired builders in the suburbs of Milwaukee or Cleveland.

Even within the often-severe economic limits of developers or individuals, it seems to me, we failed to adapt the good qualities from our agrarian past that would have provided, to name one of the less spiritual benefits, a way to live and breathe unconditioned air for the four or five months of the year when it is possible to do so in our semi-tropic clime.

Instead, builders filled the back 40 with every popular style ordained by the mass media from brick veneer ranch-style (picture window optional), split level, early American rustic on through a jumble of combinations until we are now blooming with California modern, those interesting earth-tone wooden geometrics with the periscope roofs.

If we were going to imitate California, we might have done better to pick up on Spanish mission style with its airy cloisters, white stucco and cool floor tiles.

Obviously, these assertions arc highly subjective and only one man's opinion; and it should be equally obvious that space limits have caused a complex subject to be greatly oversimplified. But it would be a serious distortion to ignore the fact that a house, after all, is only one of the three elements that go into what we might call shelter-as-self-expression. In addition to the house itself, there is the yard, the setting of the house. And then there is the space inside a house that must be furnished.

Southerners are great gardeners. Since childhood, when I watched my grandmother and grandfather working on their separate but adjacent garden plots, I have been impressed with the way Southerners can bring beauty and fruitfulness out of the soil around their houses.

From lawns—the great green sweeps up to the mansions on Valley Road in Atlanta as well as the little jewel apron of grass around the asbestos-shingle house up the street from our apartment—to all landscaping, the skillful placement of shrubs and rocks and borders, in the intricate coordination of beds of flowers, perennials and annuals, and vegetable gardens and little kitchen plots of exotic herbs, from all of this I feel a powerful force of caring and patience at work. Gardening is a joint venture of Man and Nature handled on a handshake contract. I love the sacramental hush of being shown about a Southerner's garden, responding to the outward and visible sign of a mute, profound relationship between a human creature and God's miracle of growth.

I have a more ambivalent response to the third element—the furnishings in a house. I appreciate the ever-refining good taste which affluent Southerners use these days in the interior design of their homes. And, even though acquiring antiques seems to have reached obsessive proportions, it is a legitimate and logical pursuit of a people seeking to touch an authentic past, to draw beauty and function from the best of what has gone before.

Yet, even as I rejoice in the presence of a perfect interior, even as my heart hums to the resonance of fine old wood lovingly finished and the artful balance of color and texture, of glass, brass and weave, I feel the walls of a spiritual prison closing in as if human choices were being subtly limited. My architectural ideal is a room of such rightness of space and shape and furnishings that humans gathered therein feel a maximum amount of freedom to follow the mood, to respond to the best impulses appropriate to the occasion: to kid or flirt or tell a story, poke the fire, dance a hornpipe or deliver up an outrageous free-associating polemic on some subject that just happened to drift by.

I like a room which invites human beings to be their own best selves.

When a room is too perfectly arranged with "lovely pieces," it sends a message to people that they are there as part of a tableau, that their function in the room is to be the ornamental finishing touches to make the room be its own best self.

But then, I may be talking this way because of what has happened. We found a lot in our new town (without the help of the real estate ladies). And we have hammered out a house plan with an architect that does all those things we wanted. The house establishes an amiable and useful relationship with sun and wind and light and trees and hill-slopes and the world passing by.

If we ever manage to get it built, there will be no money left over to buy antiques.

***

The (Columbia, S.C.) State Sunday Magazine
November 15, 1981

A Toast to the Bride

TING! TING! SILVER SPOON ON crystal goblet brings silence and attention from the dinner guests.

The father of the bride rises, picks up wine glass.

I rise here, tonight, as we finish this delicious rehearsal dinner given by our fine new friends, the parents of the groom. I rise to give a toast to our daughter, Anne, the bride.

A little while ago we had a practice round of the wedding ceremony.

The preacher asked, "Who gives this woman?"

And I responded, as I will tomorrow at the church, "Her mother and I do."

This is not strictly true. No one can give Anne away because no one owns Anne. She owns herself. Only an existential philosopher could truly grasp the full meaning of how she has always been in charge of her own life.

Stubborn? We often thought so. But not aloof and never spoiled. What she has always been is strong, loving, and, well, sort of wise.

Tonight, here before family, friends, new and old, I want to bring it out into the open…how it was that Anne, with that odd gift of wisdom, raised us—her mother and me—and guided us skillfully through the perils of adulthood these past two decades.

After tomorrow we will be on our own. She will have done all she can do to teach us. I think we will survive because of what she has given.

Mostly she accomplished our upbringing with the simple authority of love. No threats. Just firm, reasonable rules clearly laid down and firmly enforced.

For example, when she was nine I was going through a struggle trying to give up smoking. She resolved my floundering. She told me simply, with only a hint of sternness, "Daddy, every time I see you smoking a cigarette you have to pay me a dime."

There it was: The law. A force outside myself. And we are a government of laws. Even Daughter Laws when they are just. Especially Daughter Laws when we are blessed.

I have Anne to thank for my knowledge of history. Dates and battles and kings and empires are permanently fixed in my mind because of her.

She was beginning her senior year in that funky little private school we sent her to where the students were left pretty much on their own. We were in the worst period of the "open school" fad.

One night at supper she said, with that self-honesty that may have been the most valuable thing the school taught, "I really don't know a thing about history."

She must have known how eager I was to get it all straight in my own mind, to have a personal roadmap of time. So we set out, she and I, on the great journey to explore Western Civilization, chronologically, century by century, from Homer, to Cromwell, from Pericles to Galileo.

As the school year ended we had just arrived at 18th century France where the old regime was dying and we learned how Louis XV, sensing the floodtide of revolution coming, said, "Après moi, le deluge" (after me, the deluge).

Then came graduation exercises. Outdoors. It rained. But, in the fresh dripping afterwards the witty and literate graduation speaker got up to the podium and began with an appropriate quip. "Après le deluge, moi." We laughed our well-educated laugh, she and I, and felt it was a Sign.

He gestures his glass of wine in the direction of his daughter, continues . . .

You remember, Anne, you always did work that "open school" format around to be a learning experience for us. Like the time your creative writing teacher insisted you see that movie *Joe*—that long, lurid story about hippies and dope and angry parents who were less than honest in practicing the values they preached to their kids.

You were 15 so we had to accompany you. By the time intermission came we were stammering with embarrassment at the four-letter word realism we had been watching. You tried to reassure us that you were not being traumatized by the movie. You said, heck, your creative writing teacher uses those words all the time.

"He DOES?" We were shocked.

"SHE does," you said.

Slowly, you were teaching us the lesson that was so important to parents in the '60s and '70: that teenagers are not so inevitably corrupted by the perversions of the world. And, later, when you suggested we might enjoy *Rocky Horror Picture Show* for the wild antics of the audience, we went and felt we had survived our rite of passage. We did not worry that the kinky carryings-on had jaded your tastes. You had taught us better.

Now, I won't say you neglected our sex education just because you didn't teach us about the birds. You made up for it with bees. I learned a lot the night you received 10,000 Italian honey bees you ordered out of a catalog . . . especially when the process of unloading them into the hive exceeded your knowledge.

One false move would have meant 10,000 stings. I learned by your example the value of being cool in a crisis—just as I learned the power of patience watching you train that neurotic horse you bought that nobody could even get into a van. By slow persuasions of love and constancy you turned him into a fine hunter-jumper who would even pull a buggy full of children.

A horse and buggy you bought with your own money, earned scooping 31 flavors of ice cream, working as cook, waitress, and holding terrified cats to be vetted at the animal clinic. We may preach the Protestant ethic, your mother and I, but from you we really learned the meaning of the word "work."

Sometimes, I must admit, we thought you were wrong. When you absolutely refused to be a debutante we did think, as parents often do, that we knew more than you did. Instead, you took up folk dancing and spent your Monday nights among people of absolutely no social status:

handsome homesick Austrians in lederhosen, high-spirited buckdancing mountaineers, beautiful Greeks and Jews and other ethnic Americans, all expressing their native culture in exuberant interchange.

I won't admit you were right. But we have loved learning to dance those dances and feel enormously enriched from meeting your folk-dancing friends.

It is a frequent lament that no one ever really takes time out to express appreciation to the people who helped and taught them.

"Why bother to thank anybody any more?" we hear. Who takes time to acknowledge the debt we owe our teachers, who were loving and supportive and patient?

Well, tonight, I can say to Anne, "Her mother and I do."

He raises his glass higher. All drink . . .

***

The Chattahoochee Review
Summer 1988

Andrew Lytle: My Favorite Archetype

ANDREW LYTLE TOOK POSSESSION OF my soul one chill-gray Thanksgiving afternoon before an open fire in the late 1940s. He was in Atlanta for a literary conference, and as a friend of my brother-in-law's, he accepted the invitation to join the gathering at my wife's family home.

Several of us present that day nearly 40 years ago remember details of what happened: midway through the turkey and wild rice, the conversation took a whimsical turn toward the number seven and how, of all the digits, it seems left out in the cold, an orphan with no friends or relatives.

Until that moment Lytle had been a quiet guest, a pleasantly responding looker-on. But when he began to explain, softly at first, how the number seven was the sacred number of the Druids in their ancient courts where poets held equal power with kings, the valence of the day changed. We realized we had drifted into a magnetic force field that was drawing us into strange, compelling landscapes.

For the next three hours, through the courses of pumpkin and mincemeat pies, the coffee and cigars and brandy, on into the living room where oak logs were turned to yield fresh blazing as the afternoon slanted westward, we were held spellbound by this man standing before us in his brown tweed jacket and green vest with the gold watch chain across it. His broad brow and deep set eyes gave his head the look of a Roman bust as he stood there in front of the fire, balanced lightly forward like an old boxer, courtly and smiling, respectful of the social nature of the occasion as if he would yield the floor whenever his listener's interest lagged. But his listeners remained enthralled to the hypnotic flow of words and ideas, to the hushed intensity of his voice and his style of prolonging certain words as if in lingering love of the sound and meaning, the way Italians gather the breath of music into their thanks when they say "grazie."

From the Druids and the number seven he took us through the haunting esoterica of Frazier's *The Golden Bough* and the interconnectedness of magic, myth, ritual and art. We walked through the valley of the shadow of the world's great literature and ended lying on the battlefield with Tolstoy's Prince Andre of *War and Peace*, when the wounded Russian opened his eyes and looked up at Napoleon on his horse looming above him with the sky beyond and he saw how insignificant this world-conqueror seemed against the eternal blue of the heavens.

Under Lytle's spell that afternoon I glimpsed for the first time those wider-than-worldly horizons of mythic reality, and grasped the implications in the more-than-cousinly relationship between symbol and substance.

This vision of hidden meaning has remained with me like a secret treasure map that I have been exploring and seeking to understand ever since. The exploration has been made interesting by contradictions between some of Lytle's themes and what my own experience and instincts tell me. But there he is, an unshakable presence in my mind, my Jungian archetype of the wise old man.

***

Andrew Lytle was editor of the *Sewanee Review* when I came as a student to the University of the South at Sewanee, Tennessee, in 1943. He was a literary legend even then, before he had written *A Name for Evil, The Velvet Horn, A Wake for the Living*. I was a 17-year-old freshman, nervous and excited to find myself, one Saturday night shortly after matriculating, in a coterie of students shepherded by a merry-eyed, snorting Falstaff of an English professor named Abbott Martin on the way to a rendezvous with Andrew Lytle at Clara's, the roadside tavern popular with students and faculty. We students were impressed—as they intended we should be—with the way Abbo and Andrew took charge of the operation of putting several tables together in the festive confusion of the backroom at Clara's. And I was all but overcome with admiration at the practiced and elegant stealth with which Mr. Lytle poured dollops of bourbon from a brown-bagged bottle into tumblers he held below the rim of the table.

I had never heard of the Fugitive-Agrarians when I came out of Augusta, Georgia, that curtain-blowing summer of wartime dislocations. And long before I learned that Andrew Lytle was an important figure in this movement of Southern writers and critics, before I had been drawn into the resonant truths (and Quixotic absurdities) of the group's 1930 manifesto *I'll Take My Stand*, I encountered the full power of Andrew Lytle's fiction.

It happened one afternoon in the library at Sewanee, where I had plumped down for my routine battle between study and sleepiness. My heavy-lidded eyes saw his name on a book on a nearby shelf. I plucked it out, intending only to heft it for a few seconds of procrastination. It was *The Long Night*. I read the first sentence: His voice stopped as a clock might stop.

***

An hour later I came to myself, having been wholly caught up in the dark tale of family revenge in the years around the Civil War.

The same thing happened when I found *At the Moon's Inn* in the ward room of the ship I was on in the navy. I was lifted out of time by the seamless prose of Lytle, lost in the world of glinting armor of DeSoto and his men, sweating through the forests of 16th century America as my own ship lumbered westward in the Pacific to sweep up after the victory America had just won over Japan.

***

These two novels served to heighten my interest in Lytle and the Fugitive-Agrarians when I went back to Sewanee for my senior year in 1946. I began to learn about this famous group that flourished at Vanderbilt in the 1920s. The first essay I read in *I'll Take My Stand* was Lytle's "The Hind Tit," which I still think is the best of the lot and comes closest to expressing the common themes of the group. I read other essays and books like Donald Davidson's *Attack on Leviathan.* Also, it was possible to pick up clues on the personality and style of these brilliant, complex, outrageously well-educated intellectuals from the upper South by listening to the innuendoes and ironies that winked off the casual talk of Allen Tate, then editor of the *Sewanee Review*, his visiting friends, and his wife Caroline Gordon, who taught a course that year.

It was exciting for us—students interested in literature—to feel we were catching a glimpse of the tail of a comet whose course had burned a permanent record in American cultural history. Embracing their programs was another matter. It was easy enough to associate with their chauvinistic stance of defiance and protest of the colonial status forced on the South, to decry the commercial exploitation and spiritual debasement by the industrial north, to rage against the unfair freight rates imposed by federal regulatory agencies, to despair at the mass production culture imposed by the national ethic.

And we had no trouble endorsing the importance of civility, of custom and ceremony in human conduct. This was deeply rooted in Sewanee tradition.

But their political philosophy was very conservative, and in the South at the time, that label was identified with racism and racist demagoguery, the sort of non-progressive attitude that did not fit the postwar mood of college students. That was the year a young Herman Talmadge, scion of a Georgia political dynasty built on racism, usurped the governor's office on an electoral technicality and used state troopers to keep outgoing governor Ellis Arnall from occupying his office space. Ellis Arnall, incidentally a Sewanee graduate, had built a record of progress and reform. He even made headway in abolishing the unfair freight rates.

Yet, at a deeper philosophical level, beyond the reach of current issues, I could sense some profound truth lurking in the literary vision of Lytle and the others. I didn't understand it, but I knew it was important. Then came the Thanksgiving apocalypse which set me on a life quest to find out more about this deeper meaning.

Even as I headed into job, marriage and parenthood, I pursued the vision. I subscribed to the *Sewanee Review*, I read, I pondered, I puzzled. What did Andrew mean when he wrote that Western man had been off the track ever since Descartes spent that hot day in his tent? And what level was involved—psychological or spiritual—in the theme of the perilous separation of head and heart that was mentioned so often in essays, in the poems of John Crowe Ransom (as explained in critical essays)? And what was Tate getting at in his essay "Narcissus as Narcissus" or his poem "Ole to the Confederate Dead" when he said it was about "solipsism" and then went on to say he didn't really know a lot about "solipsism" but that the poem was about "preoccupation with self."

While I wrestled with my own bewilderment, I was still beguiled by the idea of defiance and, subconsciously, the bittersweet of defeat. I don't know if I can blame the Fugitives but I will confess that I voted for Strom Thurmond, Dixiecrat candidate for president in 1948.

But my life experience at this time was leading me away from this stance with its defense of "our way of life," the core of which was segregation. I was working for my uncle in a building supply business located on the edge of the black ghetto. This put me in touch with the rag and bone shop of real life. I could see the indignities that the system laid on blacks. In a Confederate Memorial Day address I delivered in 1955, I tried to extol the good qualities of "our way of life" as existing apart from segregation. I drew heavily on the Fugitive-Agrarian dogma. But the exercise put a strain on my intellectual circuitry.

It was a farewell speech to Augusta. The next year we moved to Atlanta. The civil rights conflict was beginning and I was lucky to get a job as a reporter with *Newsweek*, covering the South—the perfect place for observing sympathetically the struggle of blacks to achieve full citizenship. As a reporter, a Southerner, I could avoid the painful existential decision either to join the movement or sit in a coward's silence.

As the action in civil rights increased, people were being forced to take sides and something told me which side the Fugitive-Agrarians would be on. Sure enough, in my first year with *Newsweek* I covered the trail of 15 men from Clinton, Tennessee, charged with bombing a school. And, there on the battlements, making a holy cause of the defense, was Donald Davidson, head of the English department at Vanderbilt, one of the heavyweights of the Fugitive-Agrarians, a man whose books I had read and whose poems I admired.

***

Andrew moved back to his log house in the Monteagle Assembly, six miles north of Sewanee. He began teaching again, and again became a legend to a new generation of students. Emily and I would occasionally find ourselves passing near Monteagle and we would drop in for a visit with Andrew, Edna and their children, on through the years until it was only Andrew.

These visits were rich and memorable; we always stayed for hours when we meant only to stop by just to say hello. The log house—in no way a cabin, with its family portraits and fine old furniture and silver goblets used for serving good whiskey to guests—seemed to get mellower with the years with its wrap-around porch and hammock, its ancient fireplaces and, more recently, wood stoves and overpowering stacks of firewood outside. The talk and the tale-telling were always good. Sometimes a student with a guitar might be a visitor and we would get into singing and once, I remember, into a bit of mountain stomp dancing.

Whatever storm of public debate over civil rights was raging at the time, it never blew through the well-chinked logs. Civility prevailed, though Andrew would occasionally flick a benign barb at my calling; journalism was never granted high status among the Agrarians. This was part of a definite snootiness they could not suppress. It had other expressions. For example, they considered the Agrarian tradition of middle Tennessee almost in a different social caste from the coal-mining, industrialized east Tennessee with its Chattanooga smoke stacks and federally operated TVA.

On one visit in the mid-'60s, Emily had been reading a new book by Ralph McGill while I drove. The book was called *The South and the Southerner*, its dust jacket a dark and unusual shade of green.

"Hey, we'd better cover up that book," I said as we parked to go in, knowing Andrew would give us a hard time for reading McGill, the liberal prophet of the South, publisher of the *Atlanta Constitution*. She tossed her pocketbook on top of the volume so that neither the title nor the name of the author was visible. Several hours later, after our visit, Andrew was seeing us to our car. He spotted the green color on the spine of the book. Now Andrew Lytle is surely a man with the vision and wisdom of a guru; but he is also a writer of books for publication and is not a bit remote from the details of daily commerce.

"Oh yes," he said, bowing Emily into the car. "I see you're reading the McGill book."

"Well, er…" I checked the seat and nothing was visible but the color green.

"Oh, that's OK," he said, his voice whittled to lethal understatement. "We know McGill. We knew him at Vanderbilt. That's all right. He couldn't help being the way he is. He's from east Tennessee."

As we drove away I remembered that McGill *had* been at Vanderbilt with the Fugitives. Later he had written affectionate columns about "Red" Warren and he was in touch with John Crowe Ransom about the problems Donald Davidson's militant conservatism was creating for Vanderbilt's recruiting of good English teachers. McGill had been kicked out of Vanderbilt for stuffing the invitation list for a fraternity social affair with all-walks-of-life names—a bit of mischief that the hierarch-adoring Fugitive-Agrarians would certainly have considered out-of-bounds.

Much later, after the civil rights story had given way to hippies and, in turn, to ecology, we had a relaxed summer afternoon visit with Andrew. Sitting on his generous porch I tried out the idea that he and his colleagues had, indeed, been prophets, as could be seen by the number of their once-embattled perspectives that had become part of the public consciousness—ideas about alienation and wholeness, of community and the individual against the establishment. Certainly, the ecology movement was echoing what they had preached with its concept of stewardship of the earth's finite resources.

Andrew politely ignored the whole notion and changed the subject. As I recall he began to talk of John Randolph of Virginia.

Seven years ago I enrolled at Emory's Institute of Liberal Arts where I studied Dante, literary criticism, history, philosophy. I produced papers on Flannery O'Connor and Walker Percy. These two years of study opened the doors to much that had puzzled me in the writings and talk of Andrew. I learned, for example, that the New Criticism, formulated by the Fugitive group, is the respected foundation of most of today's exotic schools of literary criticism such as structuralism, deconstructionism, phenomenology.

More important, this work at Emory gave me a beggar's peek into the cathedral of thought that Andrew and the rest dwell in. I now understand, for example, about Descarte's day in the hot tent; that was when he proved his own existence by figuring that *somebody* had to be asking the question. It threw Western man off the track because it set up an ego-centered way of seeing everything, a way that makes a separate object of the external world—this, instead of man and external things all belonging to God's order.

But learning all this kind of thing only seems to set me further away from their vision. It is in my nature and out of my background to rejoice in the Renaissance instead of the Middle Ages which they so venerate. I tend to trust its rambunctious vanity to provide its own correctives rather than rely on the cool (and theoretical) stability maintained by a starchy authority. I especially like the Renaissance for its failure to enthrone man over God. I call that progress, and I don't pull out my pistol at the world even though I recognize what Sir Kenneth Clark called "the fallacies of hope." For me, progress doesn't mean fallen man holds any serious hope for perfection under the present scheme. I don't see technology as inevitably Orwellian and I don't think efforts to improve the lot of fellow human beings through government programs is intruding on God's domain.

But then, I am still on my journey. And there, in the half-light, is the wise old man. Andrew Lytle, guarding some big truth that maybe someday my experience will lead me to understand.

***

Hodding Carter: He Lit More than One Candle and Still Cursed the Dark

An essay-review of Hodding Carter: The Reconstruction of a Racist, By Ann Waldron (Chapel Hill: Algonquin Books, 1993)

Greenville, Mississippi, may not be in Yoknapatawpha County; after all, it's in the Delta, not Faulkner's hill country. But this largest of Delta cities has been mythologized by a vast literature of its own. And the myth matches reality as much as Oxford does the fictional county seat town of Jefferson.

Once a riverboat town (before the Corps of Engineers took a tuck in the Mississippi River), Greenville thrived from Delta cotton shipped from its compresses down to New Orleans. And it was nourished by ideas and perspectives that came in from the outside world. Greenville seemed to give off a special light, like some grand, brightly lit hotel, say, architecturally reflecting the majestic side-wheeler riverboats that once docked beside its levee. The mythic image is a town glowing there on the western edge of a state otherwise darkened by "The Closed Society"—the subtitle of an angry book of the 1960's that documented how benighted the race issue had made Mississippi.

When many Mississippi towns would not let Jews be members of their country clubs, the president of Greenville's was Jewish. In the violent "Freedom Summer" of 1964, Greenville was the only major city in Mississippi that did not have a home bombing, church burning, beating, or harassment arrest. When demonstrators marched in Greenville, to their own expressed amazement, they were protected, not attacked, by the police.

The source of much of this mystique about Greenville is found in the lives of two men who not only worked to set an example of enlightenment in the town, but who wrote books about their struggles, books that were read nationally and worldwide.

First was William Alexander Percy (1885-1942), aristocrat, poet, world traveler, a bachelor whose home was always filled with friends from around the world, poets, writers, theologians, sociologists. Carl Sandburg is remembered playing the guitar, Faulkner hitting at tennis; Langston Hughes came to lecture, was introduced by Percy. Sociologist Harry Stack Sullivan did significant research on black/white relations by stationing himself in Will Percy's pantry where Negro servants mingled with guests. Writer David Cohn came for a weekend and stayed a year to write his book about the Delta, *God Shakes Creation.*

"We were Delta upper-class," said writer Shelby Foote, also from Greenville. "Mr. Will was world upper-class."

Percy's autobiography, *Lanterns on the Levee*, is a lyrical, elegiac, soft-violin-at-twilight sort of a reminiscence, a melancholy farewell to old honors of manhood and courage and distress over demon furies of hate and fear that confronted them over racial policies. He recounted his confrontations with the Klan and the successful fight to defeat a Klan candidate for sheriff. Back then Percy was denounced as "liberal" and "radical" for his kindly paternalistic attitude toward Negroes. Today his stance is most charitably called quaint. He defended sharecropping as a necessary transition, and he never challenged segregation, only the brutalities it bred.

Mr. Will took on the raising of Walker Percy and his two brothers when their father—Will's second cousin—died. Walker Percy in his posthumous collection, *Signposts in a Strange Land*, wrote in great affection and appreciation of his benefactor. He credits "Uncle Will" with turning him on to art and beauty and influencing him to be a writer. At the same time, Walker Percy makes clear his philosophical differences with his older kinsman.

Mr. Will was also responsible for bringing to Greenville the second man most credited with the image of enlightenment. That man, Hodding Carter (1907-1972), was invited by Will Percy to come to Greenville in

1936 to start a competitive newspaper, one that would shake up the town when and where it needed shaking up. The then-existing daily in Greenville published only to please.

Hodding Carter was twenty-nine when he and his wife, Betty, moved to Greenville in 1936 and started the *Delta Star* with financial and moral support of Percy and some of his friends. Before that, Hodding and Betty had spent three and a half hot-blooded years fighting Huey Long (including burning him in effigy). They owned a newspaper in Hodding's hometown, Hammond, Louisiana. After Huey was assassinated, the Long machine finished up running the Carters out of business and Louisiana.

But all of this was prelude to the next thirty-six years of fighting for democratic and American fair-mindedness in a South determined to resist a growing national pressure to abolish White Supremacy.

Hodding Carter's story is now set forth in a biography by Ann Waldron, published by Algonquin Books of Chapel Hill. Ms. Waldron has done a dazzling job of research, digging out every colorful detail in the life and background of Hodding and his strong-willed and drolly witty wife, Betty Werlein Carter.

Author Waldron has masterfully assembled these stories and quotations into a smooth-flowing narrative. And if some family anecdotes seem a tad polished as from many re-tellings, it is hard to doubt the essential truth illumined by the tales. Each detail not only adds to the dramaturgy but is just plain fun. There are no boring sentences in this book.

For example as a Tulane graduate student, Hodding roomed with Cleanth Brooks in New Orleans. Hodding had met and begun to court Betty Werlein, president of her freshman class at Sophie Newcomb. One day Hodding and Cleanth Brooks drove up to Baton Rouge where each had an appointment to be interviewed for a Rhodes Scholarship. When they arrived Hodding decided not to go in. If he won it, he would be away from Betty for a year and "I don't think Betty will wait for me."

"Tinkum will wait for me," said Cleanth, hurrying inside.

Sitting in the car waiting for Cleanth (who did win), Hodding wrote a sonnet called "River Plantation," quoted in its entirety in the book. Years—and pages—later, Hodding sold the poem to Brooks and Robert Penn Warren for *The Southern Review*, which the famous collaborators had just started. All of this is fascinating history for observers of the Southern literary scene.

At the same time, a couple of problems somewhat dilute the native charm and delight of this book. One comes from Ms. Waldron's too strict observance of the famous writing-style dictum: write with nouns and verbs, not adjectives and adverbs. In other words, the author is not given to the kind of lush and textured descriptions that most writers dealing with this half-haunted land, time and people cannot resist, including Will Percy and Hodding Carter.

Nowhere, for example, is there a physical description of Hodding even as fleeting as this by Benjamin W. Griffith, Jr., in his foreword to [Carter's] Lamar Lectures Series book, *Their Words Were Bullets: The Southern Press in War, Reconstruction, and Peace*: "Hodding Carter, who has carried on his lover's quarrel with the South amid great physical and psychic dangers, is a man of impressive presence. White-haired (this was 1969, near the end of his life), barrel-chested, he reminded one of Hemingway as he stepped off the plane on a windswept February afternoon." Nor does she reveal the sad truth that at times such as this lecture series, he was too drunk to appear, and for three days Betty read his written talks.

Ann Waldron's superb research and compact writing almost make up for this absence of impressionistic visualizations, especially to a reader like this reviewer, who already knows the look and feel and smell of the places and times involved. The paragraph below, for example, begins with three uninspired adjectives but goes on to convey a remarkably full idea, not only of Betty's father, but of the tone and life-style, the pretensions and pastime of upper-crust gentlemen in turn-of-the-century New Orleans. Ms. Waldron does all this with good research, creative selectivity and crisp pacing:

> Betty's father was handsome, charming, and civic-minded. He played poker far into the night at the Boston Club and was also a member of the Pickwick Club; the Progressive Union; the Chess, Checkers, and Whist Club; the Polo Club; and the Purity League, whose goal was not to close down Storyville, the legal red-light

> district, but to ensure that white prostitutes would not be available to black men.
>
> He was chairman of the state central committee of the Democratic Party. He once stood his oldest daughter on a table and told her, "If anybody ever asks you who you are, say, I'm Betty Werlein. American. Episcopalian. Democrat."

The other problem is the title of the book, *The Reconstruction of a Racist*, which smacks of computer-generated hot-button marketing. Carter was a "racist" the way all but a few visionary white Southerners of the 1920's were, and his "reconstruction" was no more than the evolutionary response of many sensitive white Southerners—and editors—when made to see the brutal, humiliating and illegal effects of segregation. Like many journalists he was an instinctive liberal (though he supported Dewey in 1948 and Eisenhower in 1952) but was never an ideologue beyond believing, as he once wrote, that "dignity and self-respect and a common equality are the right of every man" and that "their attainment is the prayer of most Americans."

He was too pragmatic to ever editorialize for social integration, which wasn't his style anyway as his description of the young militant activists who invaded Mississippi in the 1960's shows:

> Beatniks who thought the way to be a brother to the Negro was not to bathe; boys in beards and dirty little girls in tight slacks with their hair down to their waists walking hand in hand with Negro boys down streets where this couldn't possibly do anything but antagonize the local white people and stir up violently angry reactions.

Fortunately, Ann Waldron didn't restrict her narrative by trying to prove the out-of-focus thesis of this title. But by basically ignoring it, the author was left without an appropriately large thematic framework to accommodate all her rich material.

In the flow of the story, the absence of such a structure is only subconsciously sensed. The book delivers a broad portrait of the man and his wife, their ink-stained struggles, their glamorous upper middle-class background and life, his ferocious six-shooter journalism. His words were bullets. He also kept a pistol handy and used his fists when he deemed it appropriate.

She tells of Hodding's father, owner of a strawberry farm outside Hammond, Louisiana, who was one of eleven children, five of them born in England where Hodding's grandfather sold bonds for an American investment company. This connected around to one of Hodding's aunts marrying Sir Otto Beit of a wealthy British family, who several times bailed Hodding's proud father out of financial difficulties.

Betty's wit and spunk are clear legacies from her mother, a bold-spirited American who studied singing in France, gravitated to London and, in one recorded episode, rode a balloon across the English Channel. She had her picture taken in a stylish sport dress designed for ballooning. It shocked her British heir fiancé for showing a bit too much ankle.

Shortly thereafter she wired him from America that she was going to marry Philip Werlein of New Orleans, who she'd just met.

"Hold everything I'm coming over," the fiancé cabled. "Too late," her father wired back. "She's married."

This same fast-paced highlighting of drama takes the story through Betty's first meeting with Hodding ("He's probably dangerous," she bragged to her friends), their marriage in 1931, and into incredible perseverance in starting and surviving in the running of a daily newspaper in Hammond. At one point, as the Great Depression became greater, they took their last $5 in cash, drove to New Orleans where Hodding won $400 at the gambling tables—putting them back in business with "more money than they had when they had when they started."

Hodding took on Huey Long, whose rise was built on brutal crushing of his enemies. Hodding was in a crowd of men who broke into the local courthouse and publicly burned about 11,000 ballots to be used in a special Long-rigged election. His actions were as quixotic as his front page editorial that cried out: "We have started a revolt against Longism which will not be stopped. The flames of the burning ballots. . . stand out starkly against the Louisiana sky. And, like the fiery hillside torch which summoned the Clansmen in 1876, a beacon has been lit to call free Louisiana to stand and fight. . . ."

Hodding was part of a group of armed men deputized by a local judge to resist Long's militia they heard was coming to Hammond to control an election. Waldron catches not only the air of danger and excitement of that time, but Betty's instinct for drollery:

> Ol' J.Y. Sanders lent Hodding a beautifully chased sawed-off shotgun, complete with leg holster. . . . Plans called for the deputies to split into groups of eight or ten men and begin patrolling their parishes at about midnight. Before Hodding's group left, Betty served coffee and sandwiches to some of his fellow deputies. . . .As Hodding was leaving, Betty said, with great aplomb, [how about "with arched casualness"?] "Honey, you forgot your shotgun."

Waldron ends this chapter in the book, and in Carter's life, writing: "When he next ran a newspaper, he would display fewer heroics, and more real heroism."

That's when they moved to Greenville, Mississippi, to start the *Delta Star.* While they were winning friends with the quality of his paper, and the vigorous participation in the social and civic affairs of the town, the depression along with competition from the established daily, the *Democrat-Times*, pushed Hodding once again to financial desperation.

He was borrowing money on all sides, kiting checks to meet payrolls. Then, on a hunch, Hodding spent four days in a vacant room across the street from the rival paper with binoculars and a notary public, counting the papers being run off on the presses behind the plate glass front of the newspaper building. He publicized that they had bloated their circulation figures to double the actual amount and threatened to sue.

This exposé led the way to a merger of the rivals into a paper called *The Delta Democrat-Times* controlled by Hodding.

His restless need for excitement and change led him to write articles and books and even to take on some full-time jobs away from the paper. In 1939, when he won a year at Harvard as a Nieman fellow, he was stunned when William Alexander Percy, his beloved mentor, responded coldly, saying, "If you go, you'll have to take your chances on coming back."

World War II took Hodding and Betty to Washington, then sent Captain Carter overseas to start a Middle Eastern edition of *Yank*, a magazine form American soldiers.

Betty had a lively life in Washington. She got a job with the Office of War Information where at various times she "worked with Philip Wylie, Reinhold Niebuhr, Samuel Lubbell . . . McGeorge Bundy ['a pink-cheeked Yale graduate'], Arthur Schlesinger, Jr., Adrienne Koch, and Christian Herter. She carpooled with Robert P. Tristram Coffin. She was crazy about her work, and enjoyed the camaraderie of going with coworkers to lunch every day at the Neptune, where they had a table reserved." Later, she became a personal researcher for elder statesman Bernard Baruch. She accepted invitations, gave parties and was called by Adlai Stevenson one of the two most fascinating women in Washington. The other was Clare Boothe Luce.

These years also saw the playing out of a high-stakes drama when a cold, brilliant entrepreneur named Donald Reynolds set out to gain financial control of the *Delta Democrat-Times* by outfoxing Carter. In the suspenseful showdown, Hodding, by luck, good advice, and shrewd playacting, ended up winning. Reynolds was quoted as saying of Hodding, "He's the only man who ever walked away from a poker table with me and took all the chips."

After the war, Hodding's response to racial issues put him more and more at odds with the prevailing white attitude statewide even as his stance materialized support in Greenville. When the Lions Club planned to list the names of WW II veterans from the area on a public plaque the *DD-T* newspaper joined in asking readers to report names of service people, men and women. Then some conservative whites balked at including black veterans.

"Hodding thundered out an editorial headlines 'Our Honor Roll Is a Monument to Intolerance and Timidity'":

> We fail to see any threat to White Supremacy or to segregation or to any other of the issues so useful to rabble rousers in placing the names of the Negro servicemen on the roll.

In 1946 Carter won the Pulitzer for editorial writing "on the subject of racial, religious, and economic intolerance."

But Mississippi was digging in as the pressure for desegregation increased. Hodding kept up a two-sided dialog, preaching tolerance to his fellow Southerners but criticizing the northern press for ill-informed righteousness about the South:

> Hodding denied to the Portland *Press-Herald* that he had been horsewhipped for the editorials. 'Occasionally we do lose subscriptions,' he said, 'but Southerners will take opinions such as mine from another Southerner, where they would resent the intrusions of a Northerner who spends two days in the South studying the Negro problem and then writes learnedly about its solution.

The real racial battle began with the U.S. Supreme Court's *Brown* decision outlawing segregated schools in the South. "It's about time," Hodding said to staffers. Editorially he wrote, "Keep your shirts on."

He called for punishment for the killers of Emmet Till, the fourteen-year-old black from Chicago alleged to have whistled at a white woman in rural Mississippi, but then scowled at the Chicago funeral as "too well-staged not to have been planned to inflame hatred and set off a reverse reaction in Mississippi."

He denounced the Citizens Councils, a network of massive resistance that was gaining control of much of the life in the state and of the state legislature. Of two state constitutional amendments cutting at black voter registration and authorizing closing schools "as a last resort" against integration, Hodding editorialized that "truly we didn't expect that even the most callous of our politicians would be so cynical or so humorless as to place themselves and the rest of us in the role of constitutional saviors."

When President Eisenhower sent federal troops to quell resistance to Little Rock school integration, the *Delta Democrat-Times* was one of the few Southern papers to defend it:

> On May 2, 1792, George Washington signed a law which is still on the statute books and is, in essence, the one under which President Eisenhower acted Tuesday. . . . We go along with the first president of the United States and the present president of the United States.

Among the more facile and caustic of Hodding's detractors was Tom Ethridge, editorial writer for the *Jacksonville Daily News*, who came up with such hand-flung insults as this response to a *Look* article by Hodding attacking the Citizens Councils: "While Mr. Carter profits financially and publicity-wise from such writings, it is mighty hard on the rest of the home folks who dislike sleeping in a wet bed."

Biographer Waldron keeps the reader posted on Hodding's failing eyesight and reports, if oh so lightly, his problems with alcoholism. She describes a priest at a retreat for alcoholics, trying to draw him out, asking him what was important in running a newspaper. He said, "Get the name and middle initial!"

Now and then a small omission weakens a good anecdote in this book. For example:

> Lawyer Phillips, who worked at Feliciana [the Carter's Greenville home] as butler, gardener, and general factotum, learned to mimic Hodding answering threatening phone calls: "You can kiss my ass, you country son of a bitch."

That's fun, especially if the reader *assumes* that Lawyer Phillips is black; *knowing* it would have made it that much more fun.

But, another omission, in an otherwise well-told and pivotal story near the end of the book, represents a failure of the author to settle on one of the larger themes that seem to haunt these sparkling tales of a man and his special place and time.

The first part of this story tells of Hodding as King of Hearts at the 1961 ball of the Greenville Junior Auxiliary. "No other king had ever worn a costume for the ball," but Hodding ordered one from New Orleans and went as Henry VIII, a part which, his friends assured him, he played to perfection. The royal court assembled at Feliciana before going to the local armory for the ball. Photographs show him as he wanted to be, Betty Carter wrote in her unpublished memoirs—handsome, carefree, spontaneous, gay, with a silver goblet in his hand.

"That year, when Mrs. Lawrence Lipscomb Paxton of Leland, the sponsor of the Delta Debutante Club, visited her daughter in England, she was surprised by the number of people who spoke so highly of the South's fighting editor, Hodding Carter, who lived so close by and yet whom she knew only casually."

So Mrs. Paxton invited Hodding to be master of ceremonies at the debutante ball during the 1961 Christmas season. He accepted. "[H]e felt the invitation was a seal of approval from the people of the Delta, just as the invitation to be King of Hearts was an accolade from the people of Greenville."

But two debutante mothers called on Mrs. Paxton, demanding she rescind her invitation. She refused. They said they would throw tomatoes at him when he stands at the microphone. And Mrs. Paxton replied, "If you do, you will splatter my new gown because I'll be standing right beside him."

The two ladies then went to call on Hodding and Betty with the same plea, and the same rancor. "Our fathers worked to build the Delta, and you are working to destroy it. We stand for the South, Mr. Carter. We beg of you to resign." Shaken, Hodding asked if Mrs. Paxton had asked them to ask him to withdraw. No. "Then. . . I will serve."

> The two women left, but within a day or two, Albert Lake, a lawyer and former emcee himself, and Frank Hall, a good friend of the Carters, arrived at Feliciana. They sat with Hodding on the long sofa by the fireplace in the living room and explained how Hodding's serving would adversely affect the institution. Parents would withdraw their daughters from the ball; the organization would flounder.
>
> Betty watched Hodding's face turn white. She was tense herself. If he gave in, she thought, the right to be different would be lost in the Delta. Anyone who didn't follow the shibboleths of the extreme conservatives

> would be barred from participation in the life of the community, at first just socially, but then what?
>
> "Did Mrs. Paxton ask you to come?" Hodding asked.
>
> "No."
>
> Hodding drew a deep breath and said, "I will not withdraw."
>
> Albert Lake sank back on the sofa. Frank Hall threw his arms around Hodding's neck.

At this crucial point, the show-don't-tell axiom of good writing does not suffice. The reader needs emotional guidance. If these gestures of surrender of the two men was meant only to say, "We gave it our best shot and lost; we love you anyway you old stubborn cuss," it is a minor, passing anecdote.

If, on the other hand, it carried some overtone of "Thank God, you have stood fast and broadened life for us all," the story is a significant moment that would serve to reveal that Hodding's life made a difference in opening the closed society.

But whatever larger dimensions or small detail of Hodding Carter's life that might have been neglected in the telling of his story, Ms. Waldron lets them unfurl like a banner of all the bright colors in the eulogy written by his son Phillip:

> We called him Big because he was; Hodding Carter was the biggest of his clan, a legend, first of all in his own tribe. We loved him, followed him, tried to live up to him, puzzled over and debated him, swapped wild yarns and proud old fighting tales with him, and sometimes in recent days we cried. It is better now to remember.
>
> Big cooked the biggest, richest gumbo, north of Bayou Teche and could always eat most of it, usually at 2 a.m. He was the worst one-eyed, wrong-shouldered duck hunter in

> three states and the best hunting companion a shivering young son could have. . .
>
> Big had his portion of prejudices and other failings. He always thought General Douglas MacArthur was a pompous ass and he never owned two suits that fit him, a dog that minded or a knife that would carve a turkey. He loved the smell of a hardware store and wanted to buy one. Luckily he never did, for his business sense about all but newspapers was uncannily disastrous. . . .He once tried golf and it bored him. He had read all his Bible and Shakespeare, but not two lines of the *New York Review of Books*, and if you cussed at him or in front of a lady he would knock you down. He spent most of his adult life ready to shoot, but was always glad no one dared press him to that. We will remember.

And so, if in a lesser way, will readers of this book.

***

II. Poems

Harper's **magazine**
November 1966

The Man Who Had Everything and Cried

He loved road maps and clocks, the pipe rack
In the study and to fit the steely bit attachment
Into that fat chuck of Black &
Decker's fine electric drill. On weekends golf and God.

And Monday: the feeling of the tan attaché case laid
Flat on a clean desk—then (while
Miss Laughinghouse came in the door
to walk across the carpet with the mail)

to reach each thumb to press a shiny latch
and hear the sound—snapsnap—who could ask for more?

"And yet," he told the doctor with a furrowed laugh,
"I feel depressed. I seem to want to cry . . .
          and cannot puzzle out the reason.
                    Tell me why."

The doctor heard the tale: how well
The children did in school; how Kodak
Had gone up and split and started up again.
The doctor smiled and, nodding, said to his old friend:

"Richard, listen. This is one of those strange
Things that happens in the chemistry—some
Unexplained imbalance and it seems to plague
Men just about our age. So, though tears come, rest assured:

Life is quite the same assembled set of truths
That you and I were raised to know and love. Come,
We will hunt this afternoon across the tawny
Fields of old Judge Applegate's estate."

But Richard did not hunt that field. He could not go.

He took his tilted chemistry instead,
Struck out
And fell
To find the golden meadows he'd been taught
To long for long ago.

The Family Secret
Atlanta: Peachtree Publishers, 1982

Tate Summer 1975

Hey, we have had a right good run
of summers now these last three years
or so—say, dating back some time
before the lake was drained. Can you
remember, even now, that mud-sucked year?
We had to hold off catching fish
and learned to dance the Salty Dog.
And now, when headlights swing around
our Friday late arrivals there,
the puddles in the road we see
are polliwog pavilions full
of just our kind of makeshift glee.

To keep it going is the trick.
The trick is to forget and let
the good times roll. Lord, let 'em roll!
For all things here will only stay
enchanted out of reach of time,
the ticking mind, the intellect.
It requires the strictest kind
of careless day by day neglect.

For all things here are light as air—
the butterfly, the jewelweed,
the full moon glade that litters aisles of
silver down the lake, road dust,
the crickets' kidding see-saw sound
around the dry, warm night.

And you
the young in one another's eyes,
in greenleaf laughter weaving in the
wafer light; the talk as idle
as brown pebbles plooped into
the clear, small pools along a stream . . .
the dock-tag play, the golden
fleece on flesh turned tan in sun
as unsinned limbs are lifted glistening
out of liquid-metal-colored
water, rising wet-eyed, wild,
like some unravaged Nereid.

Here only we, the grownups, grow;
and growing each year garden wise
are rich in season sense and though
we say we know of no such nonsense
such as you forget, forgot . . .
forgotten . . . still we see that all
these summer years so great in heedless
grace, so romping banjo clever,
shall be safely lost and free
to sneak alive and live forever.

The Chattahoochee Review
Spring 1983

Commencement

If home were only long enough to hold
Shredded experience: if we could take book dreams
Or faulty memory, nest in wax green
Tissue like a formal long-stemmed rose,
Then how supremely we could seem to close
Ourselves in Law, could button out the keen,
The snow-sharp blasphemies. How we would preen
Against the vulgar and the bad. But no.
We leap and learn that not all walls will fall
To mere taught truth; that home is not enough
To teach each wayward patch that will not fit
The quilting, nor instruct that half of all
Magnificence is fraud. Go, therefore—bluff
The bearded hills with jokes of holy writ.

III. Columns from the Sunday Book Page of The Atlanta Journal-Constitution

The Atlanta Journal-Constitution
August 26, 1979

Anne Rivers Siddons

ATLANTA NOVELIST ANNE RIVERS SIDDONS is in the middle of writing a new book, a big one. Could I come to her house for an interview? She preferred to come to mine.

As she curled in a chair on my porch and talked about the 325 pages she has written so far and the year's work that lies ahead, I understood. She was protecting her fledgling; no trespassing, please. She is still wrestling to get all her characters on stage which, she says, "is like taking a class of second graders to the zoo.

"I am not to that part I love yet. I'm breath-held about it. I feel it's beginning to work, but if I talk about it too much, or let myself get sidetracked again, it might go away and never come back."

So we talked a bit of old times, of those days when she was on the staff of *Atlanta* magazine in the middle 60s. She was part of that group of talented young people under the flamboyant leadership of Editor Jim Townsend who was pioneering a new integrity and glitter for the nation's Chamber magazines. Bob Daniels, now art director for *Money* magazine, was one of the brightest and funniest of the gang. Anne shared an office, desk and telephone with Bill Diehl, who is now an Atlanta gossip item for his big bucks novel *Sharkey's Machine*.

"It was terribly exciting," Anne said. "We did crazy things; we traveled in a flying wedge. We worked late, played hard, drank too much."

I remember it well. My first freelance pieces were written for *Atlanta* in those years, under the spell of Townsend. And I remember Anne Rivers (before she married Heyward Siddons) and envied her gift. She did a piece with photographer Peter Hudson called "Habersham,

Tuxedo, West Wesley and All That"—a poetic essay on the elegant old residential northwest section of town. When you drive through you encounter "a wash of sudden silence . . . an old silence . . . a dappled, underwater silence that is strangely comfortable and altogether unlike the nurtured, structured hush that belongs to the expensive new streets . . . (in this old section) power mowers, velvet-treaded limousines and Davy Tree surgeons scatter and buzz and clank and whisper around . . . but somehow the attendant outcry reaches the ear not as a noise but as a well-bred echo."

I knew even then that Anne was possessed of a writer's vision. I was glad, therefore, but not surprised when she made the leap into fiction with two successful novels: *Heartbreak Hotel* in 1976; and *The House Next Door* in 1978.

"A writer is what a person *is*, not what a person *does*," she said, sipping Perrier with lime, nibbling a ginger snap. "I could no more stop being a writer, even if I never wrote again, any more than I could stop being brown-eyed."

Growing up in Fairburn, a town twenty miles south of Atlanta, the only child of a lawyer father and school principal mother, she was always reading. Classics, trash—whatever she could get from the library that her mother would not censor (as she did *Forever Amber*). Anne was feature editor of the *Plainsman* at Auburn the same year Paul Hemphill was sports editor of that student newspaper. She came to Atlanta in 1959 and worked in advertising before joining *Atlanta* magazine.

She was well-grounded in literature, from Milton to Melville, from the King James version of the Bible to Tolstoy. But she still struck what she describes as "that truculent, half-educated stance that Southerners have that is similar to the stance a girl from Auburn might have at a Princeton reunion with her husband." The smile is from real life. And the essay she wrote on attending a Princeton reunion with Heyward was not truculent at all; indeed, to me it was the most charming piece in her book of essays called *John Chancellor Makes Me Cry.*

As we sat beneath the wood-bladed ceiling fan whirring a wash of silence on the porch, Anne talked of the process she goes through in writing a novel.

"At the beginning, I'm restless and more engaged with the outside world. But at the end, when it's coming down to the wire, I lose days,

I lose where I am. I'll start writing, say, at 10 in the morning and look up and it'll be 4 o'clock and I won't remember time having passed. You're in a time warp of some sort and it's not particularly sublime. Hemingway called it writing outside yourself and you pray for it because your best writing comes out of it and it doesn't happen every day. It seems as though it is coming from somewhere else, through you."

But, finally, she did talk about the novel. It is called *Fox's Earth*, the name of a family mansion in a middle-sized Southern university-and-textile town. The story covers five generations and a hundred years. There's a "dreadful old grandmother," Ruth Yancey Fox. And antebellum sons, educated at Yale and Harvard, who took their European tour and came home with "this Grecian classical thing in their heads and built neo-classic houses." Like Fox's Earth.

But it is really about women, Southern women, and their strength and ferocity and influence on the men and the culture around them.

"It's what really fascinates me," she says.

***

The Atlanta Journal-Constitution
June 29, 1979

Marshall Frady

The arrival of a new book by Marshall Frady signals a reading adventure; and a lively argument. Marshall Frady is a 39-year-old Atlanta writer whose new book, *Billy Graham: A Parable of American Righteousness,* demonstrates once more that he is possessed of an extravagant talent.

Few deny that. But there are sharp disputes over the product of that talent.

I declare myself with those who find his writing dazzling and delicious, who consider him a superb journalist and inspired craftsman. His detractors complain that he overwrites, that his prose is outrageously lush. "Wordy" is their word. "A style that is out of style," said one.

Well, sez I, must we all be vogue-ish?

"It's kind of ultra-telling," said Frady as we sat on his front patio in the cooling twilight recently. "The ultra-realizing of a moment, a quality, a mood." There are other ways, he notes, citing a good new novel that is "spare, terse, cryptographic." Even in conversation, Frady selects his words carefully with little nods of the head, private soundings, a hint of the creative process. "You can communicate by just giving little clues to what's out there. Invisible. In the air."

Frady's way does not leave things invisible. A Sunday morning, at one point in the Graham book, is detailed. "Sprucely groomed congregations in translucent-windowed sanctuaries, among hushed organ tones and rustling church bulletins, small polite coughs." Graham's office is "carpet-muted, clock-ticking"—inspired poetic selectivity.

Words, to Frady, are tools to use to convey the inner vision of the writer. He uses words the way The Invisible Man used bandages—to reveal the shape of what is really there. Frady is not wordy; he is explicit. " . . . a voice like a flat ring of ironware." He perceives a burly helicopter touching down "daintily." He uses simple words, not what comedian Martin Mull used to call "vocabulary words." Words like "inchoate" or "propinquity" are not Frady words. His words are selected from his fine-tuned imagination, not a thesaurus.

Frady's words "tell"—as they are commanded to do by William J. Strunk in the little book *The Elements of Style* that is catechism to professional writers. True, Frady is an adjective man and Strunk is wary of adjectives. ("Write with nouns and verbs, not adjectives and adverbs.") And he strings them out—usually in threes. But his adjectives are rarely redundant; they triangulate, give a firm fix on the noun by coming at it from three sides.

Editing Frady's copy, which I did when he worked for *Newsweek* in the 60s, was like trying to pick which leg of a milking stool to saw off. A scar on a man's face is "long and vivid and savage"; the Florida landscape is "savage, prehistoric, reptilian." OK, you try: pick which word to cut. See?

It is not by words, but the quality of his vision, that Frady should be judged. Here, it could be argued, he often waves his wand over old cliché images. One is reminded of old newsreels with music, grim for floods, war ruins, and so on.

But, more often, Frady's power of insight is so good it is downright spooky. He caught the mystique between Lester Maddox and the bicycle in a *Saturday Evening Post* article before the former governor showed it by riding backward before television cameras. In a *Life* story, Frady called Julian Bond, who, at the time, seemed a new Martin Luther King Jr. emerging, a sort of elegant dilettante, a Henry James character. It still fits. In his biography of George Wallace, Frady saw the governor, in his long, paneled office, as seeming like "the president of a venerable but slightly seedy railroad . . . perhaps a rugged little switchman or flagman who relentlessly made his way up to become head of the whole operation."

Marshall Frady should not be called a word man. He is a man with a stand; and his skill with words makes it clear exactly where that "platform of observation" is. On that he should be judged, and I say "wow!"

***

The Atlanta Journal-Constitution
September 2, 1979

Bill Emerson

SEPTEMBER-DRY GRASS AND A NEW slant of light quickens the spirit. Summer with its thousand Julys is unhooked, set adrift to fade into memory. This new excitement (and terror) is embodied in one word: School. School, as in K through 12; as in college, graduate school.

Even for people long finished with it, school sets the tone for September even as it sets the level of taxes in the county digest. Only in the after-years, in the bad dreams of hallways, do we realize how deep was the trauma; and only in that later hungry-minded need to know and understand do we recognize the feast that was available, that we scarcely sniffed or nibbled at when spread out before us.

Too often, school means "getting through material," warehousing it for a short time and delivering it back as undamaged as possible, leaving little trace of its presence.

Now and then in the long years of going to school, a lucky student encounters a really good teacher. It only takes two or three good teachers to make a student catch on to the excitement, to see the connection between life and learning.

I had about three good teachers in my years of going to school. But the most important and best teacher I ever had was not a teacher in the formal sense when he taught me. He is now. He is a professor of journalism, holder of the Gonzales Brothers Chair at the University of South Carolina. William A. Emerson, Jr.

Prof. Emerson taught me in 1957 when I came to work for *Newsweek* in Atlanta and he was bureau chief. He hired me and for several years hammered away at the task of teaching me journalism—reporting and writing.

It was a painful and exhilarating experience. He was tough; and inspiring. I would not have learned the craft otherwise.

He went on to New York in the 60s, was editor of the *Saturday Evening Post* for its last five years, wrote several books including *The Jesus Story* and *Sin and the New American Conscience.* In 1975, he came south again, to live in Columbia, S.C., and enter the teaching profession.

I talked to him about teaching and judged he is as good and tough as ever. And as generous. He always did give everything every time.

"You try to understand what's going on in your own mind and translate the process for the student. Sometimes you have a mortal struggle with the student's mind. It's combat. It's exhausting. Sometimes they refuse to let you engage with their minds."

And to Bill Emerson it is a very serious thing—teaching, engaging the student's mind. Some of his old companions might find it hard to think of Emerson being serious. He has always been without peer as a spontaneous phrase-maker, mock hurler of insults and extravagant compliments. At 56, he is still unmatched as a volcano of energy and imagination. Words and imagery pour from him like sparks and lava—enough to bury any pompous Pompeii. But when he is teaching, he is intent on a purpose other than entertaining.

"I don't think teaching is a performing art. I don't think it should win popularity contests or charm students. Sometimes you can teach them broad techniques the same way you teach somebody to foxtrot, pushing them through the steps, heaving them around the floor. But what you are trying to do is get them to move off on their own, creatively. It's like trying to start a reluctant lawn mower. You pull the cord and nothing happens. So you pull it and pull it and pull it. Finally it kicks off."

What he looks for in students that he thinks will make writers is not, he says, what most English professors look for.

"All of the art comes out of the artist. The student I look for who will be a writer is not the one who can write tidy, neat paragraphs. I'm interested in the untidy student, the obsessive student that has nightmares, who questions the world around him. Students that have had something happen to them. Who are conscious of the sensorial intake, who are not afraid of explosive, incomprehensible, unmanageable things.

"All you can do in college is ignite some of those people. Give them confidence. Criticize them, find them something to aspire to. Communicate with them."

Is it true what they say about the satisfactions of teaching? "Who can sit around being satisfied? It's the process that's exciting. Sure, it's fun to point to a student who just sold something to the Economist or got a Nieman fellowship, as I can. But the real thing is to see the awakening, the transaction begin in the mind, the spark jump...the motor start."

And that's the secret of September; the possibility that brings the new excitement.

***

The Atlanta Journal-Constitution
December 2, 1979

Writer's Workshop, Winthrop College

I AM JUST BACK FROM a two-day Writer's Workshop at Winthrop College in Rock Hill, S.C. It was for men and women from the Carolinas who wish to sharpen their writing skills. They met with us "writer-instructors."

The prevailing mood was literary with stress of poetry and fiction. I was the only "non-fiction specialist." And when I got home, I realized I had absorbed this mood so much I began to be haunted by the short-story possibilities of one of my encounters there. In real life, my "fictional" hero would dissolve in embarrassment at being written about. That's why I will call him by a made-up name—Oliver Brown.

A week before the conference, I was sent a packet of 10 manuscripts to evaluate. The writers of these non-fiction pieces would, then, meet with me in private sessions at the conference.

The manuscript of Oliver Brown stood out from the others as the most ambitious and the most badly written. It was a proposal for reform in the institutional treatment—therapy—of handicapped children. Brown obviously worked in this field and felt deeply about the need to bring some flexibility to the dogmas, some sense of unstructured play, of spontaneous creativity in the prescribed form for children with problems.

The difficulty was that Oliver Brown's writing was dense with all the ponderous, bureaucratic language, the pseudo-technical jargon that, it seemed to me, was part of the problem he was attacking. I pictured a sincere young man, intense, slender, humorless, wearing horn-rimmed glasses, in his early 30s. I would speak to him kindly, but firmly.

But then, at Winthrop College, at the appointed hour, Oliver Brown came in for his conference with me. He was a large, shaggy-bearded man with a wise, sensitive, ravaged face. If not older than me in age, he certainly was in experience. He had a slow, comforting way, a husky voice compounded of humor and sadness.

Our roles shifted and I—ectomorph that I am—seemed to be the petty bureaucrat, he the understanding father.

When I criticized his turgid prose, he absorbed it good-naturedly.

"I know, I know," he said, scratching his beard, shaking his head. "People keep telling me that . . . I keep trying." His argument that he was trying to reach people who respond to that kind of language did not hold up. He didn't push it.

He does work in the field of handicapped children. He is a doctor, psychiatrist and pediatrician. He is on the staff of a clinic for mentally handicapped children.

"You know, I write poems that are very lean," he told me later during a coffee break. I showed some interest. When I left the next day, he slipped me four poems on four white, unfolded sheets of paper. He scribbled his address on a scrap of paper, asking me please to return the poems to him when I had read them. He did not have copies.

I came home, unpacked, read through the poems quickly and went out for a run. Back at my desk, clearing up details before supper, I was about to send the poems back. Then I read them again. Slowly. Several times. And yet again. Then I went downstairs and read them aloud to my wife. I do read a lot of poetry these days, but it has been a long time since I have read poems as strong and real and good as these.

Whether by instinct or conscious craft, Dr. Brown knows how to use wit and detail to bring on a dramatic explosion in the heart. Each poem describes an episode with a "problem" child. He does it with such skill and humor that I found some difficulty reading them aloud without stumbling on a gulp in the throat.

There is not space here to quote any of them in full—the only way to convey their poignancy. But, to try: The departed child-patient had written back to thank members of the staff and tell them "how much you miss me," and the staffer's formal reply, picking up the inverted love-logic with deadpan politesse: "P.S. Please be advised/That you miss us too."

A choker was the poem of the 5-year-old who wouldn't eat and was dying as nurses rocked her day and night. Then, one midnight, she took "one green bean from Nurse O'Malley. 'One green bean,' they all whispered/And prayed for two."

I sense that Dr. Brown is too busy trying to write his reform proposal to think about publishing his poems. I wish he would think again.

***

The Atlanta Journal-Constitution
March 2, 1980

Jim Dickey

IN THE LATE 1950S, BEFORE he was the Famous Southern Poet, Jim Dickey used to come around the *Newsweek* office and go to lunch with us. He and Bill Emerson, then *Newsweek*'s bureau chief, had been friends for a long time.

Dickey was one of our best luncheon companions of those days. We would taxi down the runway with a couple of martinis and, first thing you know, we were airborne—conversationally: Doing rolls and loops and chandelles among any and every topic of talk—literary or libelous, profane or profound—from Beatnik to Fugitives, bikers to Christ, sports to sex. Dickey had been a World War II pilot and college athlete and, with his poet's natural lift and Emerson's mighty roar, we were off exploring the wild blue yonder.

Dickey was writing ad copy by day for the likes of Coke. He was working on poems at night; poems about odd things that, often, seemed to be lurking in the dark of your mind. There was one about the killer whale under the polar icecap, stalking the starving explorers, even as it stalks you under summer meadows, "turning as you do, zig-zagging."

He was getting published in prestigious magazines, and when they were collected into "Buckdancer's Choice," which won a National Book Award in 1966, Dickey sort of peeled off, swooped on up and away into national prominence. He moved from Atlanta.

He was gone. We saw him everywhere. On national TV talk shows, he delivered up that soft and faintly menacing style of Southern charm, a teasing mixture of put-on and genuine cliché. A *Life* magazine article, I recall, caught that muted macho beneath the courtliness, saying Dickey is a type you'd expect to find as a backfield coach around the Southeastern Conference college practice fields.

He was everybody's darling—the moonshot poet who gave us the inspired new perspective of ourselves with "the blue planet"; he toured with Russian poets; visited Picasso in Spain.

Then his fame turned infamous. Stories floated about of unseemly and unsober behavior, even as his popularity grew as a guitar-pickin' reader of poetry on the college circuit. The little wine and cheese faculty affairs became a legacy of Dickey trying to convert them to larger affairs with faculty wives.

He became the South's favorite gossip topic. We had need of such—a naughty native son to be scandalized by. You see, at this time all our old snorting demagogues who used to shock and delight us had mutated into being bland, boring or president.

So, if there had not been a Jim Dickey, we would have had to invent him.

But there was a Jim Dickey and he handled the job of *enfant terrible* well. I remember running into him at a conference at Chapel Hill. We had breakfast together, starting with two 12-ounce cold beers.

"That's something I learned from Cowboy," he explained. "Two tall beers start the day off right." Cowboy was the North Georgia mountaineer who played the part of the degenerate in the movie "Deliverance," made from Jim's novel.

We had lunch in 1976 during the Carter campaign.

"When Jimmy Carter gets elected, I'm going to visit him in the White House, and I'm gonna say—well, looky here—two Jimbos from Georgia in the White House!" Fun—until he passed out.

I had not seen Jim for several years—since his wife died. Then last week, he came to Atlanta to read at Emory. It was a fine reading—I think he's one of the great readers of poetry. Emily and I invited him and his new wife to lunch the next day at Fitzgerald's.

It was a cold, drizzly February 6 outside; we could see the dreary day from where we sat, mellow and warm, inside. It was one of the nicest, laidback luncheons with friends I can remember in a long time.

It was not like old times. It was like new times. Jim seemed to be a new Dickey—delightful, sipping tomato juice, introducing his new wife, Debba.

"There are a million Debbys," he said, looking at her lovingly across the table. She is a strikingly good-looking young woman with long, dark hair and a serious, sensitive face. "But there is only one Debba." We all passed around fine, old handcrafted anecdotes. New ones, too, born of the occasion.

Somehow, I thought of how critics often speak of writers in their middle years as showing hints of a new, bigger work, "Is there a new Mailer? A bigger Hemingway?" they ask, implying that there is such coming in their work-to-come.

So I have to report my instinct that there is a new Dickey coming. He is working hard these days, writing a novel, keeping up a schedule of teaching and lecture appearances.

If I'm wrong, if there isn't a new Dickey—well, we'll just have to invent one.

***

The Atlanta Journal-Constitution
March 30, 1980

Atlanta Magazine Gets the Blahs

THIS IS GOING TO BE a tough column.

Tough to write—it's about a problem concerning things I love: my city, my profession, and *Atlanta* magazine, which published my first freelance effort and some of my best stories over the years.

And it's going to be about toughness itself—heroic and otherwise.

Atlanta magazine has changed editors again. That makes six times in 19 years. But, then, it takes time for a magazine to get its vision in focus, set a tradition, establish a compact with its readers.

Atlanta was born as a Chamber of Commerce publication in 1961, leading the way nationally to a new style of really good city magazines. In late 1977 it was bought by Communication Channels Inc.

Over its two decades, *Atlanta* has been, by turns, spunky, dull, outrageous, lively, sleek, slick and blah.

Right now it seems headed for the Big Blah. This is very sad. It could as easily have become significant, important. A regional institution. A coffee table "must" from Natchez to Charleston. Fun and prosperous.

Atlanta, the city—imperial capital of the South—deserves a classy, gutsy *Atlanta* magazine. It especially needs one now, to keep fresh the memory of the great hustle called "the Atlanta spirit," that jaunty, far-seeing, buccaneer esprit that made the city great. If you study the last 30 years you will notice that, whenever Atlanta leaders dreamed of greatness, the city achieved it. This tradition needs to be celebrated by the press, in something like *Atlanta* magazine, as much as it needs to be watched and questioned with a gimlet eye. The dreams and schemes, the Omni and the stadium, along with the tough news story questioning what happened to the poor people displaced by these edifices—all of that goes into Atlanta's greatness.

That greatness may have been what attracted the New York-based publishing house Communication Channels Inc. to move its corporate headquarters to Atlanta. CC is in the trade magazine publishing business, putting out a string of successful specialty monthlies about adhesive tape, fences, shopping centers etc. In their move South, they bought *Atlanta*. It could have been a real takeoff point for the magazine, coming out from under Chamber ownership. But the Communication Channels people seem to have a hard time getting it straight that consumer magazines are not run the same way as trade publications.

The difference is crucial. Trade publications have always been more or less open about favoring advertisers in their stories. But a consumer magazine like *Atlanta* presents itself as a responsible member of the press. Press, as in "freedom of the . . . ." That makes it sort of a quasi-official institution of a democratic society—First Amendment and all that. This means that its facts and opinions—no matter how wrong-headed, biased or vulgar—are not "bought," are not influenced by pressure from companies that advertise in the magazine.

The ethics of this is, really, very practical. If readers, for example, go to a restaurant recommended by the magazine and come home sick, those readers will begin to distrust the magazine. The same principle works at other levels—stories on politics and profiles, in exposés and movie reviews. Fool me once shame on you, fool me twice shame on me. The compact of trust between reader and editor takes a while to build and not long to lose. It is biodegradable.

Larry Woods resigned as editor of *Atlanta* last week because of pressure from advertisers that was permitted by the publisher.

"There's an attitude out there of 'we've got to make it by ingratiating ourselves with advertisers,'" said Larry, a solid reporter, an experienced editor, a man of integrity. "There was pressure put on people like me to do certain things and, I'll admit, for the past two or three months, I've felt like a hooker."

What things? Well, notice the Eastern Airlines logo on the March cover. Larry was ordered to put it on. That's known in the business as "selling the cover." It is not an acceptable practice among legitimate consumer magazines.

Phil Garner quit *Atlanta* a few months ago on the same principle. "Some mornings I couldn't get into my little cubicle for the advertising people waiting there," Phil said. Another friend who worked there sheepishly answered, when I questioned an article obviously written for an advertiser, "Well, we've got to make our advertisers happy."

In my 22 years with *Newsweek*, I never heard that sentiment ever even hinted at by a reporter or an editor. It was unthinkable.

It must be said, however, that while this separation of ad and editorial is sacred to journalists, it is not always as pure as the driven snow. I remember George Leonard told me, back when he was with the old *Look* magazine, "We're whores on Hollywood pieces. Everything else is clean."

Sylvan Meyer, publisher of *Miami* magazine, suffers ad cancellations and pressures in his South Florida market as a price of staying clean. He admits it's tough. For one thing, there's the accepted practice among magazines and newspapers of doing special sections on a theme (vacation, fashion etc.) and ad salesmen push ads to go with it. "You're constantly defeating your own morality," Sylvan says. "There's so much linkage going on both ways."

But to let down on the protection of editorial integrity, says Sylvan, leads first to "running a lot of soft material and, second, you just don't get good professional writers when they know their peers are looking on them as doing something less than pure."

Jack Lange, the new editor of *Atlanta*, is a respected and competent professional. He was assured there would be no interference from advertisers. To which a former editor of *Atlanta* under Communication Channels said, "Do you believe in fairies?"

Joseph Shore is the publisher of *Atlanta* and head of Communication Channels. I saw him once, at the press conference with board members of the Chamber of Commerce in December 1977 when the sale of *Atlanta* was announced. The meeting was at the downtown offices of the Chamber.

Press conference? It was really meant as a ceremonial welcome to Joe Shore. Bob Coram was the only reporter to ask a mean question. How come, he asked, with all this happy-to-be-part-of *Atlanta,* your first move is to take *Atlanta* offices way the hell out to Sandy Springs? Chamber board members rustled with mild vexation at the breach of politeness. But Joe Shore, thickset, a silvering old gent with a sly, slow, deep-husky New York way of talking, smiled. He didn't mind the question. He was tough. As he explained with beguiling candor, he got where he is by being tough.

But, it would seem, he is not tough all around. He is bucks tough—short term. He seems to be a powder puff when it comes to advertisers, the very point at which publishers, like editors, need to stand firm.

Certainly Shore is not tough in the way Eugene Patterson and Ralph McGill were tough in the 1960s, writing flaming swords against segregation, the "sacred way of life" to a majority of white Southerners. He is not tough like Jack Tarver telling Gov. Marvin Griffin to go to hell when the governor threatened to cut out whiskey ads from the Atlanta newspapers if they didn't lay off investigating his administration. They didn't and he did. It cost the papers thousands. Short term.

And, as I think back, I see that Atlanta's greatness is the product of a lot of large and small toughness. Not just in the imagination and daring of swashbucklers like John Portman, Tommy Cousins and, alas, Jim Cushman (they are bucks tough—long term), but the toughness Ivan Allen showed, when, as mayor, he advocated integrating hotels and restaurants in 1963, before Congress could get up its nerve to pass a law. Or that Mayor Sam Massell showed when he told hippies/bikers, merchants and rednecks that they, by damn, were going to respect each other's rights in that war zone known as the Strip. Or Ed Negri, who integrated his fine downtown restaurant, Herren's, when he saw how Charlie Leb, up the block, hired goons to keep integrators out of Leb's. Ed lost a lot of business for months. But today, Herren's is flourishing downtown. Anybody remember Leb's?

Atlanta magazine, to be great, needs some of all the above kinds of toughness. Maybe Communication Channels can grasp this—that the best bucks are not always the quickest. But there's a feeling around that the only hope for *Atlanta* is that some foolish old Warbucks will take a fancy to her, take her off the street and, as they say, make an honest woman of her.

***

The Atlanta Journal-Constitution
April 6, 1980

Dante

MY WIFE AND I HAVE just been through Hell.

And, since this column is being unfolded to the light of Easter morning—I picture the newspaper being disassembled at kitchen tables, in bedrooms, on sofas, perhaps in jails and old hotel lobbies and all-night coffee shop counters—it seems the right time, Easter morning, to describe our experience. Some call it "the Dark Night of the Soul."

Indeed, it took us two dark winter months, reading aloud together at night, after supper, canto by canto, to make our way through that first part of Dante's celebrated poem, *The Divine Comedy*. That first part is called the Inferno, i.e., Hell.

The story is a first-person telling of how he, Dante, guided by the ghost of his literary hero, Virgil, enters the bowels of the earth on the morning of Good Friday, Holy Week of the Jubilee Year 1300 A.D. It is a journey into a nightmare. Virgil and Dante negotiate their way downward, through the nine circles of Hell, seeing and often talking to the damned souls of sinners who are caught in various unspeakable punishments.

At the end of two days they reach the bottom, the very center of the earth where old Beezlebub reigns. He is a giant of a giant with three ravenous heads; he is trapped to the waist in the frozen lake of Cocytus. The two poets climb down his hairy flanks, through a space in the ice, passing the center of gravity, which then makes Satan be upside down to them, his feet sticking up.

They hurry through a winding tunnel and emerge on the other side of the world, into the stars of Easter morning.

The second part of the *Commedia* takes them up the mountain of Purgatory where the sins of Believers are purged by labors and suffering. The last part of the *Divine Comedy*, then, is Paradise.

Our reading of this masterpiece is a sharing of my homework for the graduate course I am taking at Emory on the *Commedia*.

From the teacher, Dr. Arthur Evans, I began to grasp—and to take home my grasping—the true greatness of the work. It stands astride the whole of Western literature.

All that had gone before from the Bible to Homer seems to be included. Ulysses sets out once more to sail beyond the sunset. Roman poets and statesmen, the artists, poets and politicians of Dante's time are all there.

And it seems to have influenced much of the literature since A.D. 1321 when it was completed, across a range of writers from Boccaccio to Walker Percy, from Shelley to T.S. Eliot, from Petrarch to Dorothy L. Sayers.

It is not easy reading. The best of the translations . . . well, it ain't your light summer fare. Without the guidance and inspiration of Dr. Evans—a fine-tuned scholar of wit and lilt—I, for one, would have missed the main trip.

And yet, the most moving experience of the course came through a fellow student. It happened in class yesterday. She was giving a presentation of Dante entering the gates of Purgatory.

This fellow student, wife of an Episcopal priest, drives from Macon each week for the class. She is a warm, outgoing person, and a serious student of Jungian psychology. She has helped me understand Jung's theory of the archetypes which holds that there are dark forces in each of us that emerge from our unconscious in dreams as symbols, figures, "archetypes"—the Shadow, the Quester, the Eternal Feminine, etc.

To achieve a healthy psychic balance, the theory goes, it is necessary to acknowledge and not to deny these primitive forces, to "encounter them without being possessed" by them.

In the tension of this relationship with these forces they can become creative, can bring new powers to the individual. Not to acknowledge their existence is to risk their destructiveness. This psychological process corresponds very closely to the Christian ritual of confession, penitence and redemption.

For her and her fellow Jungians, Dante's trip through Hell was a journey to encounter the archetypes. In her presentation to the class of Dante at the gates of Purgatory, knocking for entrance, not on the gate but on his own breast in acknowledgement of his sins, she became overwhelmed by it all. She choked up, had to remain silent for a moment. We waited.

"I'm sorry . . . this is just so . . . powerful."

We understood and each of us felt, I think, then, or maybe later in private as in confronting a typewriter alone at 4:30 in the morning, thinking of all that dark journey and the message of Easter, felt the force of that sudden, mysterious dilation inside your chest that gives a little pumping shudder and lifts tears up and out of the eyes, spilling them uncontrollably and unaccountably in the presence of some nameless, enormous, stunning realization.

***

The Atlanta Journal-Constitution
August 31, 1980

Kanuga

THE LAST DAY OF AUGUST is what I call the End of Summer.

It is a literary sort of thing: End of Summer. An evocation, a mood, a time to bid farewell to the myth of summer, summer with a thousand Julys, summer that takes echoes from the free and tumbled days that memory makes of the long ago.

Certainly, I bear no sweet-sad farewells for this year's brutal summer—this vacationless, rainless summer, this 1980 summer with its dry death rattle of corn stalks, its rubbersuit heat, the deadly masque of politics (the Sherwin-Williams ads had more honest drama than the conventions), the wheezing, dripping window unit that kept us prisoner in two rooms.

In 1933, I first saw mountains. From a train window. Dim blue fringe on the horizon that looked like storm clouds. We clickety clacked for hours across hot, flat South Carolina and arrived at dusk in Hendersonville, N.C. Brisk mountain air, excitement of familiar faces at the train depot, hissing white train engine stream. We drove out from town—was it in a Model A Ford with baggage on the running board?—onto a winding dirt road then around a last curve, there loomed a mountain like an elephant's back, and a lake. Across the lake, in the twilight, I could see a building that seemed to hang over the water, its lights reflected like seed pearls.

That was the pavilion—a shell of musty space, basketball court, a stage, a wide, wandering porch.

Up the hill was the Inn. Green, shingled, rambling, Edwardian. Profoundly graceful. Yet the bedrooms would have horrified a slumlord: One naked light bulb hanging from the ceiling, sagging cots, plaster falling off the walls exposing wood lathe.

After supper the rocking chairs were always full of Episcopal bishops and ladies from Charleston.

This was Kanuga. Built for a sporting crowd from New Orleans in 1910, bought by Episcopalians in 1928 and made into a Church Conference Center. June and July were taken up with conferences—study groups and workshops on Christian-Episcopal topics.

August was "guest period." And this was the land of my mythical summer. In the Depression years life was rich and realized, if you had work. My father had work. To have a little was to have much. And, to have the month of August in the spicy air of hemlock and white pine, the soft brushed light, the blue-green shadows; shouting over lakes, hiking up sloping apple orchards, was to have a time to slip into my second self. I loved everyone and they seemed to return the feeling.

A few days ago I had business at Kanuga. The pavilion is gone; the old Inn is replaced by a new one. But the spirit of unspoiled simplicity is still there. And the bishops and ladies from Charleston.

Driving up across hot, flat South Carolina, into folded blue hills backlit with thunder clouds making a dreamlike Maxfield Parrish light, I listened as my wife read aloud from Walker Percy's new novel, "The Second Coming." His flipflop flashbacks set me in this remembering mood.

Percy's protagonist, Will Barrett, was struggling with Christian belief and wondering why believers turned him off so.

"But if they have the truth," Barrett is soliloquizing, "why is it the case that they are repellent precisely to the degree that they embrace and advertise the truth?—The main virtue of Episcopalians is their gift for reticence. Seldom can an Episcopalian be taken for a Christian."

That ties in with a theory I have had about Kanuga: that the people who spent June and July studying about being Christians used the "guest period" in August to practice what they learned, just to be Christians without *talking* about it.

I'm not sure that explains the sweet simplicity there. I know some heathens who come to "guest period" and are just as much in the spirit of the place.

Maybe it's the spicy air, the soft brushed light and blue-green shadows. Whatever. Goodbye, summer!

***

The Atlanta Journal-Constitution
January 4, 1981

New Year Litany

I AM WRITING THIS COLUMN the week before Christmas. You are reading it the first week of the New Year.

An interesting problem.

Nowhere else in the year's turning does the mood of the heart change so starkly as it does between those two times.

Trying to cast myself ahead from these warm-lit and ingathering hours into that wind-swept and leaden time is like hurling oneself through a wall. Or out of a bright dream into a dark dawn.

The *now*, which will be *then* as you read this, is growing in holy light even at the longest dark day of the winter solstice: The moon waxing full, children coming home from the far edges of the continent with their new mates and fates. Everything is excitement, mystery, anticipation: Presents wrapped and teasing beneath the tree; rich and prickly smells of mulled cider, cinnamon and cloves, of baking gingerbread cookies growing from the kitchen. Logs in the fireplace crackle and spark. Candles stand like acolytes among young, green boughs. Even the gray clouds hint of snow.

So the January *now* of your reading this is on the sinking side of the Doppler effect, the fall-away after the peak of laugh-sounds, songs and bowl games. Think back to those fall leaves that flamed out and then lay crisp and crunchy underfoot through November. They are twice dead now, wan and lifeless, skittering here and there over funeral home lawns blown about by a bill-collector wind.

January is the time to reinvent ourselves, to "brace ourselves to our task"—the only cure for the feeling Santayana described of having "despair before us, vanity behind."

And in this moment of meditation, I think of all who write, who, professionally or privately, seek to express and communicate by means of the Word.

So I will make a litany for this dark-dealing hour, for you and for me:

For all who sit to paper, pen-poised or Remington-rolled, with head or notebook crowded with facts or fictions ready to make the miraculous transfer . . .

For all who would pull sword from stone and with it chip and chisel that stone into a space-shape of art, a master statement for the age . . .

For all who feel burnt out and stamp-stumped from sending MSS and SASEs and seeing only their own words come back, unloved. (For those who have not tried to sell their writing it should be explained: SASE stands for self-addressed stamped-envelope. It is a recommended enclosure with manuscripts, MSS, seeking fulfillment.)

May the Muse be with you:

May you experience that magical flow that possessed Joseph Conrad when he finished writing *Lord Jim* in a 24-hour burst of inspiration, working through day and night until he sensed the curtains blowing in the light of morning.

Or know the slow surprise of inspiration that Tom Wolfe felt when he had hopelessly blocked on a story for *Esquire* until, on deadline, Managing Editor Byron Dobell told him, fer God's sake, just write out his notes, send them over and Esquire would put a staff writer on it.

And he began, letter form: "Dear Byron." But after several pages he realized something was happening. He was writing well. Sure enough, he sent it and Dobell called. He sounded excited. "All I did," he told Wolfe, "was cut out the Dear Byron."

May you find the simple, nimble word; learn the power of leaving out and the energy gained from the short sentence.

If verse be your curse may you take command of the subtle power of vowels and the opinionated strength of consonants.

And may you dry out the temptation to sentimentality with a dash of irony.

May you dare the risks of negotiating between Prescriptive and Descriptive language—the former from school rules, the latter from free flow talk—remembering that Dante, himself, employed high, low and middle styles to accomplish his *Commedia*.

May you have the confidence to know when to mix the bully metaphor and when to split the jewel infinitive.

And when we are, at last, visited by those skies already haunted with spring may we all be singing like the Dinkey-Bird in the amfalula tree.

***

The Atlanta Journal-Constitution
April 19, 1981

Fires of Spring (at Emory University)

OUT OF A NIGHT OF thunder-tumbled sleep I walked into early morning on the Emory campus. I blinked into spring.

For days I have been burning the midnight oil, reading deeply into things Greek in preparation for my master's degree examination. Not only had I studied the great works and men of the Periclean age but, from the novels of Mary Renault, I have come to feel myself dwelling in the time and place of Socrates. I have moved among the crowds of bright-minded, argumentative, proud young Hellenes, wandered in the Agora—the clattery market place of goods and ideas—in the public baths, the gymnasium, the scent shops and wine taverns. I have been caught up in the daily life of those times—the petty gossip, the painful negotiations of new love, the rumors of war.

And in that mood I found myself wading straight into the streaming sunlight, my old sleep-blundering eyes seeing the Emory quadrangle full of students, seeing as through a globule of water—a clear view down to the finest detail and yet, curiously removed as if at a great distance.

It was, I decided, a *time* distance. It came to me that what I was seeing was an ancient day in the life of the world, a tableau-in-motion from a day back in what was then reckoned as 1,981 years into the Christian era. An *actual* day. (If you check the history books you will find, for example, that the big public event of that day was the attempted assassination of the president of the United States.)

But the important news on this ancient day, as is always the case in the true study of history, was to be found in the life of ordinary people.

On the Emory campus, students were returning from the spring break; greeting each other after a short absence, confronting the stylistic problem of the medium-short-absence greeting. Some made playful caricature of the long-absent-greeting. Others underplayed the greeting almost as though no time had passed.

"So how ya doing?"

"OK. Doing fine. And you?"

"Yeah. Great. OK."

Sometimes when I'm feeling dour—or quixotic—I see Emory's marble buildings as cold monuments of strict impunity—the businesslike structures of some efficient, charmless college that could as easily be in eastern Pennsylvania; a school where students are sent for a no-nonsense track into medical school, law school, or dentistry. (The Institute of Liberal Arts where I am studying at Emory is a rare enclave or interdisciplinary spirit. I hear it is scorned as self-indulgent or, at best, subversive by some of the more vertically minded scholars.)

But on this ancient morning, this rain-rinsed day of fresh clarity, with the ground still spongy from night storms, the trees blinking pebble gold against the Aegean-blue sky, I felt something inside me burst in bloom.

The marble buildings seemed harmonious, graceful, neo-classic in their rational proportions and relationships to one another.

Every casual greeting and grouping of students before my eyes seemed of eternal importance . . . a young man admiring his friend's new beard: "Hey, getting right hairy there" . . . a plump, pale professor excusing his way through a group on the walkway of boys and girls who were talking, laughing, bearing their nervous burdens as lightly as caryatids . . . a thick-necked athlete, tanned and glossy-haired, preening along, shirt three-buttons opened, bearing his warrior's profile of victory . . . a father-visitor with son awkwardly remarking about the new chapel building still in scaffolding . . . a girl on a bench tilting her head forward to let her blonde hair fall tenderly toward the face of the boy whose head was in her lap . . .

And I, city-dressed with briefcase, stepped among the beautiful bodies sprawled on the steps of Candler Library with their heads back, eyes closed to catch the sweet sun, not hinting that I was following an impulse, breaking my planned course. I moved into the cool, empty space inside, walked into the reading room and sat down at an oak table beneath the pallid bust of Pallas and urgently scribbled after-images from this one-time-only day of long ago . . . to be a poem maybe . . . or maybe, even, a column.

***

The Atlanta Journal-Constitution
May 10, 1981

The Cocktail Party

THE COCKTAIL PARTY IS A high art form.

"But I don't really enjoy them," I said to my father once when I was young and socially self-conscious, and didn't understand that people at parties concentrate much more on how *they* look than on how *you* look.

"Of course not," he replied. "You're not supposed to enjoy them. They are far too important for that."

He was right. A cocktail party is a major secular ritual; a good cocktail party is first-rate theater. It has unity of time and place where people in costume perform in a glamorous stage setting; it has development and suspense (will it take off? Have a life of its own?); climax, denouement, and epilogue ("Now that everybody's gone, let's have another drink, take off our shoes and talk about the party.")

Of course, some find cocktail parties loud and meaningless, parodies of relationships. To which Oscar Wilde would say, "Such a view can only come from those shallow people who never judge by surface appearances."

My special interest is the small talk. Good cocktail party talk is produced out of the same demands that make first-rate journalism. Each greeting or item of news must be rich, quick and lively, and must catch the interest right off and play to a short-attention span. The basic conversational unit for a cocktail party is something between a quip and an anecdote—sort of a one-and-a-half-liner. Irony and paradox are fun, but a remark should also be open-ended, should offer comeback possibilities. The game is volley, not put-away shots.

This playful banter is serious business. People who understand the stakes have been known to give away the family secrets or confess sins they would hide from the priest, rather than deliver an inanity or a dull response.

Let me illustrate some basic types of acceptable cocktail party comments drawn from my experience of recent weeks.

Exaggeration adds lift—"It was shooting sparks long as a cat's tail . . . "

Folklore is fun—"When old Traylor was in high school, he had the gear stick of his car remounted on the left of the steering column so he could shift gears without moving his right arm from around the girl . . . "

Private outrage is always good for swelling a scene—"The Episcopal Church is slowly destroying itself . . . Did you know that someone leaves the Episcopal Church every eight minutes?"

But, as in good journalism, downright fabrication is bad form.

I was guilty of this a month ago. When Jimmy Carter was told at Princeton that the last ex-president to write good memoirs was U.S. Grant, I took a sip of bourbon and postured as literary guru. "Well, of course Edmund Wilson in his book, *Patriotic Gore*, tells how Grant had a natural gift for writing . . . a clear, crisp style. His memoirs were widely read and very influential on later writers. Gertrude Stein admired Grant's writing, for example . . . "

If I had stopped there, I would have been guilty only of stealing. I had learned all of that from a lawyer at an earlier cocktail party; I have never read *Patriotic Gore.* But I went on to make the leap from Gertrude Stein to Hemingway and found myself saying that Grant's style had influenced Hemingway's famous terse prose. And, since the South didn't read Grant and was still enthralled by Sir Walter Scott, perhaps Scott was distantly responsible for Faulkner's flashes of romanticism and turgid sentences. I was faking it.

Then my conscience drove me to Wilson's delightful book. It said nothing of Hemingway being influenced by Grant. It did quote Mark Twain's vehement denunciation of Sir Walter's "sham chivalries" for its ill effect on the South: Twain almost blamed the Civil War on the Waverly novels.

Patriotic Gore is full of fascinating revisionist items. For example, the book *Uncle Tom's Cabin* is not the melodramatic mush that it became later in stage play versions that give us our impression of it. It is nearer Dickens in it salty characterizations. In the novel Eliza was never pursued by bloodhounds across the ice.

"Let's go in by the shrimp dip and I'll tell you all about it."

***

The Atlanta Journal-Constitution
September 6, 1981

Pat Conroy

Pat Conroy, Atlanta's best known living writer, has moved to Italy. He, his wife Lenore, and their children have gone to live—more or less permanently—on the outskirts of Rome.

The reasons for leaving are private and bitter.

At the same time Pat Conroy left behind something splendid; something that he, more than any other one person, helped create in his nine years in Atlanta: A circle of writer friends with a warm feeling of love and loyalty for one another. This was no small achievement, given the prancing egos of writers. (Wilfrid Sheed once wrote, "When a writer reads an unfavorable review of a friend's book his heart leaps like a fawn.")

At the core of this group of friends are those old pros who came under Jim Townsend in the early days of *Atlanta* magazine—writers like Anne Rivers Siddons, Paul Darcy Boles, Paul Hemphill, Terry Kay, Bill Diehl; all of whom today are successful, not to say prospering, novelists.

Of course, they already were friends before Conroy arrived on the scene in 1972, comrades of many labors endured together. But when Pat hit town with his surging talent and his young writer's romanticism, I think he wanted to find a more cohesive circle of writers in the high tradition of writer fellowship than actually existed; he wanted there to be a network of writers who hung out together, who shared their troubles, supported and encouraged each other. That was not quite the picture.

But then, quite unconsciously, in going about the quixotic business of being Pat Conroy, Pat created what his imagination had longed for.

It started with his friendship with Cliff Graubart, who was also new in town and struggling to fly with his Old New York Book Store.

"One day Pat and I were sitting around wondering how Cliff was going to make a living," Cliff recalled, "and he came up with this idea of an autograph party. So we took Vern Smith to lunch and arranged the first champagne book-signing for his novel *The Jones' Men*. That first party was November 1974. Can you believe it?"

Now, after eight years and more than 30 book signing parties, Atlanta writers have formed the habit of coming together to drink and gossip and support each other by buying one another's novels in the expensive, hardback edition.

Of course, Paul Hemphill's WPA Newsletter in the late 1970s was also a point of focus for the old pros. And everybody was in on the meeting at Paul Boles' house that planned the party for Jim Townsend to honor the dying editor's valiant fight for life.

But it was Conroy who left the Townsend deathwatch at the hospital and went home to write the outrageously moving eulogy that he read two days later at Jim's funeral. "O Townsend! O Dear Heart!"

O Pat! O Conroy! . . . we will miss your Irish jig of a dance of life . . . your grizzly bearhugs, the lumberjack slaps . . . you who moved large among us even as you disappeared behind wrong phone numbers, unanswered messages . . . you who pushed your friends to write novels and connected them up with New York agents and publishers and Hollywood hotshots even as you were brooding, being elusive.

The Sunday morning before the Conroys took flight there was a gathering in Pat's honor in the floodlit yard of Cliff Graubart's house in the Grant Park neighborhood. The sweet smell of cooked pig mingled in the soft air with the ghosts of summer's end and coming fall.

It was a happy consummation of the spirit Pat has brought: Boles encouraging Bernie Schein, whose manuscript he had read; Anne Siddons and Terry Kay receiving praise on all sides for *Fox's Earth* and *After Eli*; Hemphill glinting joy that Dustin Hoffman would play Stud in the movie of his *Long Gone*.

I see Pat standing in a small circle, silent, but like an emotional tea kettle commencing to whistle, his red-rimmed blue eyes fixed on who-knows-what invisible outrage in the air before him, his mouth clamped shut against a gathering explosion. Then, with one doll-like blink of the eyes, it comes, in comic-ironic understatement.

"Hate'em. I hate 'em. Hey, listen . . . " He reaches out to touch and steps back at the same time. "You wouldn't believe . . . " His head swirls up, hurling belief to the deaf heavens. Then a centaur laugh comes galloping down from his head in self-mockery. Conroy—roughneck centaur with Pegasus wings. Conroy—immortal liar, chafing warrior, secret idealist. He is a jewel thief of good deeds; an outlaw in loyalty to his friends. In the dark of night he commits vandal acts of spilling generosity.

But his power as a writer is no secret. When he wrote of the trauma of his divorce in *Atlanta* magazine, it was so poignant that people who had never been divorced could feel it down to the far, lonely, unfurnished apartment of the heart. His wrenching "Confessions of an Ex-Catholic," I suspect, drove lost sheep home.

Writing is his real faith and, as anyone knows who had read his books, his fictional characters are in constant interchange with his real life—past and present. Of course, we all hope his Pegasus wings will fly him home some day. Until then, I'm sure the crowd at the Old New York Book Store will join me in saying: Arrivederci Conrack, Ben Meecham, Will McLean. So long Pat, good and everlasting friend!

***

The Atlanta Journal-Constitution
February 21, 1982

Bricoleurs

"THE BRICOLEURS ARE BACK!"

The heart-humming realization flooded over me one recent Friday night as I watched the bearded young man working the treadle-operated printing press, in the back of Arnold's Archives Bookstore at Emory Village.

The man, John Haydock, 37, and the press, a 1908 Chandler & Price letterpress, and, indeed, the whole new little printing shop with its "cases" of type (capital letters in the "upper case," small letters in the "lower case") produced a scene of Dickensian dignity there among the Friday night browsers at new-old Arnold's Archives.

Haydock's concentration on the task before him made him seem like some master artisan from Middle Earth. Furthermore, the freshly painted black iron press, with its gold trim and smooth-flowing motions—the type, secured in its bed and inked by rollers—seemed a mystical extension of Hobbit Haydock's own care and competence.

He was turning out a thin, crisp little booklet of poems called "Wordspinner I"—the first in perhaps a series for this new, after-hours "fine printing" operation that is called the Bricoleur Press.

And thereon hangs a chance for me to tell you about the fascinating and self-delighting group of scholars, writers, composers and intellectuals who, in the early 1970s in Atlanta, formed a sort of fellowship they called the Bricoleurs. John Haydock, of course, was one of the group.

"Bricoleur" is a French word meaning Jack-of-all-trades. Anthropologist Claude Levi-Strauss, in his book *The Science of the Concrete*, used the word to stand for an approach to art and life that uses the ideas and castoff materials and tools of the past, to create new things and ideas.

The people who formed the Bricoleurs in Atlanta were mostly students at Emory's Institute of Liberal Arts, where Levi-Strauss is an Important Name.

Bricoleurs contrast themselves with engineers. Bricoleurs love to make things and create new forms. But instead of ordering what is needed for a specific task, like engineers, they enjoy open-ended creativity, working with things at hand and getting inspiration out of the very limitations of old castoff materials.

I had some brief contact with them in those days, and it was like spending an evening with the Princes of Serendip themselves. Their dizzying scholarship would dance along the past, discovering new connections that would turn, materialize or perhaps simply vaporize into a giggle. One minute they might explore the Hopi Indian myth of creation; the next, Sir Isaac Newton's dark dabbling with alchemy.

When they gathered at night, they would invent word games on the spot, devise puzzles from the Tarot deck of cards, study the Hebrew alphabet for the symbolic meanings in each other, or ponder the secrets of the ancient Cabala.

They wrote an "opera" (work) called the "Feast of Fools," which was partly performed in our living room one night. Their most ambitious literary work was a 50-page poem called "The House that Jack Built." It is riddled with riddles, with puns upon pun. They say it was inspired by reading "Finnegan's Wake" aloud. Indeed, about the only pun within my grasp was: "He can rejoice who can read Joyce."

Then, in the mid-70s, they broke up as most members moved away to pursue new careers or cosmic visions. But not before Peter Brown (now an editor with *Scientific American*) took an old printing press he found abandoned in North Georgia and fixed it up enough to crank out a few journals. But finally, the press collapsed in a heap in the basement of Paideia School.

Then last summer Curtis Bryant, the music composer of the group, came home from New York (with a new bride and an unfinished Mass), and then John Haydock came back, after years of studying "fine printing" under a master printer in California. And, bricoleur-style, the two grew excited about restoring the old press. At this point, I knew that Don and Bonnie Arnold were looking for just such an activity for the new bookstore they were opening at Emory Village.

I put them in touch with each other. Turns out, Don's father is a retired mechanic. He helped the two Bricoleurs assemble the old press, which now hums away happily—better than new—in the free hours when John Haydock is through with his day work at Emory.

There is a poem in "Wordspinner I" by Calvin Atwood of Emory's Business School that celebrates the new-old Bricoleur press:

"*Come listen to the press/that has no sound, 1908 runs like/it's one day old, they call it Bricoleur/means handyman. Imagine that, no sound/quiet as snowfall it leaves its flakes/on the floors of time, non-melting flakes.*"

***

The Atlanta Journal-Constitution
March 21, 1982

Atlanta History Center

"HISTORY? IT BORES ME TO death. I like news! I like to know what's going on *now*!"

As a newsman I appreciate the feeling. But I don't share it. To me, news without history is like jazz without a bass, or a symphony without a timpani. I reject as non-operative the term "the dead past." I believe that the historical past pulls and pushes at our every daily move and gesture, that it lurks and whispers in our every life-shaping decision.

I could rest my case with the evidence from my recent visits to the Atlanta Historical Society. I had business that took me into these enchanted woods in Buckhead that hide the headquarters and other buildings of the Historical Society on the 22 acres of the "old Inman place." The throbbing interchange of past and present out there is downright spooky.

It is, as they say in the brochure, "Where History Is Alive." And it is alive with the special Atlanta quality that is at once jaunty and urbane. The magnificently pretentious Palladian palace called the Swan House (built by the Inmans in 1928) is no threat or put-down to the sturdy pioneer simplicity of the Tullie Smith House nearby. Then, at lunchtime in the Swan Coach House restaurant, the present is awesomely present in the pink and sunlit rooms as poised and powerful ladies meet to make an establishmentarian tableau. They possess all the lady-grace of their swan-shaped meringue dessert—along with the executive toughness of a German armament tycoon.

My business has been in McElreath Hall, the stone, glass and stucco headquarters building whose modern lines somehow blend perfectly with the woodsy setting. And, in the high harmonics of that stately hall, I have strolled with AHS president Jack Spalding, former editor of *The Atlanta Journal*, whose family history is interwoven with that of the city. And, walking with this old friend of newspaper days past the exhibit of dresses worn by Atlanta ladies 100 years ago, he would cluck small insider tidbits about this name or that grand ball as though the turn-of-the-century gossip were still fresh and dangerous.

Just last week I was rescued from a moment's loss of direction in the building by a lady of regal beauty and serene command. It was Louise Allen, wife of former Mayor Ivan Allen, Jr. It felt like being brought into line with the Pole Star. Her mother, you see, was an Inman.

There is nothing of the idle and dusty stacks of dehydrated documents about McElreath Hall. The place is quietly a-swarm with scholars, writers, historians, editors, melding past and present.

"It's marvelous," says Frances Patton Statham, who has used AHS archives and exhibits in researching her trilogy of romantic fiction of Atlanta.

The other day I found my old friend Harold Martin holed up in his cozy nook in the archives, where he is bringing up to date *Atlanta and Environs*, the great reference work by Atlanta's premier historian, Franklin Garrett. Harold read aloud to me his just-finished description of the pre-dawn moment in 1945 when Franklin Roosevelt's body from Warm Springs came through Atlanta on the black-draped train.

Does Martin's project mean that Garrett is retired or inactive? Not a bit. Garrett has his own spacious office in McElreath Hall.

Last week he was busy taking calls about the 1913 Leo Frank case, which had been in the news that morning because an 83-year-old man had come forward with new eyewitness evidence that supported the innocence of Frank in the murder of 13-year-old Mary Phagan.

Garrett chuckled as he told of an Atlanta lawyer who believes Frank was guilty and who is scheduled to address a small group on his theory.

"I'm looking forward to hearing what he'll have to say (in the light of the new evidence)," Garrett said.

My news nose gave a sniff-twitch. Or did I just hear a heart-thump on the timpani of time?

***

The Atlanta Journal-Constitution
June 13, 1982

Vacation Houses and Their Books

Books in vacation houses don't just sit there on the shelf, passive and dead, like the souvenir ashtray or the stuffed alligator from Flagler Street. They engage in a socially complex secret life more like the colony of mice behind the paneling, like the ghosts of other summers, like numberless memories.

Even in mid-July, and even if one walks through the room with brisk resolve—wicker hamper in hand packed with cheese, wine, grapes, sandwiches and "Peterson's Birds"—even then, the rows of books in the dim cool above the straw rug will seem to whisper, to tease and call out, winking a message in the soundless and not unmusical way of white clouds piling against the blue.

So it is that thunder, summer rain, sunlight, dripping afternoons, stars and crickets, a log fire (we're talking mountains here) and books on the shelves—all of these things have mythic qualities that are only truly revealed in that strange Chekhovian landscape that vacation can create.

But of these, it is the books that hold the real power. They are the very wings of escape.

The old crusader was dying in his castle; his chaplain dared remind him he would be welcomed to live his last hours in the tower of the Gilbertine Monastery of Sempringham.

"The dying baron cocked a shaggy white, incredulous eyebrow. An imprecation leaped to his profane old-soldier's tongue. 'Bleeding five wounds of God! The Devil fly away with Sempringham's tower and Geoffrey Hawkswood, too!'"

Thus begins *The Golden Exile*, a 1951 novel by Lawrence Schoonover. If there had been more time, I might have plumped myself down at the cushioned bay window and pursued the disaffection between the old baron and Sir Geoffrey in the 12th-century romance.

But we were only there for a weekend, visiting in a rambling, brown wood shingled house, a child's dream of a summer house, hidden behind the hemlocks of Highlands, N.C.

But I did take an idle hour with this rich, eclectic collection of books—this sun-faced and musty record of some family's intellectual curiosity and emotional needs that began, I judged, in the 1920s.

On the shelf with a set of Robert Louis Stevenson was *Histoire de France* par A. Malet, Faulkner's *Pylon*, H.G. Wells' *Outline of Man's Work and Wealth*, Stuart Chases' *The Tyranny of Words*, Michener's *The Drifters*, a dozen cheap detective paperbacks and 52 issues of the *Reader's Digest* dated from 1962 to 1980.

Biographies of Katherine of Aragon, Mary Tudor, Lincoln (1917 edition) stood near *Don Quixote de la Mancha* (1876 edition in Spanish) and *Revolution in Nihilism*, called "a warning to the west," by Hermann Rauschning, published in May 1939, just before Hitler's Germany invaded Poland.

My mind drifted higher as in a balloon and played across the wider view of the centuries as I pulled down Christopher Marley's *Thunder on the Left* and read the title quote from Sir Eustace Peachtree:

"Among the notionable dictes of antique Rome was the fancy that when men heard thunder on the left, the gods had somewhat speciall advertisement to impart . . ."

Then, in a preface to *The Annals of Tacitus* by W.F. Allen, published in 1890, came news that made the year 1889 seem conversationally close. "Professor Allen died very suddenly at his home in Madison, Wisconsin, December 9, 1889. The Latin text and the commentary were already in type, and now appear."

Reading this, thinking of Professor Allen and his lifetime devotion to the Roman historian of the second century A.D., and of the early owners of this house buying that book (or inheriting it), bringing the book up here to take its place in the company of H.G. Wells, Cervantes and Agatha Christie, it came to me that vacation in a summer house, with time to read, is not just a form of escape *from* the hassles of daily life.

It is also escape *into* the larger perspective of time and history, into a sense of lives connected each to each, generation by generation, through love and struggle, wars and destruction, triumph and progress—and of societies and civilizations that rise and fall and build again out of what was fallen, knowing what was there before because it was written down in books of stern record or beguiling romance.

***

The Atlanta Journal-Constitution
October 17, 1982

Camelot

I AM WRITING THIS UNDER the spell of Merlin the Magician and the Arthurian legend. I have just finished reading Mary Stewart's *The Hollow Hills*. The Mood is on me.

I feel possessed by a temporary clairvoyance by which I can observe the mythic tales of our past entering history through storytelling and treading into the strands of our real-life, value-coded tradition—the warp that is woven with the woof of daily events to make the fabric of our culture.

And I am moved, in this mood, to tell of a discovery I made in the last pages of a similar novel that I read 25 years ago. I have often told friends of this discovery, but never without risk of choking up.

The discovery is of one word, one special word that suddenly gives stunning focus to this vision of how the epic tales of heroes come to be written from dank centuries of huddled winter evenings recounting the ordeals of warriors.

The book that has this one special word is *The Once and Future King* by T.H. White—an English writer who died in the 1960s (not the T.H. White of *The Making of the President* series).

The Once and Future King is a light-hearted yet finally serious retelling of the Arthurian legend and was, of course, the inspiration for the musical comedy "Camelot." And, in show form, the story played a certain myth-making role in our times when its glow glanced off the John F. Kennedy presidency, highlighting its valiant and surging vigor, its lightness and brightness of spirit.

In those youthful years, the early 60s, one did not have to get to New York to see the original cast of "Camelot" (Richard Burton, Julie Andrews, Robert Goulet). The high moment of the play, the thing that lifted it above being merely a pretty fairy tale, is in the last song, there on the record album.

It comes in the final scene in which King Arthur is alone in camp the night before a battle that will obviously bring down the Round Table and destroy his great work—a society of Might for Right; and order in which Law rules over mayhem. He is inconsolably sad that the example of Camelot and all its noble years will be lost to time and that civilization will have to start again in barbarity.

He hears someone near his tent. He pulls from hiding a lad in his early teens who has come to join the battle, to fight for Camelot.

"What do you know of Camelot?" King Arthur asks him.

Why, the boy knows all the stories; furthermore, he understands the ideals and is willing to die for them.

Suddenly Arthur brightens. A new idea! This boy—"Tom, sir, Tom of Warwick," he tells the King—this Tom of Warwick must live, must flee quickly, away from the battle and death so that he can keep the memory of Camelot alive for the future.

"*Ask every person if he's heard the* story," Arthur charges him in a song that Richard Burton talks with shimmering emotion. "*And tell it loud and clear if he has not/That once there was a fleeting wisp of glory, called Camelot.*"

The lad obeys his king and heads for home.

Tom of Warwick? Who is this Tom of Warwick? In the book, he is described in that scene as standing there in the camplight with "the new heraldry of Malory" blazing on his tunic.

Malory. That's the word. The heart-leaping literary conceit that T.H. White has put to the reader is that this youth in mythical 5th-centry Britain is the ancestor of Sir Thomas Malory, the 15th-century English writer who compiled the tales of the Arthurian legend into that great work of our literary heritage "Le Morte d'Arthur," as if the tales were handed down in the family, father to son, in sacred trust from the legendary king.

"*Don't let it be forgot,*" Arthur sings in a voice now radiant with a new realization, "*that once there was a spot . . .For one brief shining moment . . . .*"

And he shouts after Tom:

"Run, boy, run!"

***

The Atlanta Journal-Constitution
October 31, 1982

Stephen Spender

oh young men oh young comrades
it is too late now to stay in those houses
your fathers built where they built you to build to breed
money on money it is too late
to make or even to count what has been made

Oh what a daydreaming sailor lad I was when World War II collapsed and sent me into the western sun to sweep up Japanese mines. My ship floated up the heedless Wang Poo River where, in a dusty shop in Shanghai, I bought a book of stiff cardboard cover and cheap binding called *A New Anthology of Modern Poetry* which, even now—rotting and faded—I count among my most fabulous possessions.

I kept it secret, and, in secret on the high seas home, built in the heart a house of poetry from reading Yeats, Eliot, Auden, Cummings: from learning Elinor Wylie's "Wild Peaches" and D.H. Lawrence's "The Elephant Is Slow to Mate."

On I sailed to Stephen Spender's "oh young men oh young comrades." Its cobweb-cleansing call to life sang to my blood. I didn't know until later that Spender—an English poet of near-front rank status—was beguiled by the romantic vision of Communism in the 30s which the poem reflects.

It wouldn't have mattered. I don't look for political or social philosophy in poems. I seek intellectual music. Yet, at age 19, I did respond to Spender's decrying of grubby stale materialism and extolling the human spirit and "*those riches/which begin with your body and your fiery soul.*"

In the years that followed—good years of struggle to make ends meet in a life of love, of sons and a daughter—I found equal affinity for a somewhat opposite sentiment expressed in W.B. Yeats' poem "A Prayer for My Daughter."

"And may her bridegroom bring her to a house/Where all's accustomed, ceremonious. . . How but in custom and ceremony/Are innocence and beauty born?"

And through the years I have lived with this deep-buried dichotomy. But then, doesn't everyone? Doesn't the romantic passion of youth finally have to make a sort of permanent armistice with the ironic understandings of age?

All of this came forward the other night when we attended a small dinner party for the very same Stephen Spender, who was visiting a friend in Atlanta. On an impulse, I took my battered old book, which Emily fixed up with strapping tape for its unexpected outing.

Spender is 73 now, towering, white-haired and quite charming; bearing more his earlier Oxford style of light-crust wit and anecdote than that of the humorless revolutionary of the 30s. He showed mild amusement at my book; seeing his earlier poems there on the liver-spotted page.

As we were leaving Emily said, "Why don't you get him to sign your book?"

And so I did. I went over and got him to sign the bottom of the page with the poem "oh young men oh young comrades."

"I have always admired that poem," I told him as he was writing his name. "But I have also equally admired Yeats' 'A Prayer for My Daughter' and sort of put the two up against each other, wondering where I really stood."

"Well, I was young when I wrote my poem. Yeats was old when he wrote his," he smiled, handing me back the book. Well, yes. But, no! That does *not* settle it. I still feel both ways!

But so did Yeats. At age 61, in his poem "The Tower," complaining that "old age has been tied to me as to a dog's tail," Yeats still cries out:

"Never had I more/excited, passionate, fantastical/Imagination nor an ear and eye/That more expected the impossible."

Yes!

***

The Atlanta Journal-Constitution
March 20, 1983

An Evening with my Father

I CAN FORGIVE STUDENTS AT the college where I teach for sometimes being silly and ignorant. Yeats made a poignant point with his line: "Young, we loved each other and were ignorant." And, of course, we all join Erasmas in praising folly.

But the other day I encountered students being silly and ignorant in a way that made me sad. They took being silly and ignorant quite seriously. They brought strong-willed determination to the task of remaining shallow and uninformed (beyond learning facts for grade-making) as if their social esteem were at risk.

It is sad to squint the eyes into the future years of people who separate learning from life. Students who persist in this will become dangerously bored and boring when the fluff of youth wears off. Such a dumb doom is unnecessary. Once the flame of learning catches it can, in time, become a firestorm.

And when it does, as it has in the case of an 89-year-old gentleman with whom my wife and I recently spent a rich and serendipitous evening, then, oh how majestically old age is armed to rage, rage against the dying of the light.

The evening with the learned gentleman was luminous with talk of books and ideas and things that happened long ago but are still exciting. The topics of conversation flashed like schools of silver fish invisible in the air of the book-lined, portrait-hung room.

A brief lecture on the priesthood of professions from our host ("Doctors and lawyers should have no concern with Money. They serve their profession.") led by means of some heady free-association, to a bit of role-playing, of being Cardinal Richelieu (from a French drama) warning his enemies with fixed-eye intensity: "Around me I draw the awful circle of the Holy Church of Rome."

Out of the blue but in the spirit of the evening I brought up the Whiffenpoof Song.

"To the tables down at Morey's…" he began to sing.

"Most people today sing 'gentlemen songsters off on a spree,'' I said. "It should be 'gentlemen rankers…damned from here to eternity.' It's from Kipling. Tell me about gentlemen rankers."

"Well, of course, the oldest son inherited the land; the second became an officer in the military. The third went into the church. So the youngest left home to nail down the corners of empire. He might join the army as an enlisted man—the gentleman ranker—or just work where he could. He was called a remittance man. His family paid him to go. And, usually, to stay gone."

A book of Robert W. Service was plucked from a bookcase and opened to a poem called "The Younger Son." It was read aloud:

"If you leave the gloom of London and you seek a glowing land/Where all except the flag is strange and new/There's a bronzed and stalwart fellow who will grip you by the hand/And greet you with a welcome warm and true./For he's your younger brother, the one you sent away/Because there wasn't room for him at home;/And now he's quite contented, and he's glad he didn't stay/And he's building Britain's greatness o're the foam."

As we left the gentleman ranker where "the sunlight threads the pine-gloom" the talk took a turn and, quick as a blade, we were with the Burning Bush and the voice of Yahweh telling Moses, "I am that I am." Then off the shelf came Swinburne and up rose a poem about Hertha, the force that preceded Yahweh—according to Charles Algernon Swinburne:

I am that which began—
Before God was, I am.

To which my wife commented, "Sounds like someone who wouldn't have any trouble getting into the Piedmont Driving Club."

***

The Atlanta Journal-Constitution
April 3, 1983

Gifts from the Gods: Fire and Literature

I AM SITTING BEFORE AN open fire in our mountain house on a chilly day in late March. It is my spring break. The pressure is off for a few days.

I stare at the flaming logs. The phrase "literary heritage" drifts into my mind, inspired, I suspect, by the lead sentence in an article in the *New Yorker* I read an hour ago that cleverly played on a familiar line by Shakespeare: "The marriage of art and architecture admits many impediments." Great literature of the past is with us always to enrich the jest, to strengthen a point.

As I watch the snapping hot orange tongues licking around the oak logs I muse on the mysterious miracle of fire: how burning wood is the tree giving back a piece of the sun's heat that it gathered and stored through photosynthesis in many years of growth.

At the same time I am drawn to contemplate the equally powerful mystery of literature—of all art, really—and how it addresses our dream anxieties with myth and drama and provides signals of significance in our lives. From Homer to Updike, from Oedipus to Cinderella, we have accumulated a treasured reference library for our psychic use.

I see the prim school marm enunciating "our literary heritage" to her restless and rambunctious students. A caricature of a dried-up spinster, perhaps, reciting "Hail to thee, blithe spirit." But her task is more than noble; it is essential to our humanity.

Slowly I begin to connect, metaphorically, the idea of fire and literary heritage. Fables invent themselves for my meditation.

I look into the fireplace blaze. I seem to fall weightless into the tunnel of Time, reeling down the darkness until I come to a stop where all is still. I sniff the dank, fierce savage forests of prehistory on earth. Suddenly a crashing storm is bombarding the world. I can see, silhouetted against the whips of lightning, the desperate trees and beasts, thrashing in panic.

But look there—there is one figure, alone, upright, hulking against the storm without panic, moving toward the loudest bolt of lightening with the resolute gait of a madman or a visionary.

He has left the cave in defiance of the tribal taboo, to seek out the evil Heatlight. Three times before, he has seen it come from the Skygod and possess the trees and grass in terrible roaring death. The tribal memory has taught always to flee and hide; that the Heatlight is Skygod's wrath.

But this one remembers noticing other things about Heatlight—that it does not devour rocks or dirt or water. In fact, he noted how rain water made the Heatlight spirit die. He cannot put out of his mind how wonderfully it broke up the darkness so that eyes could see when the sun was gone. Also, it felt good on the cold, wet body until one came too close and its claws began to hurt. Most of all he could not forget the good taste of the meat of the animal that had been killed and darkened by the Heatlight.

He has been possessed in his mind with a vision of how his tribe might learn to keep a piece of the Heatlight in caves by feeding it sticks but keeping it trapped by putting stones around it. It would bring light, warmth, and sweeten the meat. Of course, if he were wrong he would be driven out of the tribe and die without the help of fellow hunters. But his mind would not let him live in peace until he had explored his idea.

In my fable, of course, he did find fire and brought it to the use of his fellow creatures, making them—and us—more human. We do not forget fire in our daily lives. We flick a Bic; we blast off for space.

What would happen if we lost our literature? I think we would be like the village in the book *A Hundred Years of Solitude*. A spell was cast on the village so that people could live without sleep. At first they were delighted with the extra time for projects for leisure. But because they didn't sleep they didn't dream and slowly they began to lose their memories. First they forgot the far past; then, slowly they began to forget who they were, what food was for, what they needed to do to stay alive. Fortunately, the spell was broken; people began to dream again, to remember, and all was saved.

Hang in there, Miz School Marm. Humanity hath need of you!

***

The Atlanta Journal-Constitution
January 1, 1985

New Year's Shutdown

SEVERAL YEARS AGO A GEORGIA Power executive responded to my criticisms of some of her company's policies by saying: "So, do you want to wake up in the dark, in the cold?" No.

But, ever since, the thought of waking up in the dark, in the cold, without benefit of electricity has seemed to me one dandy idea for early January, a month whose personality seems to reflect the Dark Ages anyway.

I picture a sort of national negative holiday for three days during the first week of the New Year; the nation's power generating plants would shut down. Throughout the land the motors, switches, coils, chips, cathode ray tubes, elements and filaments that light our lives and lighten our work, would cease to function. All radios, televisions, computers, light bulbs, neon signs, subways and elevators, icemakers and ski tows, amplified guitars, microwave ovens and desk calculators would exhale a collective sign of relief and settle themselves down for a brief midwinter hibernation, leaving us to face ourselves and the suddenly unchained gods of Nature.

It would be like a fierce, brief secular Lent—a time of meditation and penitence to dry out from the Mardi Gras excesses of the holiday season. Its benefits would be subtle, but enormous, too, in ways that would prolong our national life by at least a century, much the way jogging increases the life span of those it doesn't finish off.

Yes, I know that you could never sell the Archie Bunkers of the land on the spiritual rewards of creative suffering. So the rationale for cutting off all electric power for three days would have to come from some EPA rule requiring all power plants to close down for inspection, or to clean out their scrubbers, or freshen their coolant—something like that.

The three days would become known as the Shutdown. And, while it would create some economic dislocations in the first few years, it would also liberate a long-neglected force that is akin to that impulse that, as we say, made this country great.

This contrived crisis could test the status of our national sense of community, seeing if we could pull together as in the days of the great wars, or if we could experience the sense of mutual human vulnerability as in the Great Depression, or if we still can bring off that candle-lit camaraderie so delightfully and spontaneously produced in the New York blackout of 1965.

The Shutdown would be much more than a national nostalgia trip, although one of the strong sensory impressions it would leave each year is of the smells of wood smoke, burning coal, kerosene and candle tallow that permeated the houses of our Victorian ancestors a century ago. And, as in earlier times, families would summon up entertainment out of their own resources—singing, parlor games, telling stories by lamplight and fireside. It would renew the fad of do-it-yourself music with folk, country and blues having a decided advantage over rock and other music born of electronics.

When, during the Shutdown, the Broadway-at-night glow of cities and suburban mall sprawl has dimmed and the landscape is sprinkled with windows of jack-o-lantern light from homes and neighborhood stores, the night will once more be ruled by the stars and the moon. Although it will come too late to help see Halley's comet this go-round, the turning down of the Great White Way incandescence will restore for a memorable moment the Old Testament importance of dawns and twilights as executors of day and its labor.

No need to worry about hospitals, prisons and lighthouses, for, like ships at sea, they ply under their own power in emergency conditions. As for the poor and homeless, I suspect they would welcome the company. Those who knew their way about the domain of suffering would be royalty for these three days. They might even hope that the sympathy for their plight, so often expressed in words and handouts, would mature into empathy and yield some adjustments to get them out of their predicament.

In 1947, in early January, I experienced something like the Shutdown at a cousin's wedding in a little town of elm-lined streets up east. A snow storm took out the power, and for a couple of days, life went on in heightened excitement and improvisation. The wedding took place in a church lit only by candles. We kept our coats on, as I remember. But the snow light and candles and fur-wrapped faces stand out in my memory as a time of exquisite reality.

But that was 1947—before television. Before the bowl games of early January. Which, now that I mention it, is why the Shutdown is impossible. We might fool Archie Bunker, but prevailing over the power of the bowl-watching establishment, backed by the networks and ad-bucks, would be another matter.

***

IV. On Learning and Education

Atlanta
February 1969

Review of "Education and Ecstasy"

"This may be the most important book in the history of the world," said the author modestly, smiling. George Leonard was talking to a friend about his new book, *Education and Ecstasy.*

He could be right. It *is* fun.

Fun? It illuminates like the hunter's moon and makes all other books on human seeking seem only a torch of smoky pine. It is a startling and un-angry book which deals with the human condition without despair, projects extravagant possibilities without hysteria, and calmly articulates the very purpose of life in the age that may now be beginning.

For the author treats the present time, with all its tragic waste of human potential, as the end of the Civilized Epoch—a fifteen-thousand-year period in which man was never more than a specialized component of society—limited, fragmented. If the reader can open to the notion that people are ready to move beyond the scientific-rationalist mindset of Civilization, he can begin to feel the giddy involvement with a future time that turns out to be simpler than the present in the sense that a jet engine is simpler than the old-fashioned, sputtering reciprocating job.

Near the end of the book, Leonard tells of a conversation he had with the prophetic author Aldous Huxley about the future of man. Their talk was part of what inspired Leonard to write *Education and Ecstasy.* The historical significance of Leonard's book may be that it offers an alternative to Huxley's *Brave New World.* Instead of showing how technology can dehumanize man as it does in Huxley's negative utopia, *Education and Ecstasy* details a vision of how technology can be used to help man reach his potential as a whole, unique, and joyous creature.

But Leonard is not remotely talking about the familiar conformity-vs.-individuality issue. He has conceived a whole new environment for man in which sense and sensory are not so desperately separate, one that gives play to that blood mischief that can raise the hairs on the flesh, that welcomes intuitive and illogical exuberance.

We first realize this new thing when he describes a polite visit to a classroom. As education editor for *Look* magazine he has done this hundreds of times. The principal is showing him a classroom of children, explaining the even flow of light in the room and Leonard rejoices with him. "But something disturbs me, a vinegary tingle at the back of my neck. *There is a witch in this room.*" And he spots a girl with pale skin and long black hair staring at him "bold and direct, telling me that she knows, without words, everything that needs to be known about me."

> "When it gets dark outside," the principal is saying, "an electric-eye device—here—automatically compensates by turning on the lights to the requisite illumination." The girl's eyes never leave mine. She is a sorceress, too, for already she has created a whole new world inhabited only by the two of us. It is not a sexual world. What she has in mind—she could never put it into words—by-passes the erotic entirely. But later, when those talents of hers which do not fit the scientific-rationalist frame are finally extinguished, she may turn to sex. And she may become promiscuous, always seeking the shadow of an ecstasy and knowledge that by then she will remember only as a distant vibration, an inexplicable urge toward communion.

In short parenthetical sentences in italics, interspersed in the early chapters, the underlying theme of the book is spelled out as though for subliminal reception:

> *(To learn is to change. Education is a process that changes the learner.)*
> *(Learning eventually involves interaction between learner and environment, and its effectiveness relates to the frequency, variety and intensity of the interaction.)*
> *(Education, at best, is ecstatic.)*

But the book is too full of surprises to bog down in didacticism for long. Leonard examines the evidence that man's aggressiveness and "narrow acquisitiveness" are more environmental than instinctive and comes up on that side of the anthropological and philosophical argument that holds hope in the perfectibility of man.

Then, in what seems to be a shift into science fiction, the book takes us to an American school in the year 2001. Here the implications of all that has been hinted at are seen in fulfillment. Schools are no longer rigidly fixed into classroom hours, into separated subject matter. All manner of advanced technology is used: computers that contain each child's learning history are used as highly sophisticated learning machines that can generate playful dialogue with the child.

For example, it is accepted that a three-year-old will have so learned the basics of spelling that she can launch into a whimsical game of spelling variations with her computer. Here is Sally, age three and a half, talking with CAD (Computer Assisted Dialogue), in "a session on breaking her linguistic set."

And, incidentally, Sally is sitting before a screen—well, no, not a screen, but a space in which images can be projected on the air. Pink and lavender clouds gradually take the shape of a cat. Sally identifies it into her microphone and the letters "CAT" appear at the bottom of the display.

CAD: Can you think of an alternate spelling?

SALLY: (Typing): kat.

On the display, the giant cat face recedes and is transformed into a white Angora cat, surrounded by vibrating, jagged, radial lines of many colors. A purring sound comes from the display.

CAD: How about another?

SALLY: (Pausing a moment): katte.

The purring becomes louder.

CAD: A cat is a kat is a katte.

SALLY: (Quickly): A katte is a kat is a cat.

CAD: Copy cat.

SALLY: Koppy kat.

And later, after an interval of change on the display:

SALLY: A cat hiss a kat hiss a katte.

CAD: Wild!!!

At every turn is some imaginative new approach. In a "Discovery Tent" children are presented with the exact physical equipment with which Michael Faraday discovered how to convert magnetism into electricity. The aim is to see how well the children do in discovering the laws that govern electromagnetic induction.

After two chapters on this future world, Leonard delivers another surprise. "Everything in the preceding chapters is based on something that already exists."

As the book moves on to describe how the learning process is, at best, a moment of ecstasy and that one's whole life could be directed toward keeping alive this process of learning, the surprises lose their shock value. When Leonard writes a chapter on the possibility of the best school being no school one is ready to go along.

> The most obvious barrier between our children and the kind of education that can free their enormous potential seems to be the educational system itself: a vast, suffocating web of people, practices and presumptions, kindly in intent, ponderous in response. Now, when true educational alternatives are at last becoming clear, we may overlook the simplest: no school.

It is helpful in reading *E&E* to protect oneself by laying down the blanket reservation that the book is fundamentally preposterous. Yet one cannot help but be engaged when it becomes clear that Leonard, for all his surprises, is not indulging in irony. He is writing with genuine conviction and enthusiasm.

In an afterword to George Orwell's *1984*, Erich Fromm writes: "The mood of hopelessness about the future of man is a marked contrast to one of the most fundamental features of Western thought: the faith in human progress and man's capacity to create a world of justice and peace. This hope has its roots both in Greek and in Roman thinking, as well as in the Messianic concept of the Old Testament prophets. The Old Testament philosophy of history assumed that man grows and unfolds in history and eventually becomes what he potentially is. It assumes that he develops his powers of reason and love fully, and thus is enabled to grasp the world, being one with his fellow man and nature, at the same time protecting his individuality and his integrity."

This is exactly in line with Leonard. While he seems to be pleading for a world that lies beyond Civilization and Western tradition, he is, in fact, reviving its richest hope.

***

The Chronicle of Higher Education
October 12, 1983

The Big Secret of an Education in the Liberal Arts

Every time I prepare my get-acquainted spiel for a new class, I have to struggle against revealing to my students what I consider the Big Secret—my answer to *why* they should learn.

They don't need to hear it at this point in their lives. They have enough to do keeping up with *what* they should learn and *how* they should go about learning it. The *why* can wait.

That is not to say that I think college students lack acuity or perception. I have found many of them have matured beyond the old idea that college is where you go to get good grades to get a job so you can afford the car, house, spouse, and way of living fantasized during the high school years. I have been impressed to find that most of those I talk to seem to think in terms of careers instead of jobs. And they go about picking their careers sensibly.

And yet the main point of a liberal-arts education—the Big Secret—is not career guidance. It has to do with providing some future access to that invisible world on the other side of the looking glass: the world of elegant ideas, sophisticated observation, unexpected judgments. The skills that the liberal arts teach should inform life's action with clear-minded analysis and enrich its impulses with creative synthesis.

Like most college catalogues, ours articulates the higher purposes of a liberal-arts education quite well. We seek to provide an "environment wherein each student may attain a disciplined and open mind, a capacity for self-development, and the knowledge and skills essential for living in a free society."

"Capacity for self-development." The phrase reminds me of my high school Latin teacher. When we challenged him to explain the point of studying a dead language, he would say, "It will help you learn how to learn." We, of course, felt we had been handed another of the adult world's incomprehensible, tail-chasing maxims.

And yet, even leaving aside the value of Latin as a basis for understanding the structure of language, it was a good answer. To learn how to learn. Looking back, I can see it would be a good start to explaining, "Why college?"

I look back across a quarter of a century as a journalist. The process of covering news is an experience in learning. Each new or unfamiliar story to be covered demands first a quick and accurate locating of the subject in the Great Scheme of Things, then an equally efficient exploring to discover its significance and interest.

That means a reporter must keep in mind a road map representing the "great scheme." College-acquired knowledge may do little more than provide the coordinates and North arrow of such a map. But that is a vital start. Each new subject explored in life after college is added as a landmark to the map. The picture becomes clearer. The gradual filling in of the map, the slow clarifying of connections and relationships—the process of learning and growing—is so deeply satisfying that it is difficult to describe.

When I think of the broader meaning of that process in liberal arts, I find it needs to be expressed by a fanciful myth. Somewhere between the ages of 30 and 50, it can happen that one enters what I will call the cave.

In the middle of the journey of our life I came to myself in a dark wood where the straight way was lost.

O.K.—for Dante it was a dark wood. I still prefer the cave, entered with little more than the torch of smoky pine that is knowledge acquired in college. As the years go by, the torch is held out to flicker on the walls, to explore the crevices, to reveal the unexpected passages, the hidden rooms, the connecting tunnels.

The labyrinth becomes familiar; its pattern begins to present a certain logic and beauty. Then it can happen that a light begins to fill the cave, and it is no longer a cave but a landscape that opens before the pilgrim.

Arriving at that point is not the beginning of wisdom nor does it promise worldly success. Yet with it comes understanding and confidence that can lead to the fulfillment of many long-held wishes. One can become cynical or wickedly witty. Or one can choose to believe.

***

Sewanee News
March 1984

Masters of Walsh Hill

THESE DAYS, IN MY BATTLE to teach college students, I cannot forget Sewanee forty years ago when I sat where they sit, daring my teachers—Abbo, "Fuzzy" Ware, Arthur Dugan, and the rest—to change me, to teach me, to convince me that there was a larger world for me to bear than the one I brought into class, invisible on my shoulders.

The trip back through time comes on me unexpectedly here in Carrollton, Georgia. I stand before my class in room 312 of the Humanities Building at West Georgia College and, in a subliminal blink of flashback, there I am in Walsh Hall sitting at the dark-painted pine plank that served as desk for a row of students in the 1940s. And, even as I strike my pedagogic posture in 1984, I feel the presence of those teachers, now dead or very old, who faced me in immortal combat; I think of them these days and have new insight into their struggle with our ignorance.

Oh, my teachers, how could you know that you won the battle? You fanned alive a flame in me that has not gone out but still burns, a consuming, greedy fire. How would you know you would win when all I showed you in those days were sleepy eyes, sloppy papers, and worse verse?

I am learning that a teacher can never know, in the short haul, what good—or harm—he has done to his students. So let it be.

But I would like to publish here a cry of thanks to the veil to those few who held the battle line and enlarged my life.

• You, "Fuzzy" Ware, outrageous campus character of towering bombast, scruffy beard, and battered briefcase laden with History, who bullied students in class, hurling chalk and insults, scribbling Jovian denouncements on the margins of papers we turned in. (I uncovered one in a musty pile just last month, "Dates! Dates! Give me Dates!" the red ink thundered, "...not a shopping list of names!")

Even at the time, we spotted the fraud in your anger, the joke hidden in your rampaging impatience. Yet your pyrotechnics served to impress on me for life the mythical significance of the Gothic arch in the evolution of Western civilization. I have worked the Gothic arch—not without some straining—into my Introduction to Mass Communication.

• And you, Arthur Dugan, who first startled me with the ecstasy of clear thinking, who chopped the air into neat links, dividing history into wonderful sausages, laughing at the ironies even as you shared the delight with us. I will never quite recover from the day you looked around the class and saw more blood-heavy eyelids clicking shut than irises widening and pupils dilated. You snapped shut the book you were holding, gathered up the other books you had brought to read from (with their paper markers sticking out from between the pages), and stalked out of the room. I hope to do that some day, when provoked.

• And you, Abbo, the Abbott of Martin, the raiser of consciousness long before the term was appropriated to serve a special interest, you of masterful dramatic techniques—the disdainful snorts and sudden eye-openings in mock surprise, the glint-eyed merriment; the significant final phrase delivered with insinuating and elegant English accent—you left me with an abiding love of Wordsworth and his "dark, inscrutable workmanship." And a precariously raised consciousness.

You three—all dead—are the ones I think about these days, you with your masterfully performed lectures.

While I am too much of a ham not to use dramatics, I am working on a classroom technique that has a different emphasis. I'm devising ways to induce in students in class the restless, aggressive, intellectual attitude of reporters at a news conference. I want to put pressure on them to feel responsible for producing out of a lecture—and the questions they may ask—a cogent, readable, news-like story complete with the best quotations from the lecture.

I don't know if it will work. But I hope some day a student will feel about my effort as I feel toward my Masters of Walsh Hall after nearly half a century.

***

The Times-Georgian
October 7, 1984

Both Worlds Are Real

AMONG THE POPULAR ESCAPE FANTASIES of harried executives, like sailing the Windward Islands or moving to the country, the one that is always quickened in the fall is the one that goes: "I'm going to get a job teaching at a college in a small town."

Images beckon of green-gold light slanting across the playing fields in the clear afternoon; of the bright Saturday noon before the homecoming game with a gathering of old alums, ruddy laughter, good Scotch, tweeds with leather elbow patches—all spilling into sunlight from paneled walls of books designed to muffle pipe-smoking voice to the murmur of wisdom. The imagination then flows to the stadium of splatter-colored crowds, coeds bounding in smiles, beer-leery KAs shouting down the slope of heads, of brass-glinting music thumping the cheers of earth . . .well, you get the picture.

This, as you might surmise, was my favorite fantasy. And three falls ago I figured out how to get myself and my wife beamed into this life. So, here I am, teaching at West Georgia College in Carrollton, a town of 16,000—on the surface exactly what my imagination had cooked up.

But fantasies, like travel folders, do not include details—the bugs, the heat, the insolent officials.

Nor is my fantasy-come-to-life exactly what I had pictured. It is unbelievably better. I could not have foretold the harmonies I have found: they were not visible to the mind's eye.

This is not to say we have crashed down in the land of Oz. In our town one cannot buy liquor or easily find a *New York Times.* Mail is not delivered until mid-afternoon—too late to make a difference in the day; and, for the past six months, we have managed to get only whining excuses about getting our dishwasher repaired. The repairmen who know our brand are busy in Atlanta.

But the humming fact is that we feel we have entered the right life at the right time. Indeed, I, with my job as teacher, feel in possession of two realities, each one alone enough to call the good life. These two lives correspond roughly to "town" and "gown." Do they also fit into that old division of academia and "the real world"?

Coming late to college teaching—I was 55—meant that we were entirely at home in the so-called "real world" of the town. In every way we felt welcomed—in church choir and hardware store; by the village blacksmith who made us log dogs for our fireplace and by the banker who let us store furniture in his unrented offices. We were able to plug into the circuitry of friends and gossip exactly appropriate to our taste.

The surprises came in the "gown" side. And the first surprise was to learn that the academic life is, to put it mildly, challenging. Teaching ain't stealing. It is a bit like driving a coach and six, wild horses, across Indian territory—an experience alive with danger and whahoo!

But, in the throes of this hectic challenge comes the warm delight of being among the big secrets of civilization. A college faculty is, after all, a repository of all the art, thought and knowledge of our culture. And, I confess I am a culture junkie: an intellectual dilettante who loves the idea of being close to the Big Idea. I feel like a miser living in the town of Ft. Knox, Ky., happy just knowing all that real gold is nearby.

I pass in the hallways professors who, when I get time to ask, will be able to tell me about Faulkner's *The Sound and the Fury*, or Thomistic logic, or the character flaw in the Girondens of the French Revolution. After a dinner party chat with the head of the chemistry department on the Shroud of Turin, I received a provocative pamphlet on the subject through intercampus mail. Someday I will revive my French in the language lab. My wife pores over the college catalog.

In the 30 years that I was in "the real world," I often wondered if the ideas and history that lay beneath the surface of our getting and spending were not more entitled to the label of "the real world."

Well, I don't claim to know which is the real "Real World." The question is like asking which is real water—the clear, fresh, giggling streams of the hills or the vast, dark, salty, mothering sea?

All I know is I love dwelling in the estuary—that rich nutritious marsh land where the two waters mingle in the slow tides of time.

***

The West Georgian
September 26, 1984

Greeks: Deadweights

I LIKE GREEKS—THOSE PERKY, STYLISH students who identify themselves as "pikes," "tri-delts," "kappa sigs," "fi mews," or by other such tags. They are open and friendly sorts. Their playful banter around campus provides the easy-breezy rhythm needed to remind us all that college is a very rich and special kind of coming-of-age experience. I was a Greek myself back when.

So, I was slow to believe the evidence that kept coming at me during these first three years of teaching that the Greek students—with a few sparkling exceptions—represent a kind of intellectual deadweight presence in the classroom. Not that they are disruptive or dumb. Indeed, that is the heart of the problem. They are the very students who should grasp the heady possibilities in the classroom transaction and help set the electricity humming. Yet they are the very ones who keep something from happening.

They sit with pleasant, passive-attentive expressions from behind bulletproof glass, insulated from any danger of being wounded by a new idea or dizzied by a fresh perspective. It is as though they fear that the larger concepts of the world, implied in the classroom subject matter, threaten to diminish the sense of life they depend on for psychic security. Thus, I sense, they subconsciously trivialize the classroom.

"This class," they seem to say, "is not the Big It. It is another one of life's hassles like speed limits, parking spaces and ticket lines: hurdles necessary to leap in order to get to the moment of being Me! Alive!"

It is a good and splendid thing to come alive in social comradeship, of course—to seek the security and comfort of one's peers. And I don't object, as many do, to the elitist implication of the Greek system. As a teacher, I like the idea of a little elitism. I dream of an unspoken conspiracy in the classroom in which the best and the brightest set a pace that others will scramble to match.

But I rarely get pace-setting help from Greek students. They leave outside the classroom door that enthusiasm and creative focus that I observe in their fundraising car washes and cookie sales.

My first hint of the Greek student's real priority came a year ago when I divided the class into teams of four for an exercise. Each team was to think through the attitude and actions of a different element in a public relations problem—an exercise safely beyond teacher-policing or grading and useful only to the extent of the student's desire to learn.

A student helped me understand one reason why the exercise failed. Two of the four members of his team were Greek and, as he complained, "they just weren't thinking about anything but their damn Greek stuff. They just weren't interested."

It is hard to teach people who are not interested. Last spring, a few minutes before class, I put a stack of ditto sheets on a table at the entrance of the classroom with a scribbled sign that said, "Homework for next time. Take one."

I went back to my office, since class was ten minutes away from starting. Five minutes later a student stuck his head in my office.

"Is class meeting today?"

"Of course. Why?"

"Well, K— was telling everybody there wasn't going to be a class."

I was puzzled. Then I slapped my forehead. Of course! My sign was ambiguous. It could be interpreted as meaning there would be no class. Yet half the class showed up—the half that was not Greek. All the Greek students were apparently eager to believe K—'s word that there would be no class. That was when I realized that those students who showed up had a different attitude from Greeks. They came because, being unprotected by institutional fellowship, they understand that it is up to them to get their money's worth. These are the hard-scrambling, hungry students who are my elitists!

I began to think back, then, upon many examples that confirmed the idea that was taking shape in my mind: Greeks do not help advance the main idea of college.

I have heard that Greeks insist that their members maintain a certain grade level and will go to great lengths in coaching the faltering brothers or sisters to bring up their grades.

Grades! Grades are fun and useful as a measure of what has been learned. They are like those delicious little pencil marks that parents put on the end of the closet door to show that Vera has grown faster than Chuck and Dave. But grades are the speedometer, not the speed. When grades are the focus and the goal, it is fool's goal. It is a wooden nickel that won't spend; it is plastic food that has no nourishment; it is a paper moon shining over a cardboard sea. It reduces the process of learning from a growing experience to a monkey drill of memorized reflexes.

I have heard that some Greek organizations keep a file of past quizzes and exams from professors who have a habit of giving the same tests every time they teach a course. If that is true, it stands as prima facie evidence that Greek organizations have corrupted their legitimate purpose.

The legitimate purpose of a Greek organization? To provide students a support system of fun and fellowship with like-minded comrades. It offers help and needed r & r respite from the lonely, battering, terrifying and, finally, indescribably exhilarating adventure of coming face to face with the mighty flood of knowledge and history and art and science and technology of Western Civilization that has been gathering from streams and rivers of culture, through storm and strife, for 3,000 years. And students are asked not only to learn about it, but to comprehend it enough to locate themselves in relation to it.

In such an epic enterprise, it is helpful to have a dwelling place of smaller context in order to feel human and loved. It is not helpful, however, if the voices of that smaller context suggest that the larger context is basically humbug. But that, I suspect, is the unspoken message of Greek organizations.

***

The Times-Georgian
December 18, 1986

Harvard Trip

We have just come home from five heady days at Harvard, visiting our son who is there on a one-year fellowship. Under cold blue skies, then in snow and drizzle, day after day we joined the flow of students crisscrossing Harvard Yard. With them, we entered those ancient brick buildings, dumped coats and scarves along the wall, found seats and settled forward to hear some of the great lecturers of our times:

• Ebullient anthropologist Stephen Jay Gould, pre-eminent Darwinian and protector of True Darwin from misguided disciples, explained a puzzling evolutionary gap in terms of baseball's disappearing .400 batting average.

"We've been looking at the wrong thing," he said as he scribbled a bell curve on the board. The marginally significant statistical phenomenon simply fell off the curve due to several advances in the game.

• Walter Jackson Bate lectured on Edmond Burke. Or was it the other way around? Bate is famous for his impersonations of his subjects, especially Dr. Samuel Johnson.

• At the law school, syndicated columnist Anthony Lewis concluded his final lecture of the semester by serving French champagne to his 50 students—and guests—and whimsically toasting "the Queen."

• Psychiatrist Robert Coles, whose endless pulse-taking of American life has produced books on the poor-rich-middle-black-white children of the land, talked of novelist George Eliot with such breathless rush and dramatic silences that it lifted us high enough to see the whole landscape of life and literature. This lecture was in cavernous, dark Sanders Theatre, which reminded me of the Grand Ole Opry's Ryman Auditorium.

I was interested to note that Harvard students applaud at the end of a good lecture. At West Georgia College, students don't applaud. Yet a lot of us who teach there occasionally deliver applause-worthy lectures; and certainly our students know a good show when they see one.

This is only one tiny distinction between two institutions that are so vastly different in scope, structure, and mission that it would be difficult to compare them. Yet, I find a useful and encouraging message in noting the contrast. It reflects a difference not only in age (Harvard is celebrating its 350th anniversary; West Georgia was 50 years old two years ago), but in the educational traditions of New England and the South.

Harvard's founding in 1636 expressed an attitude toward education that flowered in the New England colonies into a belief in education for all. Universal education supported the Protestant conviction that every individual should be able to read the Bible. This belief laid a foundation that produced not only the nation's greatest concentration of superior colleges, but a fountainhead of American thought and literature.

In the colonial South, the cavalier tradition believed in education for the—well, the educated classes. The private Latin academies produced brilliant political thinkers and orators, and as recently as the 1920s gave rise to a shining literary movement—the Fugitives of Vanderbilt, most of whose members were products of these private academies. But there was no solid supporting foundation of literacy beneath this glint and glamour.

The idea of universal education—even at the 3-Rs level—seriously took hold in the South only at the beginning of this century. Since it takes generations for the perspectives of the educated mind to seep deeply into the lives and psyche, into the language and libraries of a region, we can think of ourselves as pioneers. Still young. Facing a great and exciting challenge.

This is not the time for applause. This is a time to build, to grow—a time of great adventure.

***

The Times-Georgian
January 1, 1987

Education vs. Sports

THE FRONT PAGE BANNER HEADLINE on last Sunday's Atlanta paper read: "Academic push has to compete with sports tradition."

My reaction was: How come?

The story was about Georgia's "no-pass, no-play" policy for high school athletes and the anguish it is creating in small towns where football is "a way of life." Fans fear that the new rule might sideline some potential Hershel Walker.

The headline conjures up the image of an academic establishment suddenly having to "push" against a well-rooted "sports tradition" without having developed any tradition of its own—at least, none that citizens would rally to with anything approaching the fervor they display for their high school football team.

At this point, with Georgia ranking third from the bottom in the nation in SAT scores and having one of the highest dropout rates, the new policy is the least state authorities could do. It is the weakest version of "no-pass, no-play" of the seven states that have adopted it, according to the story.

But how did we get ourselves in this fix of pitting two parts of our school program against each other? It's as though no education administrators really believe there is any joy in learning, and as though sports has been the spoonful of sugar to make the medicine go down. Sports seem to have all the fun. And, since no one seems able to articulate the essential glamour and romance in the academic process, the impression is left standing that what goes on in the classroom or lab is like a Dempsey Dumpster—necessary but grim and harsh.

Of course, sports are fun—to play and to watch. According to a description in Pat Conroy's latest novel, playing football can produce an ecstasy rarely matched in earthly life. And, being a spectator in the stands amid band music, cheerleaders, and the thrill of competition—this is the kind of experience everybody needs who wants to feel fully alive.

But we need other kinds of excitement, too. Ideas, for example. And, odd as it may seem in this column, talking about football, rehashing the game, is one example of this other kind of excitement. The "hot stove" boys (Monday morning quarterbacks all winter) can be among the world's great commentators, if they know what they're talking about, if their judgment is sharp and their metaphors fresh. The elements involved are those of most classrooms: knowledge, understanding, interpretation, communication.

But knowing just sports is not enough. And the academic part of school is the normal way to get going on a dozen or more subjects. In time, they all begin to connect up and offer the best do-it-yourself plan I know of to minimize being bored or boring in later life.

Furthermore, I can't shake the idea that many of these other subjects (history? literature?) would be as easy to learn as sports, if they were bolstered by the same support-system whoopee. Certainly, understanding sports history can be as demanding as, say, getting a grasp on the War of Austrian Succession.

At a social gathering over the holidays, a sports scholar stumped me and my preacher (an avid sports fan) with a super trivia question: in 1963 the men named the most valuable players in the NFL, the old AFL (this was before the merger), the American and the National Leagues in baseball had the same jersey number. Who were the men and what was the number? (Ans: Jim Brown, Cookie Gilchrist, Elston Howard, Sandy Kofax; the number was 32.)

That was a lot trickier than the question someone asked later when Handel's Hallelujah Chorus wafted into the background music. "Was it our bad King George who started the custom of standing up when this is played?" No, it was George II. Handel died in 1759, the year before George III became king. (I had to look it up.)

But then, I recall the party when my wife fell to chatting with an ex-Auburn lineman. He was about five years out of college and into a dull job. After exhausting the subject of his knee injury and Shug Jordan, he ran out of topics. He looked across the room to where I was talking with a woman.

"Look at him. Just going at it. He never has trouble thinking what to say."

Well, that was a mirage victory of gab over heft. But it did point up that, if an athlete doesn't die young as A.E. Housman recommends, he'd better have something else going.

Come on, let's hear it for academics! Gimme an "A" . . . !

***

The Times-Georgian
January 29, 1987

Making A's vs. Learning

THE AD READS: "HOW TO become a Straight-A Student!" The secret is found in this book you buy for $6.05 plus postage. The book will reveal a "system" for becoming "test-wise…(to) know exactly what to study, when to study it, and how much to study."

As a college teacher, I am forever grateful that students are motivated to make A's. So why did this advertisement send my blood temp hurtling toward 212 degrees Fahrenheit?

Well, let's see. Suppose the National Safety Council—impressed with the number of lives saved by the 55 mph speed limit—proudly announced that they had persuaded automakers to install speedometers that would never register over 55, even if a car were careening along at 95 mph?

What would your blood do in reaction to this confusion of goals and symbols?

The point of college is to learn; it is not to become test-wise. To learn is to change, to grow; the point is not to master techniques for manipulating the measuring system. The West Georgia College catalogue states the purpose of college better than that of any other schools in the Georgia system that I have studied. Our purpose, it says, is to provide "an environment wherein each student may attain a disciplined and open mind, a capacity for self-development and the knowledge and skills essential to living in a free society."

Making A's is not one of those skills. In fact, I have found that smart students who naturally made A's are the first to understand that a collection of A's obtained without acquiring some permanent knowledge that connects with a whole is like a string of pearls without the string.

Many students leave college without ever catching on that each course they took was a piece of a larger puzzle—a truly breathtaking picture puzzle—that they could work on for the rest of their lives. This is sad.

Before it becomes sad, this failure to learn must be faced when students come to me as juniors to learn mass communication; when they sign up to develop skill as a newsperson. A reporter needs to know stuff in order to ask good questions. A good start for background knowledge of how the world works would be the facts and concepts that they should have learned from the courses they took during their first two years of college.

I have come to recognize that look of stunned disbelief on the faces of students when I reveal what they should know from past courses. It is a look that cries foul, that says, "It is unfair to expect us to still know things from courses we have finished taking."

And so, I have to start again from the beginning with students . . .

• who have taken political science but don't know their right wing from the left, liberal from conservative, Republican from Democrat.

• who have taken American history but wouldn't blink if told that Alexander Hamilton was the running mate of Woodrow Wilson.

• who have taken introductory business courses but look at each other in puzzlement at the phrase "private sector."

• students who have studied literature but snicker at the idea that everyday objects can carry symbolic overtones.

• students who have taken speech courses but can't speak up even when I'm playing "press conference" with the class.

Who is to blame? Not the teachers—we have the best I've seen. I'm still learning from them, still impressed mightily. Not the students—these are bright, serious young men and women.

The "system" then? The people, parents, politicians who buy the A's-the-thing philosophy? The administrators, ex-teachers who have failed to tell the turn-on message of education?

Let's lay it all on people who write books on "How to become a Straight-A Student!" They'll repent all the way to the bank.

***

The Atlanta Journal-Constitution
May 14, 1989

The Professor's Daring Strategy: A Mental Map of Time

OK. So COLLEGE STUDENTS ARE ignorant. They don't know if Napoleon came before Shakespeare, when the American Civil War was fought, or what the New Deal was all about. Eight years ago, when I began teaching journalism at West Georgia College, I ran headlong into that ignorance, even before it was made famous by books like *Cultural Literacy* and *The Closing of the American Mind*. The problem is known. Now it's time to talk solution.

I'd like to contribute to a dialogue on the subject by describing a course that I have developed to give students a permanent, if rudimentary, framework of knowledge for a lifetime of learning, growing, connecting up. The course seeks to make clear, without having to say it, why liberal arts are relevant to our lives—why college knowledge, contrary to the idea that it is not the "real world," is, in fact, "the super real world."

The course is called "The Language of News." It grew out of six years of experimenting with ways to minimize the harm that my students' ignorance could inflict upon them in their careers in journalism or public relations. Political commentary by a reporter who is hazy about what happened on July 4, 1776, or July 14, 1789, would be pale tea indeed; likewise, a ghost-written speech on Roe v. Wade by a public relations hiree who didn't understand judicial review and its origins in 1803.

'Will This Be on the Test?'

But ignorance of the past was only half of the problem I ran into. Most of our students have no interest in daily news. They come to me innocent of the front-page terms of politics and business. Left wing/right wing? Democrat/Republican? Three branches of government? "Sounds familiar," is the best most can manage. Concepts like public and private sector, or terms like "PAC" or "demagoguery," are as remote as Celtic mythology.

It turned out that having two blank spots—of the past and of the present—inspired a daring strategy for my course. The rationale came from my wife.

"Why is it," I asked, "that kindergarten children will memorize the alphabet with fierce glee, yet college seniors go into their zombie mode when I ask them to learn an important date like 1649?" (Charles I was beheaded—a milestone on the road to democracy. After that, no English monarch dared claim that he ruled by divine right.)

Her answer rang true. Besides the sheer delight of possessing an incantation known by all grownups, children can grasp that learning the ABCs is the first step toward a power they see all around them—the power of the written word. And the same motive leads them to recite additions and the multiplication table. The power and presence of arithmetic in the world is also apparent—in clock faces and change for a dollar. But the power and presence of liberal arts is not so apparent; at least, not to those who don't have those special glasses of liberal education that let them see the third dimension of daily reality.

Many of our students are the first generation of their family to go to college. Thus, they come without the traditional cultural schemata—those networks of knowledge E.D. Hirsch Jr. describes in *Cultural Literacy*—that are the foundation of higher (and further) education. And we seem unable to explain to these students that the idea behind taking History, English Literature, Science and the rest is to empower them with the broader perspectives and the inside jokes of educated people.

Our students know only the conventional wisdom: grades count! And the most efficient way to make good grades is by short-term memorizing. To learn for keeps, for building and growth—that's a luxury they can't afford. And if classroom material ever threatens to come alive, to be relevant, the instinct of most students is to club it to death, render it inert for easier handling. ("Will this be on the test?") As a good B-plus student said to me one day when he didn't know a bedrock concept he had encountered in a previous class, "I wish somebody had told me I was supposed to remember all that stuff."

History Starts Making News

The first part of the strategy for my course was to get them hooked on news the way most of them are on sports or a soap opera. We read stories in the newspaper and weekly news magazines and saw clips from TV news shows. Halfway through the quarter, I could see it was beginning to work. They got interested. A revolutionary breakthrough! They even almost stepped out of their bulletproof glass booth, nearly talked like *people* talking, instead of through the don't-touch-me sound system students use for class discussion.

And as they became familiar with names, faces, buzzwords and concepts, their ability to absorb new complexities grew. For example, after seeing Republican Chairman Lee Atwater cavorting with his bass guitar at an inaugural party, students then saw him interviewed by Judy Woodruff of the McNeil/Lehrer News Hour. Mr. Atwater became a clearly pictured reference point. Two months later, when he was forced to resign from Howard University's board of directors, the class knew enough to comprehend the problem that black students at Howard had with the GOP's "Southern strategy" and its coy, racist appeal.

But, more importantly, by this time I had worked the second part of my teaching strategy. I had taken them back to the alphabet of daily news: history. We had identified the origins of the political/philosophical elements hiding in most news items. I had stressed the look and feel of the historic moment of creation and the dramatis personae strutting their hour on that earlier stage. Thus, the students had enough of a mental image of the Reconstruction South to take in my description of the once-solid Democratic South and to see how this was a prelude to the Atwater story. They could fit new pieces like this into place as in working a half-done picture puzzle.

I must say that getting the picture puzzle framed in and half-coherent took some doing—a wild combination of student involvement, visual imagery and memory tricks. It included movies, slides, mnemonic doggerel and playful constructs.

John Tower and Isaac Newton

For example, I concocted a fantasy consulting firm of Milton, Newton, Locke & Smith that set up our country. A joke, but it introduced the four political/philosophical concepts that I focused upon: *democracy*—Locke's government authorized by the people, not God (1690); *free press*—Milton's marketplace of ideas (1644); *checks and balances*—inspired by Newton's balance in nature (1687) that dominated 18th century thinking; and *free enterprise*—Adam Smith's theory (1776) that was put to the test in the bustling 19th century.

These four men and their ideas took their place among other carefully selected milestones of our past, making a horizontal design that I called century blocks. This ladder-like design—a more helpful way to picture dates and the flow of history than the one-dimensional time line—I was forever slapping on the board. This way, the past five centuries became as clear, logically sequential and easy-to-remember as the rooms in a house: front hall, living room, den, dining room, kitchen.

With a firm mental image of past centuries, students could more easily connect the Eastern Airlines strike back to the theories of Adam Smith, and John Tower's rejection by the Senate to the 18th century's checks and balances. And when the American Catholic bishops told the pope that some "consider the divine right of bishops as outmoded as the divine right of kings," well, students had seen a movie of Cromwell's parliament beheading Charles I in 1649. They understood.

Did it work? Well, not all students became Helen Keller at the water pump. And sometimes "the piano" ended up in "the kitchen." But few will ever confuse the times of Shakespeare and Napoleon, the years of the American Civil War or the content of the New Deal. And from here on, I think most of them have a glimmering of why they're "supposed to remember all that stuff."

But I keep feeling a wider implication in this exercise. For one thing, because history is visual, this course serves as a useful model for all classroom learning that requires building with mental images, including math. Also, my own experience tells me that this is exactly the kind of learning we use to "catch on" (and get ahead) in the so-called "real world." But finally, the greatest value of this approach is to help us get located in the greater scheme of things in a way that reaches into the past and into the future, far beyond today's ever-changing "real world."

***

The West Georgian
September 27, 1989

Editorials as Vital Knowledge

WELCOME ALL—STUDENTS AND TEACHERS—NEW-COMERS AND come-backers. And staffers who never left. Welcome to a new school year!

This is our season. In the American dream, fall belongs to the college campus. The imagery is everlasting: football, crisp air, sporty scarves and sweaters matching the russet and gold leaves, bright talk and jostling laughter, books and classrooms. It is also traditional in the welcome-back issue of the campus newspaper to offer tips to students on such things as where to get the biggest pizza or who sells take-out coffee after midnight.

But in this column, I want to offer to all students just one monumental discovery, something I have recently decided is the Best Bargain in the West. Yes, that's "West" as in Western Civilization. We're talking big picture here.

The bargain is this: the op-ed page of the daily newspaper.

The what?

"Op-ed" is short for "the page opposite the editorial page." I would also include the editorial page in the bargain. In the *Atlanta Constitution* and *Journal*, these two facing pages are located inside the back page of the "A" section. A paper costs 25 cents (unless you want to get it on the special six-week delivery deal we use in the Humanities Building, which brings the cost down to 17 cents). Of course, the newspaper can be read free in the library.

Those two pages give the reader—in editorials, columns, and letters—enough of the latest news, opinion and rumor for him or her to be in-the-know. And, as anyone in the working world will tell you, being in-the-know ranks somewhat above dressing for success. A knowing look in the eye conveys confidence more profoundly than a glossy-page outfit.

But it is the signed columns on the op-ed page, complete with a mug shot of the author, that are the bytes that bite back. They often read like little pieces of literature, tightly written jewels of up-to-date insights from true insiders.

"The geese are overhead, flying south in V-formations as crisp as a sharpened pencil," began a recent column by Boston's Ellen Goodman. "We watched them from the porch in a Maine light transformed by September clarity. Now we follow their lead, proceeding on our own annual migration."

The column went on to ponder the quickening—almost sickening—change of pace from idle vacation to school and work, and how it is the fear of falling back in life's struggle that drives us to over-achieve. "We fight these anxieties in ourselves by making a virtue out of necessity: hard work. We fight it in our children by driving out daydreams with discipline. Our own days speed up and we teach, even compel, our children to keep up."

These op-ed pundits are the people who put buzz words into circulation ("knee-jerk"), and coin metaphors that stick and become part of the language ("cold war").

Columnist William Safire—who came up with "One small step for man, one giant step for mankind" when he worked for President Nixon, and who has written a witty book on writing—has the credentials to invent a word if it needs inventing. And he did just that, presto, right before our eyes in a column earlier this month: "Oppostablishment." It refers to politicians who say "no" to any suggestion the rival party proposes, regardless of its merit. "Let me not knock contrarianism, whose flag I so often fly," he wrote. "It provides a counterweight to Caesarism and is needed in the braking of the president."

"But in reaction to George Bush's program to reduce the narcotics traffic, I detect a lock step knee-jerk—the telltale sign of Oppostablishment on automatic pilot, mindlessly assuming criticism is always constructive."

Now, some students may not catch on at once to "flying the flag of contrarianism," to "Caesarism," "lock step" or" knee-jerk." But any college student should be able to figure out or find out what these mean.

And all college students should hunger to know what they mean, if not how to use them. The best way to learn many of these kinds of lively words is to read them, see how they are used, get the feeling of what they mean, and write your own definition.

For example, a recent column by *Atlanta Constitution* staff-columnist Cynthia Tucker bore the headline "Atlanta's Transition to Ethnic Pluralism Sets Example for New South!" A student reading that headline who didn't understand what "pluralism" meant could learn from reading the column and using simple deduction.

So, for a college student trying to learn the language and layout of the real world, reading the op-ed page should be considered an obligatory daily dip into the life of our times. Or at least a learning exercise for a greedy mind. Time spent thus, would indeed yield a bargain.

Yet a deeper response lurks in the hushed realm of the possible. If, from this self-realized learning, a light clicked on in a student's head, suddenly showing how all college courses are, in truth, in the business of offering up the exotic, backstage secrets of the real world, then studying would never again be a grind. It would be more like feeding a hunger; school work would become a compulsion to do more than the teacher assigned, to learn more than the textbook offered.

This would not be a mere bargain. It would be the gift of a lifetime.

***

The West Georgian
January 30, 1991

The Hangover and Liberal Education

"Come in—you look awful. Hangover?"

"Burn-out," said the student. "My senior year…two more quarters, and I dunno, it all seems so…pointless."

"This usually happens in spring quarter," said the adviser. "But, so it hit you in January. Have a seat."

Adviser: OK, back to basics—why are you in college?

Student: Huh? Oh, OK [picks words thoughtfully] to get a job with a future, a job that's, you know, fun…challenging. And that doesn't get my fingernails dirty.

A: Good! No petty paper-pushing for you! And clean fingernails. I like that. You want to get paid for what you know, what you think, for your judgment—not some rote manual skill. Right! That's where the money is. So, are you learning how the world works—enough to make intelligent judgments?

S: [a puzzled pause] I'm keeping my grades up. I've got a 3.4 GPA.

A: That's OK. But are you getting the picture of how it all fits together so you won't sound like a beauty queen contestant on your job interview?

S: Picture? Fits together? What picture?

A: How the real world really words.

S: But I'm still in college.

A: Lucky you. College is the last chance you get to learn what's behind all the strutting and fretting...the concept behind competition, the theories of political power, the science that produces new technologies... all that backstage stuff.

S: The real world? From college? I don't get it.

A: Few students do, sad to say. These four years are the only ones in your life devoted primarily to learning, when you can scramble around to get the background you need in order to comprehend what's going on in the day-to-day of the world. In the news, you hear of population explosion—in college you study Malthus; out there it's junk bonds, Federal discount rate, Dow Jones average—in classroom it's Gresham's Law, Adam Smith, and Keynes. You read of "fiber optics" and you can picture the band of light waves there in the middle of the electromagnetic wave chart...

S: I can?

A: Why not? When will you ever have a better chance to learn what's what? You've got a whole library of books, magazines, newspapers; and you've got a faculty of experts paid to answer your questions.

S: [Shaking head in disbelief] That's weird. You're the one who doesn't get the picture. What's wrong with a 3.4 GPA?

A: Well, it's enough to get you an interview for the good job. To win it you need a competitive edge of some kind.

S: Win? Competitive edge? Sounds like professional sports.

A: It's the real world, old son; it's tougher than football. And, usually, more fun.

S: OK, so let's say I get the interview with my 3.4. I'm cool—what's the problem?"

[The adviser sits up straight, shifts his expression to formal-friendly. He takes on the role of an interviewer with a large company, one like Coke or a big bank, and he explains, with global interests.]

S: [getting into role-playing] Global interests? Good. I've always wanted to see the world.

"INTERVIEWER": Parlez-vous français?

STUDENT: That's French. No, I don't speak French.

"INT": Habla usted español?

S: No hablo español…OK, hablo un poco. I got a B in Spanish, but I have trouble with conversation.

ADVISER: [Ducking out of role for a comment] You just lost your competitive edge. And a chance to see the world. [Returns to role-playing]

"INT": [Glancing at magazine on desk] Here's this country in eastern Europe about to privatize its industry. Might be an opportunity for us. [Pauses, inviting a comment which doesn't come.] So what do you think of privatization in these liberated Iron Curtain countries?

S: Well, er, I believe in . . . in private enterprise. Yes, sir.

ADVISER: [Charging back for a comment] So why did your eyes flatten out with the look of panic? Are you equally vague on "public" and "private sector"? Or the implications of privatization as a move toward a market economy?

S: I've heard all those words. I know what they mean. I just don't . . .

A: . . .don't have the full background, back to Adam Smith's "invisible hand" in the 18th century, confronted by Karl Marx's counter-theory in the 19th, and how the life-and-death struggle between these two dominated the 20th century—my life and yours—for 70 years, until last year . . .

S: I'm supposed to say all that?

A: Of course not; not if you know it. If you know it, you could give a short, fun answer that would get you a $2,000 increase in a starting salary offer. The interviewer would see "here's a college student with a college education." That's the competitive edge.

S: I'm lost. Would you repeat that $2,000 part again.

A: It's the short answer that shows you know.

Say the interviewer gets on the subject of Gorbachev's struggle to hold together the USSR. To test your knowledge of your own country—our United States—he makes a little joke about how Gorby is just now getting to the problems we faced after the American Revolution—you know, the Articles of Confederation and all that. So you say, "Yeah. He needs a James Madison." He is impressed that you know which father of the Constitution tightened up our restive confederation. Then to show your wit as well as your grasp, you add "or he may end up needing an Abe Lincoln." Competitive edge.

S: [Shaking his head] The pressure we're under for grades. . .

A: You could have added another $1,000 to your starting salary.

S: You don't understand college life for students, do you?

A: I'm afraid I do. Too many of you think college is where you go to make grades, friends and memories. That's fine, but it's not what you're paying for. Well, I can see I haven't cured your burn-out.

S: You've turned it into a real depression.

A: OK. Forget "job." Let's talk "human being." If you leave college turned on by what you have discovered about the world—and you can do it in these last two quarters—you'll never stop growing. Then, to put it in bumper sticker terms, you're less likely to be bored, boring and divorced by 34.

S: I wish I'd had a hangover.

***

V. Lessons Learned in Black and White

The Times-Georgian
February 16, 1997

Reporting for Work

I REMEMBER THE SPRING EVENING in 1954 when I first faced the dilemma of being a white Southerner with mixed feelings about race. It happened during a rehearsal break in the Augusta Players' production of "My Three Angels." I was the chief angel; the other two were soldiers from Ft. Gordon, non-Southerners. We were cooling off in the dusk outside when someone told the day's late news—the U.S. Supreme Court had declared "in public education 'separate but equal' has no place." Meaning: Southern schools must integrate.

This was the historic Brown decision—the high court ruling long-dreaded by the white South. It rumbled across Dixie like an answering volley from Fort Sumter.

It was Monday, May 17, 1954—"Black Monday" as it was soon labeled by the clinched jaws and narrowed eyes in Mississippi and elsewhere in the Deep South. White Citizens Councils sprung up, pledged to resist forever. Billboards along major highways called for the impeachment of Chief Justice Earl Warren.

In that May twilight, outside the theater in Augusta, the news had dropped a net around the three of us angels, relocating our show biz friendship into an uneasy national context of regional differences. They looked down, kicked at grassy stubble in a way that told me they approved of the court decision and assumed I didn't. It was for me, the Southerner and chief angel, to speak.

"It had to be," I said of the unanimous decision. "But it scares me." I was not against the Brown decision. But, as a white Southerner, I didn't welcome the turmoil and disruption that surely lay ahead.

A year later, I took a stronger stand on the by-then inflammatory Brown decision. I ignored it in the Confederate Memorial Day speech it had come my turn to deliver. Every April 26, at Magnolia Cemetery in Augusta, little girls in starched dresses would scatter rose petals among Confederate graves, to the playing of "Taps." In 1955, I, in white linen suit and genuine passion, held forth on the worthy virtues of our beloved Southland, omitting our "sacred way of life," segregation. Furthermore, I had no trouble resisting my uncle, a political hack for the city's machine boss, who had pressured me to attack the federal government for its unconstitutional tyranny.

In other words, I was a "moderate" on race, an easy label for many white middle-class urban Georgians. But moderation has no battle banner and it was no match for hard-charging racial rabble-rousing aimed at the more rural areas with their top-heavy vote-power via the county unit system. It took years to moderate the bile-stirring terms "race mixing" and "forced integration" into the more accurate "desegregation." And no counter metaphor deflected the mischief in "you can't be a little bit pregnant." So much for moderates.

But being a moderate opened the way for me to get a ringside seat at the most dramatic social revolution in the United States this century. My real break came when General Eisenhower was elected president in 1952 and came to town to play golf at the Augusta National. The White House press corps reporters came with him. They stayed at the Bon Air Hotel, an old hangout of mine a block down the hill from my house. By luck, a long-time friend, Bill Emerson, was then a freelance journalist in Atlanta. He got me to do some leg work and light reporting for stories he did on Ike—Ike's golf pro, his caddy, his cottage at the Augusta National.

For his first story, I had to contact Jim Haggerty, Ike's press secretary. I snuck into an ongoing press briefing in the Bon Air ballroom, posing as a reporter.

When I stepped into this briefing, I felt a jolt. The room was thick with a seething intelligence, a desperate energy the likes of which I'd never encountered. They were a prickly, idiosyncratic lot, these reporters, photographers, varied in shape and style—from the rumpled, harassed, overweight character Shoe in today's comics to the cool, vain, natty Agent 007 type.

For me, this was a glimpse of a new world "out there . . . a world outside of Yonkers" as Cornelius Hackl sings in "Hello Dolly." And, by 1956, at age 30, with our fourth child due, I knew I had to leave my dead-end job with an uncle's decaying building supply company. This touch of a larger world set me in motion. For Cornelius Hackl, "out there" was New York. For me, it meant Atlanta.

After a useful transition year, starving as a film salesman, I was hired by Bill Emerson who, by that time, had opened an Atlanta bureau for *Newsweek.*

I reported for work January 2, 1957, the best of times to begin this career in the South, as it turned out. The city buses of Montgomery, Alabama, had been desegregated the week before, after a year of extraordinary determination by ordinary black people, led by Martin Luther King, Jr.

On that first week of my new career, several prominent black Atlanta preachers boarded city buses, paid their fare and refused to go to the back. They were duly arrested and released on bond. That night, they were the hero speakers at a mass meeting that packed the Ebenezer Baptist Church on "Sweet" Auburn Avenue. It was my first mass meeting.

The emotional highlight of the evening was the telling by one hero of his bus experience that day.

"You know those little sideways seats up front?" Oh yes . . . The crowd, already floating, began to jostle each other with excitement, nudging, laughing, knowing what was coming . . .Oh yes, they knew those little seats. . . "I have always wondered what it would FEEL like to SIT in one of those seats," shouted the speaker, containing the gathering thunder of delight, holding off for the delicious punch line to come. "Well, today, I sat down in one…" The audience roared a-new. "And do you know how it FEELS?" Shouts, laughter and applause lifted the moments to its finale. "It feels GOOD!" And, the sound of jubilation went out in waves that night, up and down Sweet Auburn.

That is my best memory of that night. Two nights we worked until dawn, running down Marietta Street with typed pages of copy to Western Union to make the 6 a.m. deadline, before the more costly day rates went on. At the end of the week, Emerson's wife, Lucy, looked at me, a staggering, but still-standing combatant, and said, "You've seen the elephant and heard the owl." Sounded about right to me.

The Atlanta bus case disappeared into the labyrinth of the legal system, but in September, a major new integration story emerged from that system. Little Rock's Central High School was under Federal Court order to admit the nine Negro plaintiffs into the all-white school. Governor Orval Faubus blocked their entry with his National Guard until a daily morning crowd grew to a mob. He then withdrew the Guard, leaving the mob to rule. An angry President Eisenhower sent in combat-ready paratroopers who ringed the school with fixed bayonets.

This was the major story around the world. In Little Rock, I fell in with Neville Maxwell of the *London Times*. I listened, amazed, as he tested his thesis for a *Sunday Times* "think piece" on Harry Ashmore, editor of the *Arkansas Gazette* who won a Pulitzer Prize for being the gadfly to Orval's shenanigans. Harry nodded to each step of reasoning by this shy, bright Englishman; yes, Faubus had been liberal on race; yes, he was eager for a third term; yes, Arkansas voters reject third-term candidates; yes, Faubus needed a bold show to overcome this voter tradition, hence, the National Guard to block integration. And I thought, "Well I never." But, Harry nodded so I took note, and was the wiser when later, Ernest Vandiver said, "No, not one," Lester Maddox waved his ax handle at blacks, and George Wallace stood in the school house door. Each ended up becoming governor.

The last of us "foreign press" left Little Rock on Saturday, October 5, 1957, our attention fixed on a strange new story from that morning's news: Sputnik. The story of Southern integration dropped out of sight for two-and-a-half years.

At this point, there was not yet a Civil Rights Movement. That began with the sit-ins of 1960 and the Freedom Riders of 1961. It became front page news with the burning of an integrated bus in Anniston, Alabama, and the beating of blacks and whites on another bus when they arrived in Birmingham, Alabama. And this is where the second story in this series of three will begin.

***

The Times Georgian
February 23, 1997

An Irresistible Force

SOMETHING HAPPENED TO DIXIE IN the sixties that is like what happens when an irresistible force meets an immovable object—it goes through without leaving a hole.

White Southerners had been led to believe that Jim Crow was essential to happiness, was "our sacred way of life." But, across town, blacks had come to the end of enduring their backdoor half-life as people without hope of being Mr., Mrs., Miss, sir or ma'am.

Would the South change or stay the same? By 1960 change had started: the unanimous Brown decision in 1954; the Montgomery bus-boycott victory through non-violence in 1956; federal troops enforcing school desegregation in Little Rock in 1957.

But also in 1957 came a serious book on the white South by John Bartlow Martin entitled, *The Deep South Says "Never."*

Well, here we are in the South today, 40 years later, moving along nicely without Jim Crow; whites automatically use courtesy titles. Otherwise, we're not that different from then.

Did something happen? Did anybody see it? Who remembers?

Yes, something happened. A revolution. And, by the greatest good luck of having a job with *Newsweek*, I saw it as it unfolded. As a reporter, I could squeeze into packed black churches and feel a breathing air of excitement. We in the media walked beside the marches and demonstrations, and eavesdropped on confrontations. We learned to spot the smell of fear and courage, to feel the sting of tear gas, the shock of armed troops in American towns, and occasionally, we heard the sickening clunk of blows.

We covered rampaging segregation rallies and KKK cross burnings. Also, as a white Southerner, I experienced the schisms this change brought among whites, the friendships cleaved in bitter words, generations scowling across their gap in years, family Sunday dinners ruined with chairs slammed back from the table, napkins hurled at the centerpiece.

The main Civil Rights Movement began in February 1960 out of a simple existential act of four black college freshmen on their own, sitting in at a "white only" lunch counter at Woolworth's in Greensboro, N.C. It was like striking a match in flammable fumes.

Sit-ins flared up in other cities, strengthening an already-buzzing black underground network of information. It gave birth to the Student Nonviolent Coordinating Committee, SNCC, an aggressive group of students that would, from here on, be a challenge to older preachers of Martin Luther King Jr.'s Southern Christian Leadership Conference. Julian Bond and Congressman John Lewis came out of SNCC.

Sit-ins didn't get much front page play until they crossed paths with that year's presidential race between John F. Kennedy and Richard Nixon. In October, King was arrested leading a group of students on a sit-in at Rich's in Atlanta. But, when he ended up, mysteriously, alone at Reidsville's maximum security prison deep in rural Georgia, his friends and family were seriously alarmed. Presidential candidate Kennedy made a phone call to King's wife, Coretta, expressing his concern, and pressure from Democratic Party biggies secured King's release. This gave Kennedy the black vote and a narrow victory.

The Kennedy connection became crucial when, the next year, the biracial Freedom Riders, testing segregation on interstate buses, arrived with much advanced notice in Montgomery, Alabama. They were met by a vicious mob that beat them, knocked out teeth and broke jaws. Neither police nor other lawmen were in sight.

That night at a mass rally at Ralph Abernathy's church, I stayed at a front window in the foyer looking out on the street. I could see a turned-over car ablaze and a mob approaching. A line of U.S. marshals, thanks to Attorney General Robert Kennedy, stood between the mob and the church.

"We jes' wanna go to church with the n—ers," said a pot-bellied mob leader, holding a 2x4 taller than he was.

The head marshal ordered his men into gas masks. Then they began to roll and lob spewing canisters of tear gas at the mob, driving them back and into a night of random destruction.

That was my first experience with tear gas, but not my last. The worst was at the Ole Miss student riot when one black man, James Meredith, was admitted as a student in 1962. That night-long barrage sickened the air around Oxford for several days. More vivid was the tear gas canister tossed through an open window of a black church mass meeting in Greenwood, Mississippi. It almost brought on a stampede until the crowd saw it was a dud.

Looking back, I see a three-act play pattern in how the Civil Rights Movement played out. Act II begins with King's children crusade in Birmingham in the spring of 1963 . . . the mass arrests, Bull Connor's police dogs and fire hoses and King's eloquent "Letter from a Birmingham Jail." The nightly news pictures of dogs and fire hoses against black youths heighten national sympathy for the young people's cause. This reached a high point with King's "I Have a Dream" speech before the multitudes in Washington in August.

Then came the defiant answer: the bombing of the 16th St. Baptist Church, which killed four young girls. It showed what one writer calls "the mystifying and unconventional power of the race issue." Two months later, President Kennedy was shot in Dallas. But, Act II might end with President Lyndon Johnson pushing through the Civil Rights Act of 1964 in July, showing his sympathy by quoting the Movement's famous song: "We SHALL overcome."

Act III would open in the wild, surreal happenings in Atlantic City, more formerly known as the Democratic National Convention of 1964. Large placards bore the pictures of the three civil rights workers slain in Mississippi earlier that year. Alabama and Mississippi both had alternate delegations seeking seating. The Mississippi Freedom Democratic Party ousted the old line Democratic delegation before the Credentials Committee, largely from the testimony of abuse—from Fannie Lou Hammer, a natural leader out of the Delta cotton fields.

On the boardwalk, blacks from the South stood out in all-night shouting matches in a sort of impromptu Speakers Corner that TV flood lights made a show of shows. I only remember fragments:

"You just think you're alive," said a lanky black man, playing with some of the existential ideas that made their way into Movement philosophy. "But, you just walking around."

And, I remember a passionate young Republican in coat and tie, shouting until the vein stood out in his neck. "I'll tell you what I'm talking about. I'm talking about Adam Smith and the Wealth of Nations. That's what I'm talking about."

The final scene swings to Selma, Alabama, in 1965 where a voter registration drive is gaining momentum, but no registrations. Sheriff Jim Clark likes his job, wants to be re-elected and sees himself gaining favor by his strong-arm tactics against blacks. On Sunday, March 7, when blacks began a march, Sheriff Clark's mounted posse charged the marchers, cracking skulls in front of TV cameras. It was called "Bloody Sunday."

Clark intended for this to be seen on TV. Local TV. That's where his votes were. But, he miscalculated. The national stir from "Bloody Sunday" led to the passage of the Voting Rights Act.

By the time Clark ran for sheriff, enough black voters had registered to defeat him. End of play and, in the real world, the beginning of political empowerment of Southern blacks. That's when change began down deep.

***

The Times-Georgian
March 2, 1997

Unforgettable Characters

YEARS AGO, WATCHING A TV special on the Civil Rights Movement, my 15-year-old daughter asked, "Why didn't you tell us about this?"

Why indeed? It's about us. It is a story that should be told especially in the South, where most of it happened. If the Civil War was our "Iliad," The Civil Rights struggle was our "Odyssey," our epic narrative of how the South, in a struggle with itself, shed the leaden burden of official segregation, enforced by law and silly ritual. Of how we, black and white, could finally shout, "Free at last!"

It is told in books now, good books made from digging, interviewing, putting together what happened deeply in those Shakespearean days. They tell what went on behind-the-scenes and hidden-in-the-heart's-core that we reporters missed in our "history in a hurry," as my boss at *Newsweek* called journalism. Such books now number in the hundreds; I have 25 or more on my shelves.

Here are some of my favorite people described in these books, individuals who made personal, life-changing choices that influenced the triumphant outcome of the story and helped save the sum of things:

• Charles H. Houston, Dean of Howard University's Law School, whose obsession with over-turning *Plessy v. Ferguson* (1896) for its mocking "separate but equal" doctrine lit a fire in the belly of Thurgood Marshall and his classmate law students. Richard Kluger's *Simple Justice.*

• Diane Nash, SNCC leader in Nashville whose clear vision and steel nerve got up a replacement team of Freedom Riders when the first became too battered to go on. "If they stopped us with violence," she said, "the Movement is dead." Taylor Branch's *Parting the Waters.*

• Floyd Mann, head of Alabama Public Safety, who pointed a pistol in the ear of a white man beating an unconscious black Freedom Rider, saying, "Hit him once more and I'll kill you." Fred Powledge's *Free At Last?* That black man was John Lewis, now a U.S. Congressman. I arrived on the scene just after that beating and had it described to me by an eyewitness reporter, our stringer, Stuart Culpepper, now a leading Atlanta actor. He was convinced the assailant would have killed Lewis without the intervention of Mann.

• E.D. Nixon, key black leader in Montgomery who turned Rosa Parks' bus seat arrest into history, a bus boycott that he then maneuvered 26-year-old Rev. Martin Luther King, Jr., into leading. Nixon had heard King make "a heck of a speech" to the NAACP months before and told a companion, "I don't know how I'm going to do it, but someday, I'm gon' hang him to the stars." Howell Raines' *My Soul is Rested.*

• Richard T. Rives, a federal judge in Alabama whose ruling on the three-judge panel broke the tie in the bus boycott, giving the landmark victory to the blacks. The ruling began the enlargement of the Brown decision's anti-separate-but-equal by applying it to busing. Rives, deeply-religious and a respected leader in Alabama politics, was socially ostracized for his swing-vote role in the ruling. This happened to other Southern-born federal judges whose moral rulings were made at the forfeit of their own and their families' good lives of honor and prestige. Jack Bass's *Unlikely Heroes.*

• Mae Bertha Carter, Mississippi sharecropper whose gutsy decision to buck the system became a book called *Silver Rights,* written by Connie Curry, a white worker for the American Friends Society who helped the Carter family survive.

When seven of the Carter children dared to integrate the all-white public schools, their lives became something out of the Book of Job. They survived and prevailed. Of eight Carter children who broke the barrier, seven graduated from Ole Miss and all made it into the sunlit uplands of a decent middle class life.

This powerful new book takes the reader into the Carter family and the savage heart of Delta apartheid. The toughness of their courage shines like a golden thread that did not break.

In 1990, Mae Bertha, a Civil Rights leader in Mississippi, and a friend, Winson Hudson, were in Washington to speak to a class taught by Julian Bond. Connie was working there then. Julian and Connie, knowing that both women hero-worshiped the late Robert Kennedy—had known him from his trips to Mississippi investigating hunger—arranged a visit with Kennedy's youngest son, Max, a law student at the University of Virginia. "Your daddy could have spit you out whole," exclaimed Mae Bertha at the son's likeness to his father, after they'd exchanged warm hugs of greeting.

Then Mae Bertha and Winson sang a song they'd worked up for the dashing 25-year-old Max. It was the poignant up-dating of the old folk hymn "Has Anybody Here Seen My Old Friend Abraham?" that goes on to verses for fallen heroes: Medgar Evers, Martin King, John Kennedy. Then finally, "Has anybody here seen little Bobby Kennedy?"

Connie wrote of this later, though it is not in the book—how everyone cried, tears streaming down cheeks . . . Max's . . . her own. "In a rush, I felt my own tear-stained days of 1968, when most of my own dreams died along with Dr. King and Robert Kennedy. . . we saw the closing of a twenty-five-year period of history and the fusion of moments that move America a little further along in the search for its soul."

***

LaVergne, TN USA
01 February 2010
171642LV00002B/4/P